Nick Skelton was born in Warwickshire in 1957. Having won team gold in London at his eighth Olympic Games in Rio, 2016, he won the individual gold medal, the first British rider ever to do so, proving himself to be one of Britain's most durable sports stars. He was made CBE in the New Year's Honours List in 2017.

Co-author Bernadette Hewitt is a writer and media consultant who, as an award-winning equestrian journalist, covered four Olympics and numerous championships. She is the author of several books including, with Carl Hester, *Making It Happen* (Orion 2014).

NICK SKELTON

Gold

MY AUTOBIOGRAPHY

W&N

WEIDENFELD & NICOLSON

A W&N Paperback
First published in Great Britain in 2018
by Weidenfeld & Nicolson

LONDON BOROUGH OF SUTTON LIBRARY SERVICE	
30119 028 443 99 4	
Askews & Holts	Oct-2018
798.2509	

ISBN 978 1 4746 0734 6

Typeset by Input Data Services Ltd, Somerset

Printed and bound by CPI Group (UK) Ltd, Croydon, CR0 4YY

Weidenfeld & Nicolson

The Orion Publishing Group Ltd
Carmelite House
50 Victoria Embankment
London
EC4Y 0DZ
An Hachette UK Company

www.weidenfeldandnicolson.co.uk
www.orionbooks.co.uk

Contents

The beginning of a new day

This is the beginning of a new day. God has given me this day to use as I will.

I can waste it or use it for good. What I do today is very important because I am exchanging a day of my life for it.

When tomorrow comes, this day will be gone forever, leaving something in its place I have traded for it.

I want it to be a gain not a loss – good not evil.

Success, not failure, in order that I shall not regret the price I paid for it.

Heartsill Wilson

Sent to the author by Ed Smith on the morning of the individual in Rio, 2016

1

Bowing Out

The first grand prix I ever won as a showjumper was at Royal Windsor Horse Show. It was on St James, in 1981, and together we won it for three consecutive years, which was a bit of a mark. I've had numerous wins there over the years, with Showtime, Cartagene, Jalisco, Russel and Pandur to name a few. When I made the decision that Big Star and I would retire, it was just a month before Royal Windsor. That would be the place to do it, I thought.

I rang Nick Brooks-Ward, the Operations Director at HPower Group, which runs Royal Windsor and Olympia, and the 'man behind the microphone' at plenty of other shows. Hands-free is one thing but Nick had to actually stop his car when he heard what I said, that I was calling time on my competitive career, finally, and that Big Star was joining me. I always said we'd stop together and the time had come.

I didn't have much time to think about it beforehand, the retirement ceremony. I knew they'd have some master plan as that's what they're expert at. Nick and his brother Simon Brooks-Ward are born and bred to run shows. Their late father Raymond was commentating on TV before I was born and his boys have carried his show and sponsorship organisation to a different level. They didn't tell me much more than the timing, which was probably just as well. We went down to Windsor on the Wednesday as Laura – that's my partner Laura Kraut, the US showjumper – had several horses competing, and Big Star came too.

I'm sure Big Star knew pretty quickly he wouldn't be jumping there. He is so intelligent. He must have been thinking: I haven't been jumped at home, what am I doing here? I hadn't ridden him much but on the Thursday I got on him and walked him up the short distance to Windsor Castle. Simon Brooks-Ward had asked would I take Big Star up as the Queen would like to have a meeting with him and see what he looks like. It's not every day you get a chance to do that.

The Queen is so very knowledgeable about horses and when she said thank you very much for bringing him up I replied that it was a bigger honour to be asked to bring him. There we were, right in front of the castle. She asked all about how Big Star was bred, his bloodlines, what he'd been like to ride and general questions asked by someone who really knows and has a genuine love of horses. We're very, very lucky in our sport that the Royal Family is so horsey, especially the Queen. We were talking about Big Star's character and I told her how well behaved he is, how his character is unbelievable, and then we just chatted about horses, about racing generally and what my boys Dan and Harry were doing. I told the Queen we actually have a horse that she bred at Dan's stables, and before I could tell her who it was by she already had it! A mine of information, she must be an 'encyclopaedia of horses'. Naturally we talked about her horse Barbers Shop that the day before had won the show class for retrained racehorses. It was a great moment and I appreciated being given such a rare opportunity.

Bowing Out

The following day, I worked Big Star in the main ring. He was quiet and I was even more sure then that he knew he wouldn't be jumping. Several people asked me how I felt about Sunday being my last time in the ring wearing white breeches and my team jacket, and my reply was I'd be sticking them all on eBay on the Monday morning. I didn't, but apart from a few bits and pieces most of my tack had already been offloaded to Dan Skelton Racing. I'd got my head around it, the thought of never competing again after forty-three years. I'd made the decision and I was sure I'd be able to speak when Nick interviewed me in the ring. But would I when it got to reality?

There was plenty to keep me busy; an autograph-signing session for which the queue was huge, a talk at the Pony Club stand and as normal helping Laura, who had a great win in Friday's speed class and would go on to a respectable fourth in the Rolex Grand Prix that final afternoon of the show. On the Saturday I was honoured to receive the BHS Queen's Award for Equestrianism from the Queen. I did think she might be a bit sick of seeing me by then, but that she would be present for our retirement ceremony as well topped the lot. I'd just have to hold it together.

It was time. Mark Beever, my groom for more than thirty years, brought Big Star from the FEI Stables to the collecting ring where we waited outside for the Household Cavalry Musical Ride to finish, then the presentation of the awards for the Land Rover Driving Grand Prix. All those cavalry horses charging out, then the drivers from four-in-hand to ponies. Big Star's never minded that level of excitement, it's just better to be on him. A cute little kid on a chestnut show pony had followed him up from the stables and was right next to him. Unusually for a stallion, he's not bothered by ponies. Lots of people wanted photos, so a bit of posing was going on. I'm guessing the kid on the pony photobombed most of them.

Then it was happening. They played the Spandau Ballet song 'Gold' as we walked into the Castle arena. Was Big Star going to neigh or not? Throughout his career, every single time that I've ridden him into an arena to start a round he has neighed. I'd have thought something was wrong if ever he hadn't. But this was different. There weren't any jumps as we walked in, none, just people, lots of them, lined up in a guard of honour. Big Star has done a lot of parades and appearances, he's used to them, he walked calmly between the line-up. Those faces were representatives from every part of the showjumping world; the course design team led by Bob Ellis who designed the London 2012 courses among many others, and Kelvin Bywater, Jon Doney and the international ground jury, John Roche and the FEI delegates, the stewards, international riders present, past and past it – Geoff Billington and Malcolm Pyrah among them – the band I'd opted to join. Liz Edgar, who had been so instrumental in my career and had been with me the very first time I jumped at Royal Windsor, was there too. At the top of the line-up stood Gary Widdowson, who'd been with me on my very first show abroad. Without him and his wife Beverley this story wouldn't have happened. And there was Dad, same applies in a different way, with Laura and my son Dan, ditto. If I was the type to say literary things like 'my life spread before me', this would be the time for it, but reading this you're going to have to go with great. It was great.

The stands were packed, Big Star soaked up the applause. Mike Tucker, who'd hung up his microphone at Badminton after forty years as the BBC's equestrian commentator, came out of retirement to introduce us, and Nick took over to interview me. When we came to a halt beside Nick, Big Star neighed. Then when the music had stopped and Nick asked over the microphone would I stay on Big Star, he neighed again and the crowd went wild. I don't know what he was saying but our time had come and there was no going back. As the crowd cheered and laughed, Big Star bucked, jangling the medals round my neck, making the point that it was his day as much as mine.

If I'd been going to break down it would have been when Nick Brooks-Ward read out the text he'd had from Harry. Nick shared it with the sell-out audience at Royal Windsor so I know Harry won't mind me sharing it here:

Dad, I'm so sorry I'm not there, but when I asked you if I should go racing today or come down to Windsor, you said, 'Go and do your job and try and ride some winners.' I thought, that is what has got you to where you are: your hard work, dedication and determination. My first great memory of you in the ring was when Dollar Girl won the World Cup final in '95. You went through so much from then to Rio 2016, and when you finally reached your childhood dream to take individual gold it was the best day of my life. I am the proudest son alive and so glad you've stopped at the top. I hope I will make you as proud as I am of you one day. See you later, love you, Harry.

Harry had just ridden a winner at Ludlow: Azzuri, in the two o'clock, trained by Dan. The boys had produced a winner every day of Royal Windsor. Needless to say, I am proud of both of them already. I'll miss winning, but they'll do it for me.

I took my team jacket off and replaced it with a tweed 'civilian' one. There was a huge round of applause from the crowd; hopefully they didn't think it was part of a striptease. Then I took the saddle off Big Star's back in the time-honoured ceremonial tribute to a retiring horse. Mark was there to take it from me. Then John and Michael Whitaker, my teammates from Rio, with Scott Brash from London 2012, walked in on their horses and followed me and Big Star round the ring to the strains of 'Auld Lang Syne'.

Big Star lapped it up. Everyone was on their feet, the applause was massive. He gave a huge buck which made the audience clap harder. He really showed off – and why not, he is a Big Star; I've said it so many times and I said it during that retirement ceremony. From the day we bought Big Star when he was five years old, I had it in my mind that he could win an Olympic gold medal. He's been an outstanding horse, and he has never let me down. I have an amazing team around me, and I have been very lucky all my life. I've had the most wonderful horses, great owners and great sponsors, and I am very proud of what I have done. I would do it all again if I could. But I can't – there's not enough time, for a start – so I'll just tell the story instead.

2

Jumping into Life

I jumped my first fence before I was born. I'd been due on Christmas Day, hence my parents' choice of the name Nicholas. On Boxing Day, Mum and Dad arrived at a family party and Mum, carrying the oversized bump that was me, was having a hard time getting to the front door past the randomly parked cars. Dad suggested she jump the wall as it might help me get a move on. She jumped clear but I stayed put until five thirty in the morning on 30 December 1957 when Mum went into labour.

As they did in those days, Dad called the midwife. She came round, pronounced Mum would be a few hours yet, and went off to do her washing. A few hours later she came back, and after checking Mum, announced she was off to do her ironing. Back she came again, but Dad wasn't letting her go a third time. He was at the end of his tether by this stage and when the midwife announced she was off to get tea ready, Dad barred her way. Just as well he did, as not only had she made nearly as many calls as the BBC has shown series of *Call the Midwife* by then, it was teatime when nine pounds' worth of fair-haired baby me finally made an appearance. When my sister Sally was born on 12 June 1965, it was in hospital. I don't think it was just that times had changed but that shattered nerves couldn't take another home birth. At least I made up for it by sleeping well at night, a talent that has stayed with me through most of my life, with a few exceptions.

I might have been a good baby but by the time I started growing up another talent that has stayed with me was beginning to show itself, the one for getting into scrapes. Dad was cleaning the windows at our house and at the age of two I was 'helping' him. I'd climbed on to the stool Dad was using to have a go at the nearest window while Dad had gone off to fetch something. Naturally I couldn't reach and so I fell off the stool.

A couple of days later we all went off to Blackpool on holiday, me with a big bump on my forehead and one side of my face black and blue. Some kind soul asked me how I'd got the bumps and bruises. 'My dad hit me,' I replied. That didn't go down too well. These days it would probably have had more consequences than a severe look. I don't remember saying it – well, I wouldn't at that age – but Dad does and he knew the truth: the colourful bruises were the consequence of a tiny boy biting off more than he could chew.

When I was very young my favourite pastime was riding my grey rocking horse called Mobo. This was no gentle rocker but a fearsome beast I would make rear and buck. Mobo was a model horse (the name came from the company that made them) attached by springs to a metal frame and I would ride it and have it leaping all over the place. It was the first horse I fell off, and I did that often, but I'm convinced that riding Mobo taught me to stay on and stay in balance for when I graduated to riding live equines.

The first of these was Oxo, the pony Mum had bought for £40 from a friend when he was two and I was eighteen months old. Sounds like a recipe for disaster, but Mum knew what she was doing as we learned together. Much later, my boys Harry and

Dan would learn on him too. Oxo would be in our lives for nearly forty years.

Mum taught me to ride and she and Dad were my grooms as well. She used to put out my riding clothes for me: jodhpur boots and those Bedford Cord jodhpurs with balloon sides, the ones you associate with cavalry officers. I think they're known as shitstoppers. Anyway, it was long before stretch fabric came in, don't forget. She'd also get Oxo ready – he lived in a field at the back of our house – as I couldn't reach much further than his legs and feet, which I would brush and pick out. My introduction to competition was at local gymkhanas like Exhall and Bedworth, Ansty and Shilton, first of all on a leading rein. It wouldn't be long before I got the bug for winning. Dad would even recruit the fastest runners to lead Oxo and me in the gymkhana games. Thanks, Dave Docker and Roger Abbott!

Oxo was just as competitive as I was. We won hundreds of rosettes together. Red for first, blue for second, yellow for third, green for fourth; but it was only the red ones I wanted and some-times I'd come away with a haul of five in a weekend to add to my growing collection. It wasn't always an easy ride though. Oxo hated brass bands, as I found out to my cost when I entered the ring for a fancy dress class dressed up as Ivanhoe. The band struck up and Oxo reared up. I fell off, screaming my head off, while Mum rushed in fearing I was injured only to find the pins she'd used to stick my outfit together were stuck in all over me. That was a lesson learned for later life!

It has often been assumed that my parents were not horsey, but Mum rode and her great-grandfather, who was a coal merchant, had a stable of dray horses and the finer kind of driving horses known as high-steppers. It was a tradition that he would drive the family in a four-in-hand from Coventry to Stratford at Easter. He also had a horse-drawn hearse for funerals. It was probably because my dad worked in and later took over the pharmacy in Bedworth, which had been in his family since 1852, that the myth arose, or it made a good story, but Dad also rode when he was young and while he was doing his National Service in Egypt, and his great-grandparents had their own pack of foxhounds in Yorkshire. He's always been into racing and these days he'll be up every day at Dan's to watch the first lot, armed with his copy of the *Racing Post*.

I decided very early on that I was going to be a jump jockey. I'd get the day off school every year for Gold Cup Day at Cheltenham. Grandad Brindley, Mum's father, took me, and of course my dad, who would put me up on his shoulders so I could see the action over the heads of the crowd. I've been every year to the Cheltenham Festival and the Gold Cup; these days it's to support my sons, Harry, who did become a jump jockey, and Dan the National Hunt trainer. I can safely say we're a horsey family!

My schooling began at Coventry Preparatory School, where it was pretty obvious from the start that I wasn't at all academic but very good at winning in sport. I had a keenly developed taste for winning by then and was always the first back from cross-country runs. The school's motto was *Confide Recte Agens* – 'Have the confidence to do what is right' – and winning was right for me. I was, however, sometimes spotted getting on the bus, but in those days it was all about winning, not how you did it.

One day, Mr Phipps, the headmaster, called my dad in to complain that I didn't train hard enough or put enough into it. But come Sports Day I'd win and one year I won five cups, so Dad's retort to this was that my effort went into winning when it mattered, which was what counted. Just do it on the day, that's what I thought. The school merged with King Henry VIII Junior School in 2008, so there's a chance my 100-yard sprint record still stands.

When I was six we moved from The Cedars in Exhall to Holly

Lodge in Berkswell, a spacious red-brick Victorian house with 24 acres of land and a huge garden. I was in heaven! So was Oxo, who had a field at the bottom of the garden and a stable up near the house. Oxo and I jumped everything we could, including the privet hedges in the garden, and bombed round the fields. It was great. When we got back from Cheltenham races I'd rush to go and tack up Oxo. I'd hike my stirrups up short and race him all around the place jumping everything we came across. Every time I went over the privet hedge into the garden Mum would yell out of the kitchen window, 'You're going to hurt yourself!' but I never took any notice, I just raced on.

My parents would take me to gymkhanas and shows every weekend and I'd meet Stuart Crutchlow at Exhall and Bedworth. Stuart was a few years older than me and just as pony mad. His parents owned the bakery in Bedworth and lived a mile down the road, so the two of us became inseparable. When we moved to Holly Lodge, Stuart would bring his pony and come and stay or I'd take Oxo to stay at his during the school holidays, plus we'd see each other at gymkhanas. Stuart was as good at getting into scrapes as I was. Whether it was the first time we met or another year I don't remember, but I do remember us wandering off to climb trees between classes. We decided to try to cross a stream by climbing some overhanging branches. The inevitable happened and the bough broke, dropping us into the freezing cold stream. We emerged soaking wet from head to jodhpur boots and received a proper telling off from both sets of parents. My parents were never a pushover; you couldn't get away with stuff, although I did lead them a bit of a dance.

When I was seven years old, my parents took me to the Horse of the Year Show at Wembley. It was the year they had a parade of Grand National winners. I vividly remember Dad took me to the stables and he asked the lad if I could have a sit on Nicolaus Silver.

The lad took me into the stable and put me up on the striking grey Irish horse that had won the 1961 Grand National. It made my day.

I never used to go inside at Wembley to watch the classes; I would be outside watching David Broome and Harvey Smith riding on the black ash warm-up arena. They were my childhood showjumping heroes, but it never occurred to me that I would be going there jumping one day myself – I wanted to be a steeple-chase jockey. Pat Taaffe, Arkle's jockey, and Terry Biddlecombe, who was champion jockey three times in the sixties and had posted 900 winners when he retired from riding in 1974, they were my jockey heroes.

Arkle was my horse hero and I saw him win all three of his Gold Cups in 1964, 1965 and 1966. I thought 'Himself', as he was known, was the most fantastic horse I had ever seen. Later in 1966 I was devastated when Arkle fractured his pedal bone while racing in the King George at Kempton Park; he struck a guard rail while jumping an open ditch but still went on to finish second. I sent him a get-well card and a box of sugar lumps and I was thrilled when I received a letter and a photograph from his owner, Anne, Duchess of Westminster, thanking me for the sugar lumps. They were his favourite. When she visited him at the yard of his trainer Tom Dreaper he would come galloping across the field for his sugar or, if he was in, would bang on the stable door. Arkle recovered but never ran again and he became her hack until he was put down in 1970 at the relatively young age of thirteen. In later years I have fond memories of seeing her at the races and reminding her I was that little boy she was so kind to write back to. She must have written a lot of letters as Arkle was a national hero. She was one of the nicest ladies you could ever want to meet and enjoyed her racing until she died in 2003 at the age of eighty-eight.

Oxo and I had won pretty much everything we could in classes for ponies of his height – just 11.2 hands, which is about 113 cm in today's currency! Moving to a new area opened out our choice of shows and we hit some new ones: Crackley, Tile Hill, Keresley and Kenilworth. Towards the end of one afternoon at Kenilworth, Oxo and I had pretty much cleaned up in the classes for smaller ponies so we decided to have a go in the open classes. They had much better prize money as well! Oxo was lining up alongside rangy thoroughbred-type 14.2s ridden by much older boys and I was trying to elbow my way into pole position when somebody in the crowd shouted, 'Give the little 'un a chance!' to which someone else answered, 'Nah, hold that little bugger back!! I've seen him at Exhall and Bedworth!'

Inevitably the time came when I outgrew Oxo. And when my sister Sally, then five, decided she wanted to learn to ride, she seemed the obvious heiress. One day we were in the garden playing together and I put her up on Oxo. I led them round the garden then decided to let Oxo go. I hadn't bargained on the privet hedge, about three feet high, which Oxo and I always jumped. Well, as I let Oxo go he spotted that privet hedge. Off he trotted and over he went. Poor Sally didn't go over but hit the floor as he took off. She got up and fled into the house crying her eyes out. She never got on a horse again, so I was responsible for ending her riding career before it had begun. I don't think Mum was too pleased.

That little bay pony was amazing, he used to jump anything, and he'd jump and gymkhana all day long. The first pony I had after Oxo was a bit of a liability. He used to bomb off with me and he frightened me one day by running away and ending up on top of the muck heap. He was sent back and my parents secured a stunning black 13.2 pony called Prince Tarquin for me from Major Long.

Tarquin was my first proper jumping pony. He was about 20 cm taller than Oxo. I would set up courses in the paddock with anything I could find; oil drums were a favourite for using as jump wings in those days and I'd use 45-gallon drums and anything else that would support a pole. The rails were made up of bits of wood, telegraph poles – anything I could get my hands on. Tarquin could jump quite well so we joined the BSJA – the British Show Jumping Association which is now British Showjumping – and started going to affiliated shows. He was also good at cross-country, so we entered Hunter Trials as well. One day at Meriden show we were doing the cross-country and somehow Tarquin fell at a fence. As he got up, he must have clipped my collarbone, breaking it. After that I was lucky enough not to be injured in a riding accident again until 1999 when I shattered my collarbone in a fall at Solihull. Meriden show is long gone but Meriden Business Park, between the village and the A45, is now the home of British Showjumping.

I was doing a lot of travelling with Stuart Crutchlow who by then had a 14.2 pony called Seamus. Stuart's dad, who I called Uncle Fred, used to drive us in an old Thames Trader horsebox and we were going to a lot of affiliated shows further afield. Tarquin was doing well and winning a lot of 13.2 classes. It was with Stuart and Uncle Fred that I made my first ever trip to Hickstead in 1968 when I was only eleven years old. Stuart had qualified for the Junior Foxhunter Finals with Seamus and there were also 13.2 classes down there, so I took Tarquin. Getting to Hickstead from the Midlands was a major adventure in those days of very few motorways. There was just the M1 and a short stretch of what would become the M40, but certainly no M25 or M23 so it took about six and a half hours to get there. Arriving at Hickstead in the dark we had to unload, muck out the lorry and bed the ponies down by torchlight. We had an old gas ring for a cooker and a canister of water for washing and drinking. Uncle Fred slept on the Luton over the cab and Stuart and I had sleeping bags in the back on the straw, so it was a good job we mucked out the lorry before turning in.

Stuart finished second in the Foxhunter Finals that year and I had some good places in the 13.2 classes. I was annoyed not to be winning at that level, but a couple of years later I qualified Tarquin for the 13.2 Championship, my first ride in the main ring at Hickstead. A lad called Jonathan 'Jonny' Haynes came first with Ballyshan; I think he won the 13.2 Championship of Great Britain three years in succession. Jonny also wanted to become a jockey and after starting on the flat he turned to jump racing and had a promising career ahead of him until, at the age of twenty, he had a bad fall and broke his back. He was paralysed and confined to a wheelchair, but he pushed aside those barriers, bought a farm in Cumbria and took out a training permit. I used to see him sometimes at the Horse of the Year Show at Wembley.

School, meanwhile, continued to take second place to ponies. After Coventry Prep School I went on to Bablake Boys School, also in Coventry, which is one of the oldest schools in England and is, and was then, a fine academic school. I had to pass an entrance exam to get in. God knows how I did that. I didn't get into trouble at school but I did play truant . . . a lot. Dad used to take me to school every morning and when he'd safely driven off to go to work I would go and find a telephone, call Mum and ask her to come and fetch me because I wasn't feeling well. She fell for it every time and always used to turn up, but somehow I'd miraculously recover when I got home and manage to get out riding.

In the summer of 1971, when I was thirteen, my parents separated. Holly Lodge – paradise to Oxo, Tarquin and me – was sold. Dad bought Odnaull End Farm, still in Berkswell, which had six acres of land and stables, so my ponies and I went to live with Dad. Sally, my little sister, was only seven years old so she went to live with Mum. Sally and I are very close despite being separated when we were young. After my parents divorced the following year, Mum subsequently married Derek Jones and they had a son, Michael. Mum and Dad were still living close by after the separation and within a few years became friends again. All our lives would intertwine and still do.

When Dad and I were living on our own at Odnaull End Farm he no longer drove me to school; instead I was supposed to go on the train from Berkswell Station. We lived by the old disused railway line and I would walk down the track to the station. Sometimes, however, I would hide behind the hedge and watch until Dad went to work. Once the coast was clear, I'd dash straight back to the stables and go and ride my ponies. Dad never came home from work until after I was supposed to be back from school, so he had no idea I'd played truant until many years later. Thank heavens he never forgot anything and had to turn round on the way to work!

After a year or so Dad's partner, Janette Southall, moved into Odnaull End Farm with us. Janette was horsey too and had a thoroughbred mare that had bred a foal. Janette quite fancied the idea of the two-year-old going flat racing, so a friend of Dad's, Lol Weaver, suggested that we take it to trainer David Nicholson, who was known as 'the Duke' and was based at Condicote in the Cotswolds. The two-year-old duly went into training and ran on the flat at Doncaster. It was useless. But Dad asked David to look out for another horse for him to buy. David found Christmas Comet, who went on to win a couple of races over hurdles for Dad. In the meantime, going over to David Nicholson's strengthened my resolve to become a jockey, and when I got the chance to occasionally ride out I was all the more convinced that was the life for me.

My course-designing skills were greatly helped by our handyman, who would cut holes in the hedge and build fences for me to jump the ponies over. I had post and rails, ditches toward, ditches behind, the lot. What an asset he was!

My friend Greg Parsons lived just up the lane in Balsall Common and we were always coming up with some new moneymaking scheme to supplement our pocket money. We decided to use the two biggest chicken sheds for rearing cockerels and bought a load from market to get them fat for Christmas. I was less soft-centred when it came to dispatching them and Greg and I did it quickly and painlessly. Plucking and dressing was another matter. Apologies to all those customers who ended up with feathers in their Christmas dinner!

In the winter I used to go to indoor shows at Balsall Common Equestrian Centre where I met the Clawsons and was offered the ride on three 13.2 ponies: a roan called Kimberley Rook, a grey pony called Bullet and a coloured pony called Hanky Panky. I had to get myself over to their place at Leire in Leicestershire, about thirty miles away. Stuart was seventeen by then and had his driving licence, so drove me over in the evenings to ride the ponies. I took Prince Tarquin too when we went to shows with the Clawsons, so I had a string of four ponies to ride – even more chances to add to my red rosette collection.

I made a lot of friends at Balsall Common. There was Lizzie Harris who had a 14.2 pony called Just William. Dad and Janette became friendly with Lizzie's parents and we used to spend a lot of time at each other's houses. Lizzie eventually got married, had two children and moved to California. I called in to see her at her home on Malibu Beach one time on my way back from New Zealand. Then there was Johnny Wrathall, who was, like Stuart, a few years older than me. Me, Stuart and Johnny became like the three musketeers and those two would get me into all kinds of scrapes. I understand why my headmaster used to write on my school report: 'Nick is easily led.' I was.

Johnny's family lived about ten miles away from the Clawsons. His dad, John, was a farmer and a good producer of young horses, including Pennwood Forgemill, who had become a household name. John took 'Forgie' to Grade A for owner Fred Harthill before Paddy McMahon took over the ride. They won lots, including the 1973 European Championships, until Paddy set up on his own and Fred Hartill didn't want to let the horse leave home. Fred gave the ride to Geoff Glazzard, who rode his novice string, and 'Forgie' made Geoff's career.

Stuart and I used to drive over to Johnny's on a Friday night. They always had a yard full of ponies and horses, and Saturday morning we used to help milk the cows and then we would go hunting with the Pytchley. Johnny's dad used to wake us up at six o'clock in the morning with the strongest tea I have ever tasted; it was like drinking black tar. On a Saturday night Johnny, Stuart and I would go over to the Clawsons and go out. I was only thirteen, they were four years older. Enough said!

Prince Tarquin was sold when I moved out of 13.2s at the age of fourteen. Tarquin was a great pony for me but the inevitable happened and I outgrew him. He went to Scotland when James Aird bought him for one of his children who had come out of 12.2 classes. Tarquin stayed in the family as a succession of brothers and sisters rode him. He was a champion in Scotland and, as far as I know, he stayed with the Airds for the rest of his life.

Uncle Fred, Stuart's dad, told my dad about a nice pony whose girl rider wasn't getting on that well with it. We went to see the pony, Calibas, at Balsall Common, where I tried it out in a class and jumped double clear. With Dad's approval, Uncle Fred set about buying Calibas. Louise Spencer was the rider and Uncle Fred knew the family. He approached Louise's dad and asked would he sell Calibas. Mr Spencer replied that he would, 'as long as I get my money back'. He didn't name a price. Uncle Fred told Dad to write a cheque for £400 to secure the pony, and dropped it off at Spencer's. The deal was done and when Mr Spencer asked Uncle Fred how he knew how much he had paid for the pony, Uncle Fred told him: 'I know everything sold in this area and for how much!'

We were travelling to shows more and I got the ride on a good pony, a 14.2 piebald called On The Move, when his usual rider Nigel Wood broke his leg. We went off to Hickstead four times a year which was *the* place to go. Stuart and Johnny had both graduated to horses by now and were good riders. Ken Clawson was training me and was strict with it. On a couple of occasions when I'd gone badly in a class he locked me in the caravan, but with hindsight that was probably less due to my performance than to stop me hooking off to the pub with Stuart and Johnny, which I managed by escaping out of the window. We three musketeers used to go up the Castle Inn and, because I was under age I would get thrown out every night by Terry Sherman, the landlord. He would see me out of the front door and I would go straight round and come in the back door, burying myself in the thick of the crowd so he couldn't spot me. It was always busy. Afterwards we'd go back to the horsebox park and continue the party. I was growing up.

Going to shows with the Clawsons, Stuart and Johnny, meant missing school – a lot of it. The headmaster, Mr Burroughs, is credited with bringing 'a more liberal and relaxed atmosphere' to the school. He didn't mean it to be that liberal and relaxed, so he called my parents in to tell them my mind was too much on ponies and not enough on school work. It didn't make any difference. I couldn't wait to turn fifteen so I could leave school and become a jump jockey, but that plan was going to change, thanks mainly to Calibas.

3

The Gopher

Calibas and I were not seeing eye to eye. There wasn't one specific thing he'd do, rather he'd just express his own opinion by having a fence down, running out, rushing his fences, the odd refusal. And I couldn't hold him. Other than that, everything was fine!

Lol Weaver, who'd introduced Dad to David Nicholson and, incidentally, was Chief Steward at the Horse of the Year Show and Olympia for many years, suggested that Dad took Calibas and me over to some friends of his, Ted and Liz Edgar. Liz, who is David Broome's younger sister, and Ted were both professional showjumpers, very well known, and Lol thought they could put me and Calibas on the right track.

So we went off to their yard, the Everest Stud at Leek Wootton. Ted was away but Liz gave me a lesson, putting me right on what I was doing wrong, but also putting me right on Calibas. He simply wasn't up to the job. Apparently, that evening when Ted got home he asked Liz how 'that kid' had got on with his pony and she had told him that the pony was useless, but she thought the kid had potential.

When Ted rang up to ask would I like to go and help them at

shows at weekends if I wasn't away jumping myself, I decided to give it a try. I wasn't all that bothered as my sights were still firmly set on becoming a jockey. And it was nothing like being at the Clawsons, where I'd picked up those extra rides; this was cleaning tack, polishing Ted's boots, holding horses, just generally helping. I wasn't there to ride.

The first show I went to with the Edgars was a two-day show. As it was at Nottingham Racecourse some way away, we stayed up there. Ted and Liz had a caravan. I was sleeping in the front of the horsebox and their groom, Fenella Power, known as Hob, was sleeping in the horsebox as well. Suddenly, in the middle of the night, the door burst open and an older lad walked in. He picked up my sleeping bag, with me still in it, and dumped me out on the grass, then he slammed the door shut and locked it. I didn't get back in until feeding time at seven o'clock the next morning. Just as well it was a summer show. I curled up in my sleeping bag and slept on the grass under the horsebox. I had no other option. It wasn't exactly an introduction, but it was my first encounter with Tim Grubb, who'd be a teammate a few years later. He was only a couple of years older than me but on that occasion seemed a lot older.

That same summer we went to the Bath and West Show at Shepton Mallet; again I was just helping. I was everybody's gopher; even the grooms treated me as their gopher. One lunchtime in the caravan, Ted was having his lunch and he said, 'Pass me the salad cream.' I said, 'We haven't got any salad cream.' So he told me, 'Well, go and get some off Banky, next door.' 'Banky' was Trevor Banks, a big owner and dealer and a big man in every way. I was totally intimidated by the idea of knocking on the door of this big, bluff Yorkshireman's caravan and asking for salad cream, but I was equally intimidated by the idea of telling Ted I wouldn't go.

The Gopher

I knocked on the door in trepidation and this voice growled 'Come in'. As I crept in, Banky snarled, 'What d'yer want?' I asked had he got any salad cream and he replied: 'Aye and it's got "please" written on the fucking label!' Oh shit, I had been that intimidated I'd forgotten to say please.

Over the following six months I helped at the Edgars on the weekends when I wasn't riding myself and gradually I was given the odd horse to walk round the collecting ring at shows. Then there was a breakthrough and Ted sent me a horse to ride, The Red Baron, who was brought over by Australian rider John Fahey. Ted said I could keep him at home and ride him in a few Young Riders Classes, which I did. He was a nice horse; not too careful but not difficult to ride. Ted then sent me a dun horse called Timmie on which Liz had competed quite successfully. He was a good horse for me at that time. Dad still took me to local shows and on the weekends I wasn't competing I 'gophered' for the Edgars; helping, leading horses up, cleaning tack, that sort of thing, including at the Horse of the Year Show.

The winter that I celebrated my fifteenth birthday, Ted and Liz were going to a show in Switzerland at Davos where the jumping was on snow. It was the first time I had been abroad, I had my first passport and I was very excited to be travelling with one of my childhood heroes, David Broome.

We set off in the horsebox to Davos taking Everest Make Do and Boomerang for Liz, with Everest Peak and Snaffles for Ted. David was riding Manhattan and Ballywillwill. Pam and Lionel Dunning made up the team. We arrived to cold I'd never before experienced in my life. The horses were stabled in an indoor school in standing stalls made of poles slung together with rope. You wouldn't get that these days. Outside, the air froze the hairs in your nose and made you gasp for breath. I was glad I'd had a shower before I left home because I wouldn't have another until

I got back. It was too cold to even think of washing. All I did was put more clothes on each day.

The diesel engine in the horsebox froze solid and Ted had to get a mechanic out with a pair of heating bellows to thaw it out. When it got started we left it running for four days and four nights until it was time to come home. The grooms and I were sleeping in the lorry and my thought was please don't let's have a repeat of Nottingham Show as I'd have ended up frozen. But I was OK, I was sharing with a lad who wasn't that way inclined.

To jump on snow, the horses had to have four studs in each hoof and the back stud was a two-inch long spike. Guess what my job was? Yep, you got it. I was up at five o'clock every morning studding six horses up, so that's four studs, four feet, six horses, total ninety-six studs. Classes started at eight o'clock in the morning, before the sun came up and melted the snow, and the last class was over by three in the afternoon. And then it was back to the studs, taking them all out again. I now consider that to have been my apprenticeship in studding, or should I say putting in and removing studs.

Well, my studding must have been up to scratch because Ted and Liz asked if I would like to go and work for them when I left school. Anything rather than school, I thought, and it would do until I could get myself over to David Nicholson's and start being a jockey.

First, I had to go and see the headmaster. This was the last visit and his words were: 'As you have missed so much school with shows, I think it is better that you pursue your outdoor activities rather than continue your academic career, if that's what you want.' I thought, That's good enough for me. So I left school at the end of the Easter term in 1972 without having sat a single O level. What I did not realise was that this was to be the start of twelve years' hard labour.

The Gopher

My first wage packet was £7 per week. Dad had to drive me to work at the Edgars' every day, and that was seven days a week. It was years before I discovered there were only five working days in a week, I always thought there were seven (and, by the way, I still think there are seven).

I would arrive at seven o'clock; it was like being in the army, everything happened by the clock and everything had to be clock-work. Seven o'clock feeding and mucking out the straw beds, every horse had one clean bale of straw every morning. There were eighteen stables and they had to be finished by eight o'clock. Feeding, mucking out, bedding down, buckets washed, all done by then. We had three horses each to do. The muckheap was stacked properly, the barrow contents thrown up the heap and the layers squared off so when it got big it looked like a staircase, definitely not a heap. Each stable had high banks of straw around the walls and the floor straw tossed and fluffed, water buckets filled, hay nets filled – good old-fashioned stuff. Neat; I always have liked neatness.

In December of that first winter at the Edgars' I turned sixteen. I was now old enough to legally ride a moped and that would save Dad driving me back and forth every day, so we went to Halfords and bought one. It was yellow and I was very proud of it. The first thing I did was ride over to Mum's to show her. She inspected the moped and then gave me the mothers' talk about being careful and watching what I was doing, and as I drove away, I turned around to wave goodbye to her and ran smack into a tree, tipped the moped up and fell off.

Come rain, hail or snow I always managed to get to work on that moped. But if I was even five minutes late Ted would greet me with, 'Good afternoon, having a half day, are we?' and walk off. The problem was that, if it was raining, it took me five minutes to get all my waterproof gear on in the morning so I was often five minutes late. Should have got up five minutes earlier, I suppose. At seventeen I got a car licence and my first car, a Ford Escort. I didn't have to get wet any more.

The horses had to be done in time for breakfast, no question. In the house at eight o'clock sharp, and if I was a minute or two late Ted would deliver one of his famous bollockings, but Liz always made sure I got my breakfast. Breakfast was a bowl of cornflakes and a piece of toast with marmalade, and the tea was much better than Mr Wrathall's black tar! I was still very much the gopher and I'd have to clean Ted's boots and fetch his Woodbines. I can remember that shout: 'Oi, kid, fags. Go and fetch my fags.' And off I would go to fetch his horrible Woodbines. If ever the drains were blocked in the stables, Ted would shout, 'Where's that kid?' and I would have to roll up my sleeves and put my arm down the drain.

Ted always referred to me as 'that kid'. He gave me the dirtiest, messiest jobs on the yard, jobs that the grooms wouldn't have done. I like things neat and tidy – very – and I wonder if having to do all those revolting jobs reinforced that trait in me. Liz had a big peacekeeping role; she kept the whole thing going and deserves a medal as big as a dustbin lid. The only reason I stayed there so long was that Liz was so good to me. It was great that she was in the ring at Royal Windsor when Big Star and I retired.

At 8.45 it was everybody out back on the yard tacking up and riding. I was still riding Timmie but The Red Baron had disappeared somewhere; probably sold, as John Fahey had sold his Munich Olympic hopeful Warwick to Tony Newbury before heading home to Australia.

In those days the Edgars had a small indoor school with a flat roof approximately 12 feet high, 80 feet long, and maybe 40 feet wide. The surface was dirt and shavings. It was very small and if there were three or four of us in there riding it was a bit like a fairground wall of death. Mostly we worked the horses outside on the grass on a field with a very sandy surface that drained well. We only rode indoors when it rained.

The horses had a set but varied routine. Monday was a rest day and they went out in the paddocks. Tuesday would be hacking, riding round Ted's farm of around 350 acres. Wednesday was flat work and fitness work, and then on Thursday they had a jump. Friday we were off to a show for the weekend. It is a system that I still use. The great thing about being there was that the discipline and tidiness instilled in me by Ted has stood me in good stead throughout my life.

Monday may have been a rest day for the horses but it was a bad day for me. The first bit was all right, apart from missing breakfast. My first job on Monday morning was to tack up two horses and Ted and I would ride around the farm and round up all the sheep. We would put them in a pen and Ted's farm manager, Fred Wilson, who was there for years, would pull out the lambs that were ready for market. The lambs would be loaded into the lorry and Fred would take them off to Rugby market with me helping. Going to the market was like having a few hours off; as soon as we arrived, we would have a cup of coffee as we'd had no breakfast.

We would be back at the yard by eleven when my day went downhill. Every Monday morning without fail my job was to wash the horseboxes. They had to be immaculate; washed inside, outside, polished and hoovered. I also had to wash Ted's car, a red Mercedes coupé. Washing the car was OK, but I hated hoovering those hairy car seats where their three Corgis had been sitting. The dogs would sit on the rear parcel shelf and rub their noses on the back window, so every week I had to clean the glass. Why Ted didn't just have one of those toy dogs that nod their heads in the back window, I don't know. At least that wouldn't have made such a mess. And then I had to hoover the pile of cigarette ash up from the past week because Ted refused to use the ashtray. He used to flick it on the carpet on the driver's side. That was why I didn't like Mondays. Mind you, I got to like those Corgis because they were a great early warning system. Whenever Ted was coming down the yard, those dogs would start barking so I knew it was time to get to my feet and start looking busy.

4

Maybe a Showjumper?

My first team call-up and my first trip abroad to compete was in 1973. I'd been selected for the junior team at Dublin Horse Show with a horse of Ted's called Everest Himself, a black Irish-bred gelding. One of my teammates was Gary Widdowson, who was riding a horse called Jeremy. We became friends instantly. Gary and I went for a night out and we stayed out way too late. The next morning we got a summons from our chef d'equipe, Tinka Taylor, to 'come to my room NOW!' We got a serious talking to for not taking it all seriously; in fact, we nearly got banned.

It's ironic, to look back to the start of my career then to the end when Gary's was the last horse I ever rode. Himself didn't come home as Eddie Macken bought him. Himself wasn't so easy and I remember Eddie telling Ted a few years later: 'You forgot to send me the handbook when you sold me that horse!' Eddie would go on to become a legend in the jumping world with his star horse Boomerang.

Ted had spotted a horse called Maybe in the collecting ring at Southport Flower Show. Harvey Smith and the Irish rider Paul

Darragh were trying it. Harvey allegedly said: 'It'll never be a jumper as long as it's got a hole up its arse' and didn't buy it. Neither did Paul Darragh. Ted did. Maybe was Irish bred, by a stallion called Love and Marriage out of an Irish draught mare. He wasn't the easiest of horses, he had a nappy streak in him, and Ted always said he paid £500 for his jump and £1,500 for his nap, but Maybe was to be my first great horse. He would put me on the road.

It wasn't an easy road and we used to have some fun and games with his napping. Some days he would go and some he just wouldn't. I remember one time going to Shrewsbury Flower Show – yes there were quite a few flower shows with showjumping back then – I rode into the ring and went to go through the start . . . and that was it. Maybe glued himself to the floor. He just stood there, wouldn't go forwards, backwards, nothing. I had to get off and lead him out.

Ted decided Maybe should go hunting to get him going and so Maybe became Ted's hunter during the week and my showjumper at the weekends. That routine kept the horse fresh and got him going, although we still had the occasional hiccup at shows. He was a strange one, either brilliant or immovable, but I was starting to win those red rosettes again, as I had back in the Oxo days, and it got me thinking that maybe showjumping wouldn't be such a bad job after all. Ted was keen for me to give up the idea of being a jockey and stay with showjumping. The idea was more appealing now that I was winning.

Another horse that really taught me to ride was Tycoon, an American-bred palomino. If I wasn't right at a fence, he would stop and fire me off head first. Ted decided we would take a team to the first-ever Team Chase. Douglas Bunn, 'the Master of Hickstead', was also a master of invention and he came up with the idea over lunch with a leading BBC Sports producer of the day, Alan Mouncer. He invited twenty teams of four riders to take part over a mile and a half course of around thirty fences. It was pretty fearsome; the second fence was a ten-foot drop hedge and there were five-foot solid rails in and out of the railway crossing. It was televised live that Good Friday in 1974 and was for years until the Hickstead meeting changed dates. Dougie had the idea that Team Chasing would catch on and it did.

Ted rode Maybe, Bob Ellis (who went on to become the course-builder) rode Sweet Charity, I took Tycoon, and Rowland Fernyhough was on a point-to-pointer that looked a serious contender. The first three home would count for the time. Ted set off strongly until Maybe knocked himself and had to be pulled up. I couldn't hold one side of Tycoon and was flying blind as I couldn't remember the course, while Rowland wasn't much help as he'd already flown for home. The last thing I remember was Tycoon putting both his front feet in a ditch in front of a fence, the pair of us turning a somersault and ending up out cold. Someone pulled me out from underneath Tycoon. I woke up in the ambulance tent next to Ray Howe, who'd broken his collarbone, then was taken to Cuckfield General Hospital where I spent four days under observation. It was the first of the very few 'holidays' I had while at the Edgars and I was grateful for visits from Carol Newton, who later married the former jump jockey turned race-starter Steve Taylor. Their son James was a popular member of the England cricket squad until diagnosis of a serious heart condition forced his retirement. I've never forgotten Carol brightening up my days in Cuckfield General.

Once I was up and about and Maybe had recovered from his injury, things started to look up. Maybe won a few Young Riders qualifiers and in that year I made my championship team debut when we were selected for the Junior European Championships in Lucerne, Switzerland. My teammates were Cheryl Walker riding Wishbone, Lynne Chapman on Mandalay Lass and Debbie Johnsey riding Assam. It was a good start to my team career: we won the silver. Two years later, Debbie became the youngest showjumper to compete at an Olympic Games and narrowly missed out on a medal in Montreal, finishing fourth with Moxy. Later she married the footballer Gary Plumley and I used to see her a lot when my boys and her kids were riding ponies.

The following year Maybe and I were again selected to represent Great Britain on the team for the Junior European Championships at Dornbirn in Austria's alpine Rhine valley. My teammates were John Brown riding Paddy Connelly, Marion Howard on Top Rank, Sally Mapleson with Waterbrook and Vicky Gascoine with Extra Special. I was really looking forward to it.

Then two days before we were due to leave there was a problem. I was competing Maybe at the Royal Show, Stoneleigh, when he reverted to his old bad habits and flatly refused to go through the start. I had to get off and, with a very red face, lead him out of the ring.

A new horse with a hogged mane had arrived from Belgium. His name was O.K. Ted told Gerald Barnes, Chairman of the Selectors at the time, that Maybe wouldn't be going to Dornbirn but I could take another horse, O.K.; Gerald Barnes wasn't too happy, but it was too late to change the team and, besides, Gerald wasn't about to argue with Ted.

I was disappointed not to be taking Maybe as I knew it would be a real work of art to try and get O.K. to win a European Championship. He wouldn't have been selected on form; he had only won a couple of speed classes and he wasn't the most careful of horses.

Maybe a Showjumper?

We set off to Dornbirn with all five horses in Sally Mapleson's horsebox, and all five of us young riders in there as well. It was bedlam. I didn't have a groom in those days, I had to do my horses myself at shows, so the one positive point in his favour was that I didn't have to plait O.K. I arrived at the show convinced that my best chance of a medal was eating grass in a Warwickshire paddock.

It turned out that O.K. liked the warm August weather. If he thought he was on holiday it was obviously the active type he liked as he was in a great mood and suddenly found his form. For some reason in those days the individual came before the teams and on competition day it was very hot. I got up early in the morning to work O.K. and give him a few jumps to sharpen him up. There were sixty-seven starters in the individual and instead of kicking the rails out as usual, O.K. tapped his way around but left the poles up. I was astonished! A third of the field jumped clear and in the second round O.K. jumped clear for me again. I was now feeling a bit more confident.

There were nine of us through to the jump-off. Italian Guido Dominici produced the first clear round, then John Brown followed and tore round the course to take 6.7 seconds off Guido's time. I was last to go and O.K. jumped the round of his life, fast and clear. We won the gold! O.K. and I were European Champions! It was an amazing achievement for an average horse – and it wouldn't be the last time a horse would surprise me.

On the Sunday in the team competition, O.K. again jumped clear in the first round. The second round did not start for three hours, by which time the weather had broken. It was pouring with rain, lightning was flashing around the mountaintops and the grass football pitch of an arena was cutting up badly. O.K. didn't like this weather one bit and had two down, which was more like his usual form. Marion and Top Rank were clear and four, Vicky had four and clear, and John Brown had four and four. Mine was the discard score in the second round.

The gold medal went to four girls from Belgium: Veronique Vastapane (later Whitaker, she was with Michael for sixteen years); Daniella de Bruycker, who had won the individual silver; Hilde Goris (who I see a lot of as I buy horses from her husband Emile Hendrix); and Marlene Marteens. We were equal second with the Germans and the Polish team, who had shown remarkable form. I didn't hear of Marion again but John Brown is now based in Florida, Sally came to my post-Olympic party and Vicky I see around as her nephew Jake Saywell is a very promising rider.

Back on the home circuit, we did the rounds of qualifiers for the Butlins Championships: Skegness, Bognor Regis, Clacton, Filey, Pwllheli, Minehead – day-trips to good old British seaside resorts and a far cry from today's trips to Cannes, Estoril and Monaco. The rings were always tiny and getting in and out was invariably down narrow roads, but those were good shows and good fun. We'd get our lunch in the canteen with the holidaymakers, who'd all turn out to watch – along with stars like Eamonn Andrews and Diana Dors. It was real Hi-de-Hi!

Maybe had qualified for the Grade C final, the Whitbread Young Riders and the Butlins Championship at the Horse of the Year Show, Wembley, and I was so excited to be riding there. Whether I'd got a bit cocky as Junior European Champion, I don't know, but I had decided I was going to make an impact. Monday night was Butlins Gala Night. It was a big charity night in aid of the Army Benevolent Fund (now ABF, The Soldiers' Charity), foreign riders were invited to take part and it was televised live on BBC.

It was a dream come true when Maybe jumped clear in the first round, my first time in the Wembley arena. In the jump-off, some fella called Alwin Schockemöhle went into the lead riding a big grey mare called Santa Monica. I didn't see him go as we were warming up. Ted told me to go for a slow clear as it was my first time, Maybe was a young horse and I would end up fourth or fifth. Yeah right, I thought as we went into the arena and the famous red curtains closed behind us. Bollocks to that! If I win I'll be a hero – and who the hell's Alwin Schockemöhle?

I set off at a fair clip, totally ignoring Ted's orders. Maybe jumped the first few fences. We were clear and flying into the last line. I'd learn later this was a typical Alan Ball course. This was a triple bar off the corner, four strides to a double, vertical in, one stride, then an oxer out. All I had to do was jump it. I turned Maybe to the triple bar on two strides and I missed, and I mean really missed the stride. We took off a whole stride too early and jumped straight into the middle of the triple bar. Instead of taking a pull before the double I kicked on for four strides which were way too long by then, so we took off early. We crashed the vertical and crashed the final oxer. That was that over.

As we headed out of the arena I looked back at that line. Not only were all the poles on the floor but most of the wings. We'd made the impact of a demolition squad.

Over all the years Alan Ball built courses at Wembley he only ever built two final lines, and ever since I've trained my horses to jump triple bar, four strides, vertical, one stride, oxer. Alan built the course for the 1988 Seoul Olympics and mentored Bob Ellis, who took on his mantle. Alan died in 2016, just a couple of days after Big Star and I won gold in Rio.

Alwin Schockemöhle won that class, on Santa Monica, two years running and he won the Butlins Top Score on Rex the Robber that year. He'd won both the previous year on different horses. He was also the European Champion, had two Olympic medals under his belt, and would win the individual gold the following year in Munich. I think it was safe to say he was rather well known and had a bit more experience than me, something Ted was about to make abundantly clear.

Ted Edgar dragged me off Maybe and, waving his finger in my face, shouted, 'You stupid little fucker, who do you think you are?' and more. The BBC camera at the back of the collecting ring filmed the whole tirade and, every night for the rest of the show, the BBC programme would open with that clip, thankfully without the commentary. It wouldn't be my last serious bollocking from Ted.

For the rest of the show I kept a low profile, keeping my head down and getting on with my job, but things improved. I was still ambitious but a lot more careful. Maybe and I won the Grade C Final and the following day won the Whitbread Young Riders Championship. Two more red rosettes and I'd got my confidence back. Ted was pleased, but he never really forgave me for making such a Horlicks of that first night through not listening to him. Thanks to Maybe, however, it was less of a maybe and more of a dead cert that I would stay in showjumping.

It was when Ted had a big break in 1977 that I got my big break. Ted had broken his knee and had the kneecap wired together. The first thing he did when he came home with his leg in plaster from ankle to thigh was get me to help him cut the plaster off so he could get in the bath. When he'd finished his bath he just bandaged it back on. Then when he started to heal, Ted thought that now he was walking about a bit he might as well go down the field on his motorbike to get the sheep in. He fell off the bike going through the gate and broke his knee again. Ted was off riding for a long time.

Ted had decided when the first break happened that I would ride his string of horses. With Lastic, Orchid, Jumbo, Louisianna and a few other good youngsters, together with Maybe and O.K., I had as good a string as anyone in the country at that time. We were winning every week on the county show circuit. The county shows were great fun back in the seventies. Everybody stayed, it was like a holiday campsite, and there were always barbeques and parties in the stockmen's tent with all the farmers.

The Bath and West was always the best for after-hours entertainment. They had a big stockmen's tent there and they would have a band on every evening. There would be beer everywhere, farmers in their wellies and a few birds about. One time there was a hot-dog stand next to the little stream that ran through the showground. One of the lads pulled a bird who showed donkeys. They went off behind the hot-dog van to do whatever came natural to them and while they were at it the hot-dog van packed up and drove off, leaving him with his backside going up and down like a fiddler's elbow in full view and everyone cheering him on!

Meanwhile Ted, unable to ride, was keeping a closer eye on my training. Some of his methods were far from orthodox. I was riding Maybe in the Young Riders class at Burley-on-the-Hill one time and in the collecting ring Ted kept telling me I wasn't sitting forward enough over my fences. We kept jumping the practice fence, but Ted wasn't satisfied with my position. He shouted for me to go over to him. Everyone always knew what Ted was up to when they heard him shouting. He called me over, got hold of my tie and tied it to Maybe's martingale saying: 'That'll stop you sitting back.' Off I went with my nose practically on Maybe's neck, to jump the practice fence. Fortunately, I didn't have a fall at the practice fence and Ted undid the tie before I went into the ring. I did get his point though. My style's always been forward over my fences.

Since winning the Junior European Championships, O.K. had

shown flashes of brilliance every now and then. He had stopped kicking rails out all the time, and water jumps were now his favourite thing to play with. He kept paddling in them instead of jumping them.

The major championship at the Great Yorkshire Show is called the Cock O'the North. The big class was on the Thursday and for the previous two days O.K. had jumped into the water. I kept wondering how the hell we could clear that water, otherwise we'd have no chance. Ted had the bright idea that we would get up as soon as it was light, four o'clock in the morning, and school over the water, which is not in the rules. Along with Lol Weaver, Ted and I got up, tacked up O.K. and went down to the arena. The whole place was asleep – animals, people; it was so still you could have heard a mouse fart.

At that time of the morning the gates to the arena were locked, so I jumped in over the hedge at one end of the arena. Lol and Ted built three or four poles into a triple bar over the water so O.K. would have to jump higher over the water rather than in it. He soon got the hang of it and was jumping over the water nicely, so we finished up and I jumped back out. We were all walking back to the stables when a security guard came round the corner and saw us. We thought we were in trouble for a moment until he said: 'Can't beat an early start can you, mate?' Whew.

We all went back to bed but having been up at four then got up a bit later than normal. Ted was normally first man up on the showground every morning so everyone else guessed he must have been up earlier. In this game, everybody knows everybody else's business, so it is safe to say everyone assumed we'd been up to something. We walked the course for the Cock O'the North – there is a famous double of walls which is a characteristic of the course. They looked fearsome. Getting up early worked as we cleared the water, but O.K. didn't clear anything else.

Maybe a Showjumper?

Later that same year, I returned to Austria for the first time since winning the Junior European Championships with Lastic and Maybe. This time we headed to Laxenburg south of Vienna, a town famous for its castles. I was there on my first Senior Nations Cup team. Becoming a jump jockey was no longer part of the plan. I was a showjumper.

5

For the High Jump

The British High Jump record had stood for forty-one years. It was set by British rider Donald Beard riding Swank in 1937 at Olympia. Don and Swank had jumped a fence measured at 7' 6¼" (2.28m). Apparently, some felt it was a bit of an injustice and he should have been given the world record as the fence could have measured 7' 8". I don't know how they measured things back in 1937 but the record had been set and in 1978 there was to be an attempt to break it, again at Olympia.

The Puissance was the warm-up for the high-jump attempt and I just happened to win it on Lastic. There were about ten of us trying for the record. It was late in the evening, the arena was packed. The high-jump fence was built on a sloping wing so from take-off to the top rail it was quite wide. The bottom part of the fence was solid with heavy poles to the top. The whole thing was about eighteen feet wide and very imposing. Lastic wasn't a big horse and this looked more daunting than the puissance wall. It was built exactly in the same way, the same fence design that Don Beard and Swank had jumped to establish the record.

It started at 6' 6" and each time we jumped we cleared it, up to about 7' 3". Then it came to the record-breaking height and Lastic had had enough. Out in the collecting ring Ted put up a big vertical, a single rail with a ground line. It was about 5' 6" or 8", so not as big as Lastic had been jumping, but with all that air between the ground and the rail Lastic saw the easy way out and just ducked underneath it, leaving the rail balanced perilously on my arms. That was pretty dangerous. I could have broken both my arms with them hitting that rail at speed, but each time we tried again, each time he ran under that rail. This preparation clearly wasn't working; in fact it was hopeless. Eventually, Ted put the fence down low enough that Lastic couldn't run under it. Over it he jumped and into the arena we went.

That obstacle in the ring was now standing at 7' 7⁵/₁₆". I rode Lastic in thinking there was absolutely no way we were going to be able to jump it. As I came down for the first attempt I got a bit of pace up, plenty of leg on and holding him together. He couldn't run out as there were huge wings but I didn't want to let him stop. Down we went and Lastic took off too early. He jumped straight into the middle of the fence, legs everywhere. He broke two poles but somehow he managed to land on all four legs. Thank God for that, I thought, I can get out of here now.

I'd had enough, Lastic'd had enough. I walked him back towards the gate. Harvey Smith and David Broome were standing there and they both said I'd better come out as I was going to kill myself. Ted wasn't having any of it. He was there, leaning on the gate, and wouldn't open it. 'Don't take any notice of them pair,' he said. 'Get back in that ring and jump it.'

There was no arguing with Ted, otherwise I would have been facing another public bollocking, so I started to canter up the side of the ring. I knew I needed a better stride this time and as I rode Lastic down to the fence we hit the take-off point just right. He hesitated a bit on take-off – hardly surprising when he'd crashed through the same obstacle only minutes before – but he bravely left the floor. He cleared it in front but he just clipped it with a hind leg to dislodge the top pole.

Off we headed towards the gate. This was surely enough. Not for Ted it wasn't. There he was, leaning on the gate again. He said, 'Get back in there and get it jumped. You're riding like a fairy.' There was no way out, I would just have to jump the damn thing. There was only one more attempt and either way, that would be that and we could get out of that arena. Not even Ted could make me stay.

But first we had to face that obstacle again. I turned my stick upside down and gave Lastic a refresher on his backside; we got up a rhythm and a fair bit of pace. Whether or not God was looking after me I don't know, but we took off in the right spot. When we got airborne, and it did feel like that, I remember looking down in mid-air, at the top of the fence, to see if everything was still intact. Lastic did rub the top rail behind but it stayed in place, it didn't fall.

The whole arena erupted. As I left the arena on that brave horse Lastic the audience got to their feet and gave us a standing ovation. That was a terrific feeling. This was the first big stepping stone in my career as a showjumper. Breaking the high-jump record made my name back then. In we went to the prize-giving ceremony, Lastic with gold tinsel round his neck. Don Beard was there too. He was a legend who rode on lots of Nations Cup teams in the fifties on his horse Costa and would sometimes come along to Nations Cups with Ronnie Massarella when Ronnie was chef d'equipe of the British showjumping team. Don was awarded an honorary life membership of the BSJA for his services to showjumping in 1989 and died in 2004 aged eighty-five.

Olympia has always been the big pre-Christmas show, so this all happened not long before my twenty-first birthday. Ted was pleased, naturally, but he wasn't giving me any of the £2,500 prize money. In fact he told the newspapers that if I was lucky he'd give me a tie for Christmas!

I celebrated that night by going to Nikki Caine's twenty-first birthday party. It was at her father Michael's restaurant, Langan's Brasserie in Stratton Street, Mayfair. We've been friends since forever and Nikki came to my post-Rio celebration party. Back then I just remember the hangover I woke up with the next morning. I had to go back to Olympia and pose beside the fence for the press photographers. I felt a bit off colour, to say the least.

6

My First 'Olympics'

The Olympic Games were scheduled to take place in Moscow in July 1980. Maybe was going very well. We had every reason to be optimistic he'd be selected for the Olympic Team with me – and that was what happened.

Earlier that year, however, US President Jimmy Carter called for a boycott of the games in protest at the Soviet invasion of Afghanistan and Mrs Thatcher's government put pressure on the British Olympic Association to follow suit. The BOA voted by a large majority not to boycott Moscow, but the decision was left to individual athletes. For all the equestrian teams the big problem was that if there were to be trouble out in Russia it would be very difficult to get the horses home. The International Equestrian Federation decided to hold 'alternative Olympics'. It was completely different to the Olympic Games, but I didn't know that at the time and wouldn't for another eight years realise that Rotterdam was just another horse show. The disciplines weren't even in the same place, as dressage went to Goodwood, eventing was at Fontainebleau and showjumping went to Rotterdam.

We set off for Holland; me with Maybe, Graham Fletcher riding Preachan, John Whitaker and Ryan's Son, and Tim Grubb riding Night Murmur, an American-bred horse owned by his then wife, US showjumper Michele.

The course for the team competition was absolutely huge and by far the biggest track I had ever seen or jumped in my life. I was staggered. The chefs d'equipe, including Ronnie Massarella, weren't too happy and there were a lot of complaints. I particularly remember the combination – an oxer, one stride that was a little bit long to a vertical and then two very short strides to a triple bar. That distance of two strides was so short a lot of horses were going to the triple bar on one stride.

I was the first to go for our team, fifth to go overall. Of the four that had gone, two came out leading their horses and two came out on stretchers. Ronnie Massarella was standing with me as I waited at the gate, as he always did. As we were about to go in, Ronnie put his hand on my knee and said: 'Now then, lad, go out and enjoy yourself.' I looked at him and said, 'You must be joking!'

But Maybe was good at taking short strides; I practised that a lot with him as it was the best way for him to keep his jump. We went to that triple bar on two short strides.

Maybe did the job and jumped the first clear round.

He went clear again in the second round. There were only three double clears in the whole competition: us, Austria's Thomas Frühmann on the mare Donau, and Mark Laskin, who became chef d'equipe for Team Canada, on Damuraz. That was quite an achievement. We got the silver medal, which was good going against the world's top teams, especially on that difficult course. Canada took gold and Austria the bronze.

In the individual competition, Maybe had two down in the first round. There was no point in going on with no chance of winning. John Whitaker and Ryan's Son jumped brilliantly to take the silver. Hugo Simon and Gladstone, who'd won the World Cup the previous year, took gold for Austria with Melanie Smith with Calypso taking bronze for the USA.

Not a bad show for my first major senior championship. We had come home with a good result so I was pleased. I even invited a couple of the American girls over to stay with their horses as Hickstead was scheduled to take place the week after Rotterdam. I had a different kind of result on my mind there.

The day after they arrived I turned on the charm and took them hacking around the farm. We were riding back to the yard through a field where some horses were turned out. One of them, feeling a different kind of excitement, galloped past me, bucked and gave my left leg both barrels. There was a loud crack followed by agonising pain.

Off we went again to Warwick Hospital. My leg was broken. I was off for a week before going back to yard chores with the aid of crutches. You know Ted's philosophy – and I did still have a leg. That loose horse certainly tried to put the mockers on my courting strategy but no amount of plaster of Paris was going to stop that!

I went to Hickstead on crutches and what happened was a classic case of every cloud having a silver lining. If I had been riding, I wouldn't have been in the right place at the right time when a Rolls Royce pulled up beside me as I hobbled between the Main Ring and Ring Two. The driver's side window purred down and the occupant asked, 'How's your leg doing?' 'OK,' I replied. He went on to tell me that he wanted to buy a top horse for a top rider to ride and asked who I would suggest. I was hardly going to say David Broome or Harvey Smith, was I? I said Ted would be in touch with him.

I hurtled off as fast as I could on my crutches in search of

Ted, who was in the top ring about half a mile away. I was bursting to tell him that Terry Clemence, the property developer, wanted to buy a top horse for somebody to ride. Ted straight away replied: 'That's not a problem, I'll find him one.' He did. Ted bought St James from David Broome, but it was for Liz to ride, not me. At least it wasn't for Lesley McNaught who had joined the Edgars. The atmosphere on the yard had become very competitive.

My leg mended quickly and just seven weeks later I was riding at the Horse of the Year Show. The first night at Wembley was the Butlins Championship and this time Maybe and I won it, with John Whitaker second on Ryan's Son and my old hero David Broome third with Queensway Philco. I'd laid the ghost of that over-ambitious introduction to the Butlins.

I didn't go to the World Cup final that season and by all accounts it was pretty low-key and an American whitewash, so I didn't miss much. But when Birmingham, so close to my home, was chosen to host the 1980/81 Final, I was very keen to qualify. I now needed 45 points to qualify and a fourth place at the Dublin indoor show in November got me off to a good start with 13 points on my card. The horses had two months off after Olympia, so my next stop was Antwerp in the New Year. I was raring to go.

John Whitaker drove Ted's lorry as I didn't have an HGV licence and we set off on a six-week tour around Europe. These days, riders fly in and out of shows while supergrooms truck the horses and organise everything on the ground, but back then we all went in the horsebox: two riders, six horses and two grooms.

The show was held at the Sportpaleis Antwerp, which is right beside the E19 motorway. The horseboxes were parked directly underneath the motorway flyover to provide some shelter. We arrived to find our hotel was only booked from the following day, when the show actually started. No problem, we could bunk down in the horsebox. Being early meant a free night and John and I were on the loose.

Off we went into the town, John and me, ready to let our hair down. We met up with Kevin Bacon from Australia and a few others, found a bar and started on the beer. As the night wore on we got stuck into a local beer with pink elephants on the label. I always thought it was called Elephant beer but we'd discover later why its real name was so apt. After two months off we were fairly fit but clearly not up to staying the distance.

I was faring slightly better than John as I half-carried him back to the lorry. When we got there, he plonked himself on a bale saying he didn't feel well and was going to sleep right there, outside the lorry. It was March but it was freezing.

John has a very placid, quiet nature, but once he digs his toes in he can be as stubborn as a Blackpool donkey. He was determined to sleep outside on that bale. I was equally determined that if he slept outside he'd freeze solid. I managed to drag him into the lorry and get him on to the mattress on the Luton, then clambered up beside him. I remember the clunking noise as lorries went over the motorway flyover above me, every two bloody seconds; clunk-clunk clunk-clunk, but the beer took over and I fell asleep.

The lorry smelled rank when I woke up the next morning. I found out what it was when I nudged John to see if he was OK. He'd been sick in the night. I thought, 'I don't believe this!' For a start he could have died, then what the hell was Ted going to say when he saw the mess. At that moment I was wishing I had left John outside on the bale all night!

After getting John showered and cleaned up, we just managed

to get the sheets down the launderette and the mattress cleaned up before the boss arrived. We survived to pick up points in the World Cup qualifier; 6 points for my eleventh place and 8 for John in thirteenth. Sunday night was the last night of the show and the next day we were due to move on to 's-Hertogenbosch in Holland. After the grand prix we headed out on the lash again but this time steered clear of the pink elephant beer. I found out later the beer's real name is 'Delirium Tremens'.

Malcolm Pyrah is a bit older than us and was being responsible the next morning. He decided John wasn't sober enough to drive the lorry to 's-Hertogenbosch so I had to, with no licence. I got us there and picked up another 15 points for third in the World Cup qualifier. On we went to Gothenburg via Dortmund and Vienna.

I was watching the puissance in Gothenburg. In came a guy called Lionel Collard-Bovy riding a little strawberry roan, a French-bred horse by Nankin. It was tiny, only 15.3 hands. The horse had no mouth; Lionel had no control, nothing. They hurtled down the middle of the ring to a 5' 9" square oxer and left the ground one stride too early. For whatever reason, the horse gave it a foot and landed a stride away on the other side. What a jump for a little horse! They then turned around and galloped down to the wall at 6' 6" and popped it just as easily.

I got straight on the phone to Ted and told him I'd just seen a horse here which was small, difficult, but could jump anything. Ted was interested. He tracked down the owners and bought that little roan, which was called Epsom. When the horse arrived home we changed his name to If Ever.

Birmingham beckoned. I had 46 points and a place in my 'local' World Cup final for the 1980/81. The late Raymond Brooks-Ward masterminded the event in Hall 7 of the National Exhibition

Centre. It was televised to at least a dozen countries and over the five days there were 50,000 spectators.

I took Maybe and If Ever and was second to Franke Sloothaak on the opening day. On day two I crashed and burned, picking up twenty-eighth place and we continued to fade after that, finishing in fourteenth place overall. Again, the Americans took six places in the top ten, although Harvey Smith and Malcolm Pyrah managed seventh and eighth respectively. Michael Matz won it on Jet Run with Donald Cheska second on Southside and Hugo Simon third on Gladstone.

On the Sunday, Liz had taken St James to his first show, the Heythrop Hunt Show at Richard Sumner's in Chipping Norton. She arrived that evening in Birmingham to watch the World Cup and told me I'd got myself another horse. There was no way she could ride St James as he gave her a bad back.

I would soon discover what Liz found difficult about the way St James jumped. Whenever he jumped into a double or a combination he wouldn't land far out after each fence; he didn't make up much ground so you were always a long way away from the second or third element. The good thing about St James was that he always made up the ground in his jump and had enough ability to pick up from wherever he was.

St James was a 16.1 liver chestnut, allegedly an Irish-bred thoroughbred type. A lot of people claimed to have bred him, but we never found out his actual breeding. He was certainly a blood horse, fizzy but rideable, and he had a big heart but was a difficult character, a nervous sort, especially in the stable.

He was rideable once you got on him but very difficult to get on. I couldn't just put my foot in the stirrup iron. I had to develop a plan of attack. I'd make sure the groom had his girth done up ready, rugs off, lead rope off, everything off, and then I would walk towards St James and the groom would leg me up without me breaking stride. I'd grab the martingale, reins, whatever I could and off he would go. The minute your backside hit the saddle he was off in a canter. After that you could rein him in and he would be fine and stand, walk, whatever, but you could never just get on and have him stand still.

St James used to jump off nervous energy; the busier you were on his back, the better he jumped. The more adrenaline you had in you, the better he went. He was a very, very careful horse. He was a bit untidy with his front legs; in fact they could be all over the place, but he always knew where the poles were and tried to clear the jumps. And he was fast. He was going to be a good horse for me and I still think of him as one of my all-time greats. Back then there weren't many better around.

He'd had a few different names. When Fred Broome, David and Liz's dad, first saw the horse at Bicton with Bina Ford, he was called Sunny Side Up. David went to try him in Somerset in a small indoor school with ground that was six inches deep. Allegedly, David paid £5,250 for him with another £500 due when he won his first class. They won twenty-one classes together one year, although the horse was always a bit on the small side for David. As David was sponsored by Harris Carpets, Sunny Side Up was renamed Harris Homecare. When Terry Clemence bought him he approached Peter de Savary to see if he would like to buy in too. Peter saw an opportunity to promote his St James clubs – he owned several around the world and one in London – so the horse was renamed St James. Peter told me years later that it was quick, simple and very worthwhile!

My first time out with St James was at Amberley, which was the first big outdoor show of the season. It used to be held in Cirencester Park, home of the famous polo club. I was second to David Broome riding Heatwave in the grand prix. Then in May St James won his first big class with me, the grand prix at Royal

Windsor. We would win that for three consecutive years and Royal Windsor would always be a special show for me.

St James went on winning. He won the big classes at all the county shows, such as Surrey County, Suffolk County, Bath and West, South of England, Bucks County, Royal Show, Kent County. At the Royal International in July he earned nearly £10,000 winning the grand prix and the John Player Trophy. That was good going by any standard.

When If Ever arrived at the yard I started jumping him outdoors. He had no mouth at all and would run to every fence you turned him to, but he'd jump anything despite his small size. Ted gave him a lot of work to basically try and put a mouth on him. Maybe Ted's weight wore him out but seriously, Ted was brilliant at working a horse on the flat. It's a knack. I don't think you can teach anybody how to do it. Another great master of working horses on the flat was Alwin Schockemöhle – I knew more about the German maestro by then. I think Ted watched and learned from him. It's about getting the horse in balance, working from behind and up in the wither – carrying itself, as the dressage riders would say – and responsive to the rider. It took me several years to learn and it probably wasn't until after I left the Edgars that I picked up what to do and how to do it properly.

When I got on a horse after Ted had worked it the feeling was like driving a car with power steering instead of one without. Whether it was Maybe, St James or If Ever – and they were all different – I think Ted was ten years ahead of his time in his way of working them. His horses won so much, they totally dominated the British scene in the early eighties.

In 1981, I was on the Nations Cup team for my first visit to Aachen, the mecca of European showjumping. It is Germany's official equestrian show and arguably the biggest horse show in the world. I rode Maybe, along with Liz on Everest Forever, Malcolm Pyrah with Towerlands Anglezarke, and Fred Welch on a grey mare, Norstar. We won the Nations Cup.

The following week I went to Dublin with St James and rode him in the Nations Cup and then we flew to Spruce Meadows in Calgary for the first time ever. St James travelled on the livestock transport plane, and I flew separately on a passenger aircraft. St James had never flown before but he coped well and arrived in good shape.

I hadn't been to any of the North American horse shows and when I arrived my first impression was that Spruce Meadows was just a big field, with a ring, one building at the side of the ring where the judges sat, and the secretary's office.

That is all it was. There was no indication of Ron and Marg Southern's hidden agenda that Spruce Meadows would grow to be the biggest horse show in North America, attracting crowds of nearly 200,000 throughout the show and covering 315 acres of prime Alberta farmland.

On Saturday and Sunday a few local folk turned up to watch and there was a bit of a crowd there. Why had we come all this way? For the inaugural Du Maurier International, then the world's richest grand prix with a prize purse of 85,000 Canadian dollars. David Broome won it on Queensway Philco, pocketing a tidy C$30,000.

Nowadays, Spruce Meadows ranks with Aachen as one of the top horse shows in the world, offering fantastic prize money of C$1.5 *million*! And that's without the Rolex Grand Slam – but more of that later. The show attracts an audience of around 500,000 people and the stands and sponsors boxes – all the facilities, in fact – provide every possible comfort for horses, riders, spectators and officials. It is phenomenal and a huge tribute to the late Ron Southern and his wife Marg, who wanted to build one of the greatest jumping venues in the world and had the vision to achieve that dream.

7

If Ever

Over the winter Terry Clemence's daughter, Sarah-Jane, who had ridden successfully in ponies and was now ready for Young Riders, had been eyeing up St James, knowing a horse with his form would give her the best possible chance of making the Young Riders team. Despite protests from me and Ted, blood being thicker than water, Sarah-Jane took St James back home to Epping in Essex.

In all fairness, she was going quite well with top three placings and showing well in Young Riders classes, until St James started to have the odd stop. Horses like him that are very, very careful over a fence and bit fizzy need an accurate rider.

Meanwhile, If Ever became my top horse. He has always stuck in my mind as a good one even though we only ever won five classes together. He got off to a fine start by winning at the May Hickstead meeting. I was equal first with David Broome on a horse called Mr Ross in the grand prix – we dead-heated to share the prize money of £9,500. Before that, I'd got engaged.

I had met Sarah Edwards at Arena North in Lancashire, where the show had the added advantage of a good nightlife. Geoff

Billington and I took that advantage one night and I hooked up with Sarah while Geoff hooked up with her friend. Ted was never happy about it. Firstly, he thought me having a serious girlfriend was a distraction from the 100 per cent dedication he demanded and, secondly, Sarah's dad Charlie was a horse dealer, and Charlie and Ted had fallen out several years before over some deal. It didn't bode well.

My first trip abroad with If Ever was to Lucerne on the Nations Cup team with Liz riding Forever, Malcolm Pyrah on Chainbridge, and Pam Dunning on Roscoe. The weather was awful, it never stopped raining. In the first round I had 24 faults and Liz was clear. Then in the second round Liz had 24 faults and I was clear! Despite 48 faults between the two us, the team was able to discard the cricket score in each round. Pam and Roscoe went clear and I remember feeling very pissed off later when the *Horse & Hound* report said how badly Liz and I had gone and how brilliantly Pam had led the team to win. It was as if Pam had ghost-written it!

We went on to Aachen. The following year the format was changed to three rounds but in 1982 the Aachen grand prix was run over four rounds: two complete rounds, then a puissance round of eight big fences, and after that all the clears went against the clock in the final round.

The rain that had followed us from Lucerne was now torrential. The grand prix was a gruelling course and it was entirely down to If Ever's temperament and strength that he kept going throughout those four rounds. How brave and tough he was! The stamina that saw him through was due to Ted's work on the flat, hour after hour.

In the final jump-off If Ever took a second off Frédéric Cottier's time with Flambeau C then Hugo Simon completely mistimed the second last fence on Gladstone while Paul Schockemöhle (Alwin's brother) took Deister too short to the wall. Their mistakes left me as the third consecutive British rider to win the Aachen grand prix, one of showjumping's toughest competitions. My name went up on the famed Roll of Honour for the first time. It was a great feeling and I now had a crack at a place on the team for the World Championships.

Back in England, we went to the July Hickstead meeting. In the grand prix at Hickstead they had a very wide fence; the poles were ten feet long, and either side of those were two very narrow walls, about three feet wide. The flags were on the outside of the walls, so in effect the walls were part of the jumpable part of the fence. If Ever had a habit of cocking his jaw and running right-handed whenever I held him up and that's what he did that day. He had actually run out at the fence but, just in time, I managed to haul him back in and got him to jump the narrow wall, just inside the flag. We won the grand prix and £8,000. If Ever was on a roll.

The team for the World Championships in Dublin that August was announced at Hickstead. On the team were Malcolm and Anglezarke, John and Ryan's Son, David with Mr Ross and Pam Dunning with Roscoe. I was picked with If Ever as non-travelling reserve. Tragedy struck quickly when Roscoe fell at the dry ditch in the Derby. He broke his leg and had to be put down. As reserve, I was automatically on the team.

Sarah-Jane Clemence was riding St James in the main ring in the Young Riders Championship. I can still see him now – there were three verticals in a combination going towards the lake and he stopped and was eliminated. Sarah-Jane came out of the ring and said she couldn't manage the horse, she thought she would ruin him. She got off St James and generously gave him back to me. He came home with us.

Then I was off to Dublin for my first World Championships with If Ever. What a disaster that turned out to be, although we did come home with team bronze. The course for the team competition sticks out vividly in my memory. I walked the course with Malcolm Pyrah. There was a wall positioned on a dog leg of five and a half strides to a pretty big double of oxers. Malcolm said to jump the wall then go on five forward strides to the oxers. Malcolm, quite rightly, was walking the course for Anglezarke and I was listening carefully, taking advice and thinking I'd pay attention to a more experienced rider. I automatically took his advice and thought oh well, five strides it is. What we didn't discuss was that his horse Anglezarke always jumped slightly to the right. If Ever would always jump to the left.

I was first to go for the team. The wall was fence five or six and as I went round Malcolm's words were echoing in my mind: five strides forward to the oxers. We jumped the wall and, as ever, If Ever jumped to the left over it. We landed and I set him forward to the big oxers counting one, two three, four, five. Of course we were a mile off but I still gave If Ever a big kick and expected him to pick up. There was no way he could do it. He stopped, sat down on his backside like a dog, obliterated the fence and I fell off.

I got back on. The arena party rebuilt the fence. I jumped the double of oxers, turned right-handed and continued the course, knocking down another three fences. We had lost all our rhythm, concentration, everything. We turned back left-handed towards the entrance and a gate. If Ever stuck his head in the air and just ran at the gate. I was fighting to keep him under control, but he'd reverted to his old ways and Ted's flatwork had gone to pot. As we hit the gate he stopped, sat down and off I fell again.

It wouldn't happen these days as a fall of either horse or rider means elimination, but on I climbed again and we continued to finish the course. Adding the time faults, I ended up on 56 faults. When I left the ring I continued to blame Pyrah for telling me to go on five strides, but it was my own fault. From that day on

If Ever

I learned an important lesson: make your own mind up for the horse you are riding, walk the course for your own horse and not somebody else's.

In the second round, we made an incredible recovery – I guess I had If Ever under more control and applied my lesson learned when walking the course. We just clipped the last fence to finish on four faults. Amazingly, our team ended up with the bronze medal.

The final test for individual World Championship medals, until the FEI changed the rules in 2016, was that the top four riders each had to jump a round on the other three horses as well as their own. John Whitaker got the bronze, Malcolm claimed the silver behind Germany's Norbert Koof. It was hilarious watching Malcolm ride Norbert's horse. Malcolm's only about 5' 6" and the dark chestnut, Fire, stood 18 hh. Malcolm looked like a pea on a drum!

After the Dublin disaster we went to Hickstead, where If Ever excelled himself to win his fourth grand prix in succession. At Olympia I was thanking my lucky stars to have St James back. Going last in the jump-off he shaved 0.6 of a second off Norbert and Fire's time to win the grand prix.

Coming up to the World Cup final the following spring, John and I were first and second in the European league. John just pipped me for first place as European league winner. At Gothenburg, the last qualifier before the final in Vienna, If Ever won the grand prix. I didn't know it at the time but that was to be it. He only won five classes for me the whole time I rode him. He was sold, but I can't remember who to.

I felt quite confident heading to Vienna along with Malcolm, David Broome, Steven Hadley and Liz. I took St James as well as If Ever. I rode St James in the first leg, which was a disaster, and then jumped If Ever in the second and third legs. We ended up equal first in the third leg, with John Cottle from New Zealand riding Arturo and American Norman Dello Joio who won the final with I Love You. I finished up sixteenth overall, equal with Stephen Hadley and Sunorra.

I'll never forget the nightmare that show was. On the second morning, after that bad day with St James, I was in my hotel bedroom when Sarah phoned. She had some terrible news. Stuart Crutchlow, my best friend from my pony days and one of the 'three musketeers', had been travelling on his own the night before when his car came off the road and crashed into a tree. Stuart was killed.

It was an appalling tragedy, especially for his wife Cheryl and his young lad, Nick, who was named after me. I used to see Stuart's lad quite often until he got married, had kids and moved away. I always thought him the spitting image of his dad. The family donated a handsome trophy in Stuart's memory which is awarded each year to the winner of the 1.05m class at Weston Lawns August Bank Holiday show.

8

All Change

Sarah and I got married in October 1982. I had never lived any-where other than at home before and when we moved to Oak Cottage at Beausale, a couple of miles from the Edgars' yard, I found a new vocation. If I hadn't been a showjumper I could have quite easily been a builder. The low-beamed cottage was quaint but it needed renovating and a new kitchen and bathroom. It also came with about an acre of paddock, where I built three or four stables so Sarah could have her horses at home. She brought a few horses from her parents' place in Shropshire so she could bring on youngsters and do a bit of dealing.

As I was in the middle of a busy showjumping season, our honeymoon was a trip to the Amsterdam show. As usual, John Whitaker drove Ted's lorry, but now we both had wives with us – John had married Clare Barr a while before, one of the few mar-riages I can think of from that era which was to stay the course.

As we drove out of the docks at Hook of Holland we were low on diesel. John and I thought we had enough to get us to the show, but we were wrong; we ran out. Stranded on the side of the motorway, we were getting a lot of verbal abuse from the women, who had suddenly become expert mechanics, or so they thought. They kept telling us what we should have done, what we shouldn't have done, how we should bleed the engine.

John and I soon had enough of this so we left them to it and walked to a garage we could see along the road. We came back with a can of diesel, but how were we going to get it into the tank? We didn't have a funnel and the filler cap was right underneath the lorry. Then John had a bright idea. He brought out the hollow aluminium table leg from the living area. We stuck that into the tank and poured the diesel down the leg of the table. Instant funnel, it worked a treat.

Then we had to bleed the engine, which is where the women really came into their element. Despite their constant (and useless) interfering, John and I succeeded in getting the engine started and we drove down the road, filled up with diesel and made it to the show in Amsterdam. Not much of a honeymoon, and not a good start to a marriage.

Back at the Edgars' the atmosphere slowly began to deteriorate and the rot set in. As a married man with responsibilities and bills to pay, earning a pittance was no longer on the cards. I was now going home at lunchtime, which was unheard of. I was still as committed to winning as I ever was, but Ted knew he no longer had me under his total control. I was in love with Sarah and my daily life no longer revolved entirely around the Edgars' yard. That caused friction between Ted and me.

The arrival of Lesley McNaught on the yard had brought another set of problems, as Ted started giving more of his attention to training her. As Lesley lived at the yard full time she was better placed to give that 100 per cent dedication he demanded. It wasn't that I wasn't giving jumping 100 per cent, just that there were other things in my life. It was over a long period of time, but the relationship between Ted and me started to fracture.

Lesley was now the up-and-coming stable jockey. She'd won the 1981 Junior European Championship with One More Time and she would become very successful. With Liz, Lesley and me riding, there were a lot of jockeys for the number of horses we had. The rift in the Everest Team slowly became more apparent as I started to go off to shows with Liz, while Ted took Lesley under his wing. We ended up going to different shows.

The bonus was that going to shows with Liz taught me a lot. She was especially helpful as the job of showjumping became more technical, which it did as courses changed over the years. Liz was one of the first people to work out how to stride related distances between the fences and how to judge those distances. Liz is renowned as one of the best showjumping riders. She was fantastic to watch and learn from and was a big influence on my career. She won a lot of classes and if she had had a first-rate horse like Milton or Jappeloup, she could have been European, World or Olympic Champion, she was that good.

Slowly an internal competition developed within the Everest Team. It became all about who did best, and if we did end up at the same show and I didn't go so well, Ted would give me another bollocking. He was also tough on Lesley, but not in the same way. She was a girl.

I was riding a horse called Barbarella, who'd been going well but then lost a bit of form. Ted decided Lesley would do better, so he took the horse from me and gave the ride to Lesley. It made me feel very protective towards St James, and later Apollo. If either of those horses were being left at home while others were going to a show, I would put them on the lorry and take them too, just for a day out, because I wouldn't have put it past Ted to have given the ride to Lesley. In the end, though, I would outlast her by two and a half years as she left to go and work for Willi Melliger in Switzerland and later rode for the Swiss team.

Meanwhile I made my second trip to America for the fall (as Americans call autumn) circuit of Washington, New York and Toronto. I took St James and a chestnut mare named Arabesque. I was on my own for that tour, no teammates with me. The horses flew on ahead while I took a British Airways flight. I remember thinking as we took off that, as I had my best horse with me, at least Ted couldn't take him off me while I was away.

Washington was a really bad show for me. I didn't win a thing in seven days. St James was competing in the bigger classes as he was my best horse, but being very, very careful he didn't like trying to cope with the American courses. The fences were wider and the distances longer than he was used to. It meant you were always going forward to the fence, but the distance would be too short to put in an extra stride. St James hated hitting a pole and these poles were much heavier, the fences more solid with fillers than the light, airy English fences. St James wasn't happy.

Every day I was calling the yard and every day I had to report that I hadn't won anything. It was starting to annoy Ted. Arabesque won a bit, but not much, and by the end of the show, with no big win, Ted was not happy.

On we went to the six-day New York show at Madison Square Garden. I hoped my luck would change. The stabling was up on the third floor and the horses had to be walked up a ramp, like in a multi-storey car park. The ceilings were very low and it was extremely hot for the horses. In the stable area, every two minutes, night and day, over the Tannoy would come the announcement: 'Please extinguish all smoking materials by order of the New York City Fire Commission.' It drove us all completely mad.

Exercising the horses was difficult. You could hardly go for a hack down 7th Avenue. There was a rota system for exercising, and sometimes your allocated time would be four in the morning! Jumpers, hunters, high-steppers (hackneys to us), Tennessee walking horses – they were all allocated different times to exercise before the show started each day. Competitions started at nine o'clock in the morning, although the showjumping never took place until six or seven at night. You couldn't swing a cat in the collecting ring and the two pillars didn't help. The main ring was oval and very small.

Day one I drew yet another blank. It was painful to have to report that and I was starting to hold the phone at arm's length so I didn't have to listen to the barrage of abuse down the line from England; how Ted had sent me all the way to America at vast expense but I was so useless I couldn't win anything. Blah blah blah.

Then on the Friday I was warming up for a class and across the collecting ring there was Ted. No warning, nothing. He came storming across that tiny collecting ring, roaring at me that I was useless. Everyone could hear. He was giving it to me, same as he had on the phone, but now he had an audience. My patience snapped: 'Why don't you fuck off back home?' He turned on his heel and I never saw him again, so I assume he did just that.

Nevertheless I thought I'd better sort out a different tactic. The distances were the same as Washington, so St James wouldn't manage. The only thing to do was try Arabesque in the bigger classes and use St James as my speed horse. Arabesque had a bigger stride, she was scopey and would cope better with the wide fences and the long distances. So that was the plan, Arabesque would do the grand prix on Sunday.

Someone upstairs was looking out for me. Arabesque went and won the grand prix! I was only too pleased to pick the phone up and call home, but it was Liz I told about the win. I was not in Ted's good books. It was good to hear the delight in Liz's voice. St James, however, didn't like the speed classes, the damage was already done. America was not for him.

New York was a very sophisticated show. I'd never before seen anything like the way they all dressed up for the evening; men in white tie and tails, ladies in evening dresses and loaded down with jewellery. Every night after the show finished, there would be unbelievable parties on the top floor of the New York Penta across the street on 7th Avenue. Bands, food, dancing and as much drink as you wanted. They were fantastic evenings.

After the party, it was back to the stadium to exercise your horses if you had an early slot in the rota. A few years later, I remember John Whitaker turning up one morning straight from the party, still wearing his evening suit. Everyone else had changed into boots and chaps, but not John. He just got on and exercised his horses in the arena and then went off to bed for the day. I think it was on that same autumn trip, in Toronto, that John and I were there for seven days and never saw daylight. We jumped all evening, partied all night, and slept all day.

Back then we had the best chauffeur in the world because the Hungarian rider Joe Turi never drank. So when we finished jumping at midnight we would get Joe to take us to the parties and on to the nightclubs. And then we would emerge at four, five o'clock in the morning, go to the stadium and exercise our horses from six till seven and then go to bed before it was light. Then the next day we would do it all over again. It was like being on British time!

Joe was a one-off. He had defected from his native Communist Hungary by jumping off the lorry carrying the Czikos trick riding team he was part of when it stopped at traffic lights in Dover. It was tragically ironic, given all that, that he would be fatally injured in a motorbike accident in 2003 – but more of Joe later.

Our next stop was the ten-day Royal Winter Fair in Toronto, a huge agricultural show. You could have knocked me down with a feather. I walked in and there was Alan Oliver, the English course-builder. Alan used to ride himself and had the distinction of riding no less than six horses in the 1953 Leading Show Jumper of the Year class. It was at Haringey back then. He won it on Red Admiral and told the story of how he went into the ring and, looking up at the leader board, thought, that's funny, there's no one else up there. He just kept jumping his horses off one after the other!

Alan was a real character and very approachable, so I asked him what he was doing in Toronto. Building courses, he said. That was the best news I'd heard in weeks and I told Alan St James was going to be glad to see him. Was Alan going to build in his style, not the North American way? I asked optimistically. Definitely, he replied.

From then on St James was a different horse, back to his old self. He won two big classes and ended up winning the grand prix over good old-fashioned English courses. St James loved Canada but he still hated America.

At Olympia that year St James won the grand prix and the World Cup, so no long-term harm had been done by those long American distances. I had redeemed myself in Ted's eyes, but although with time he forgave me for swearing at him, he didn't forget, he only forgave.

Geoff Glazzard had been riding a 17 hh gelding by Erdball for owner Linda Jones. She had bought the horse in Holland for her nephew to ride but it proved too difficult. She took it to Steve Hadley (another top showjumper who later commentated for the BBC for years) for some help as the horse was stopping badly, but as Steve was moving house at the time he suggested she send it to Geoff Glazzard. This big, white-faced, Dutch-bred horse was named Apollo.

Geoff got Apollo going well and won a lot with him. To this day, I still don't know how we ended up getting the horse but all of a sudden Apollo appeared at our yard and I was always thankful that he did as he ended up being a fantastic horse for me, one of my great horses. Apollo was so versatile; he could win the fastest speed class, the biggest grand prix and he would eventually jump 7' 5" in the puissance at New York.

The first class I rode him in was at the Royal Show here in Warwickshire. Apollo used to jump to the left, so I put a small brush on the left-hand side of his bit, to help him keep straight. In we went to the main ring at the Royal. We jumped the first fence then Apollo bolted with me. He did not like that brush at all. We did two laps of the arena before I was able to pull up. That was the end of the brush idea.

Apollo was a completely different character to St James, although they did share one thing in common. They were both tricky to get on. You could never get on Apollo with a rug on, you always had to take it off. If you didn't, he'd be off. And you had to be quick about it, no hanging about, otherwise he'd go. He was also impossible to turn out. It was nerve-racking. If he knew he was going out in the field, as he came out the stable he would gallop straight down the yard to the paddock. Then he was fine, he'd just stand and graze. And he did know the difference between an indoor rug and an outdoor rug, he was clever. If he had his New Zealand rug on, once the stable door was open he'd be off.

One day I thought I'd stop him. I put a strong headcollar on him and a rope. My idea was to hook the rope over the gatepost to stop him when he bolted. He bolted and it flipped him over. Apollo simply got up and carried on. It didn't make a blind bit of difference, he just went. After a while, we gave up trying. We'd open the field gate and then open the stable door and let him get on with it.

Apollo was strong, very strong. He was scopey but not as careful as St James. Apollo used to give the old poles a bit of a rub, but he was brave, really brave. He had a big stride and won a lot of classes as he was always quick getting away from a fence. With a lot of horses, it takes them a stride or two to get going when they land, but he was always quick off the mark and gone for the next fence.

He was brilliant for the big occasion, a real showman. The bigger the occasion, the better he went. You could always bring him out after the winter break and go straight to a big show. He didn't need a warm up, so I could take him to a show like Rome and pretty much guarantee he would win the first class. He often did.

I wasn't allowed to go to the 1984 Olympics because I was sponsored by Everest and in those days a sponsored rider was classified as being professional. So the 1984 team of John Whitaker and Michael Whitaker, Tim Grubb, and Steven Smith (Robert's younger brother), went off to Los Angeles and won the team silver medal. Steven later suffered a dreadful motorbike accident that severely damaged one arm and finished his riding career, although he went on to become a successful trainer.

That year Ted was training the Australian team, who were based in Stow-on-the-Wold at the late Laurie Connell's. Laurie owned the horses ridden by Jeff McVean, one of the Australian team. Being of a similar age, Jeff and I struck up a friendship and I was sorry when he left in 1989 for New Zealand, where he set up a training facility with his wife Vicky. We kept in touch though, and I saw him and his family again some twelve years later.

Laurie Connell had racehorses in training with David Nicholson, who was still at Condicote near Stow-on-the-Wold. One New Year's Eve, Jeff and Vicky had a party at their house and I was there with John and Michael Whitaker and David Nicholson. As the evening wore on, somebody suggested that it would be a good idea to get up very early the following morning and go and ride out at David Nicholson's. David thought that was fine and told us to be sure to be there at seven o'clock in the morning.

We didn't go to bed until about three in the morning. Both Whitakers are very sound sleepers so I knew it was going to be difficult to wake them up, but sure enough I woke up at half past six. I looked out of the window to see torrential rain and began to think that maybe this wasn't such a good idea after all, but I knew we couldn't let David down as he would have four horses tacked up for us that morning, waiting. Only Michael and I got there, but I think David was surprised to see any of us. He didn't think I looked well enough to ride, but I managed. Michael rode What A Buck over the 'chase fences. He took to it like a natural! He would have made a good jockey. Riding on that cold, wet morning, with no indoor school in sight, made me sure of my decision not to be a jockey but to take up showjumping instead.

9

Arrivals and Departures

In August of 1984 when we'd been married for nearly two years, Sarah became pregnant. It was good news – except to Ted.

We were all packed and loaded up to go to the Horse of the Year Show and Sarah was coming with me in the horsebox. When Ted came out of the house and saw her in the passenger seat he made some remark to her like, 'Haven't you got anything better to do?' which upset Sarah. Ted clearly wasn't in the best of humour. A great start to the week, I thought.

On the first day, Monday, I drew a blank and won nothing, neither did I win anything on the Tuesday, or the Wednesday. The show was turning out to be a disaster on the scale of the American Fall Circuit. This didn't do much for Ted's temper and I felt he was blaming my marriage for my lack of success. My luck changed on Thursday with a win on Halo in the Grade B final and from then on I started winning, big time; all four classes on Thursday, all four on Friday and two more on Saturday. Ted's temper improved.

The grand prix was the last class on Saturday night. St James was clear in the first round and last to go in the jump-off. I was going for win number eleven. We were clear to the last and I made the fatal mistake of thinking I was home; I was a little bit too far off the last oxer and he just clipped it with his back legs. We finished third as the fastest four faulters. To be fast and clear and then knock the last fence down is unforgivable, and nine times out of ten it is the rider's fault. You're anxious, you're going too quick, and bang, the last fence comes down.

Those ten wins in a row were forgotten as Ted bollocked me all the way home up the M40 about that final class. I just sat there, at one o'clock in the morning, taking all this abuse, thinking, what do I have to do to please him?

After the Horse of the Year Show we started chasing points on the indoor World Cup circuit. St James was second in the Berlin qualifier and ended the year winning the grand prix and the World Cup qualifier at Olympia, just like he had the year before.

We started off the new season by winning in Antwerp, but we drew a blank in Dortmund, and in Paris only picked up a minor place. By now Sarah was heavily pregnant and no longer able to travel to shows with me.

It was getting very difficult at the yard, the friction between me and Ted was worse than ever and in the back of my mind was the thought that Sarah was about to give birth to my first child. Daniel was born in Solihull Hospital on Tuesday, 9 April 1985. Sarah didn't want me to be at the birth so I was at home in Oak Cottage, waiting by the phone. As soon as she called me I went in and saw them both. It was a wonderful moment when I held my first child.

The very next day we were due to leave for Gothenburg. I flew out as the horses had gone on ahead in the horsebox. John Whitaker, Malcolm Pyrah, David Broome and Liz were all riding there. On the first day our horses didn't go very well and then

Arrivals and Departures

Ted arrived, not in the best of humours. He was giving out to Liz in the collecting ring, telling her she was bloody useless and couldn't ride. I got the same treatment. He was in a real temper and I knew I couldn't do or say anything right. My friends were all congratulating me on Daniel's birth, but there wasn't a word of congratulations from Ted.

You could get tea, coffee and snacks between classes at the Riders' Club. I went in there to keep my head down; Ted was talking to Eddie Macken but I didn't see Eddie at first. I walked in and sat down to have a drink. I didn't bother saying much to Ted because he wasn't speaking to me. Eddie had no idea what was going on, so he jokingly said to Ted, 'You'll be getting a cot in the lorry now, will you?' Ted replied, 'That little bastard's not coming in my lorry.'

I heard that, got up and walked out. I was seething. I went back to the stables and sat down thinking, enough is enough. I'd had my fill of him. I knew I had to think about my future. Ted had been shouting at Liz all day, he had been shouting at me all day, and now that spiteful remark was the straw that broke the camel's back.

I took my boots off and left the stables; it was between the afternoon and evening performances. I walked into the hotel foyer and Ted was sat on a sofa in reception, talking to Liz. As I walked across the foyer towards the lifts, he called, 'Where are you going, you useless fucker?'

I didn't respond. I totally ignored him and took the lift up to my room. After a while I went to see Malcolm Pyrah in his room where he was watching the racing on television. Malcolm could see that I was absolutely furious about something.

He asked what the matter was and I told him that if Ted said one more word to me I was going to knock his head off. Malcolm tried to calm me down. 'You don't want to be doing that here,' he advised. I was having none of it. I'd had enough. I couldn't take any more abuse. I watched a bit of racing with Malcolm and then went back to my room. Then it was time to go to the stables for the evening performance.

I took the lift down to the foyer and I saw that Ted was still sitting with Liz on the sofa in reception. As I walked across, he came out with another comment, I can't even remember what it was but it infuriated me. I was seeing red, my mind was a blank. I walked over to him and told him to say it again. He did. I lashed out and punched him twice, a left and a right.

We ended up brawling on the floor in reception and for good measure I gave him a kick while we were down. At that point the hotel staff came and threw me out. After that it was a dismal show. I walked down to the stables feeling much better, but I knew this was the end. I never saw Ted again during the show, he left and went home. Liz came down to the stables and we talked. She could understand how I felt.

I rang Sarah and told her about the fight, but not what started it: that Ted had insulted my newborn son. It was years before I would tell anyone the real reason. I believe people can abuse you as much as they like, but abusing your family cannot be tolerated.

I moved on to the World Cup final in Berlin. I was worried. The consequences of what I had done and the repercussions when I got home weighed heavily on my mind. But I had another week or ten days of the trip and I thought maybe it would all settle down. How wrong I was.

St James was in good form at Berlin. In the first leg, we finished equal fifth with Malcolm Pyrah on Anglezarke. Michael won on Warren Point. When I telephoned the yard to report what had happened I had to talk to Liz; Ted wasn't speaking to me.

I won the second leg, beating Malcolm who was second on Anglezarke, and Pierre Durand with Jappeloup, a horse I would meet again at the World Championships. St James and I were leading going into the last day. It meant a lot for me to win this and redeem myself. In the first round of the third leg, St James jumped clear but I still had Conrad Homfeld and Abdullah breathing down my neck. Abdullah was another horse I would meet again at the following year's World Championships.

In the second round I only had to jump clear and I would win. The tension, with the Americans coming up behind me, was tremendous. If I won, I would be the first European winner since Hugo Simon at the inaugural World Cup. Conrad had jumped a double clear. I was only three points in front of him. I had to jump clear. I couldn't make a mistake. I was last to go.

Before the final double was a line of fences on a related distance of four strides and three strides. Both distances were a little bit long. St James was very, very unlucky. He just clipped the pole as he went up. We had the last but one fence in that line down.

The first person I saw as I headed towards the competitors' stand was Frank Chapot, the former rider turned US chef d'equipe. He was jumping out of his seat with his arms spread-eagled. Another American World Cup win. Conrad Homfeld had finished on three faults and I had finished on four. I was gutted. Second is never good enough.

It was time to go home and face the music. The day of reckoning had arrived. I turned up for work as normal at 7 a.m. to a frosty reception. Ted wouldn't speak to me at all, everything came via Liz. New rules were being laid down. There was no way Ted wanted anything to do with me, so from now on I wasn't allowed in the house, not even for breakfast, and I wasn't allowed on the yard when Ted was there. I did everything with Liz. Ted never spoke a word to me the following month and there seemed to be no way of smoothing things over.

I realised then that this was it. I would have to leave and set up on my own. The first thing I did was to call Terry Clemence, who owned St James, and tell him what had happened and that I would be going on my own. If I was going on my own I would need some horses with me. Terry stood by me and said wherever I went, his horse would go too. It was a great relief to know that I would have one of my best horses with me. Then I rang Linda Jones, who owned Apollo, and she agreed the horse could come with me as well. I don't think they rang Ted and told him, they kept it to themselves.

Then I made a mistake. I suppose I should have stopped at two but I called Lady Inchcape. I explained what had happened and asked if she would let me take Radius and Domino. She was less understanding. 'Certainly not,' she replied. What I hadn't realised is that Lady Inchcape has a loyalty streak as strong as mine. Her loyalty was to Ted. She and the late Earl of Inchcape did a lot for the sport over the years, and for dressage, but she wasn't my greatest fan.

Ted had got wind of what I was up to, that I was ringing up the owners asking for their horses, and it annoyed him, rubbing more salt in the wound. More new ground rules were laid down. I still don't know to this day why he didn't just kick me out. But he didn't, he made me work on.

The latest set of new rules were that I would I arrive at the yard at 8 a.m. when Ted went in for breakfast and then leave again at 9 a.m. when he came back out. The only two horses I could ride were St James and Apollo. Our paths never crossed. I would still go to shows with Liz, as normal. At shows, Ted would have nothing to do with me whatsoever. This went on all summer but only working an hour a day gave me lots of free time to plan my future.

Dave Dick, a friend of both Ted and me, tried to intercede. Dicko went one day to speak to Ted, pointing out what a good winning team we had been, and couldn't things be sorted out between us. Ted agreed to let bygones be bygones. I went into the tractor shed where he was working and apologised to Ted while Dicko was there. We shook hands, I said I was sorry and we tried to get on as well as we could. But the rapprochement only lasted a couple of weeks. The damage had gone too deep and the rift never healed.

As I got going with plans to set up on my own, Sarah and I went house-hunting for a place with stables and a bit of land. We didn't have much money but our luck was in and we found an old farmhouse near Tapster Valley, in the heart of the Warwickshire countryside. It was in a quiet lane with decent hacking for road work, although even then the M40 extension was planned. It would eventually ruin the lovely view.

We sold Oak Cottage, took out a mortgage and bought Sandall House Farm. It was pretty run-down, virtually derelict, but it had lots of potential. It had about ten acres of land with a stream running through the fields and a few old wooden stables along the side of a cracked concrete yard, plus a couple of pigsties. The farmhouse wasn't fit to live in, so Sarah, Daniel and I went and lived with my father and his wife Janette, back at Odnaull End Farm.

In the meantime, I had said nothing at the yard, but word soon got out. I was in the lorry going to a show with Liz. I told her I would have to leave, that I couldn't go on like this any more. I offered to work to the end of the year and finish after Olympia. I asked her to tell Ted for me and she agreed to. Liz, as always, completely understood.

We were a professional showjumping team though, so despite the problems, it was business as usual. The 1985 European Championships were held in August at Dinard in Brittany and I was on

77

the team with St James. John Whitaker had Hopscotch, Michael took the inexperienced but talented Warren Point as Amanda had trodden on a stone ten days before and was lame, and Malcolm Pyrah rode Anglezarke.

We absolutely thrashed the opposition and won the team gold medal by yards – our team finished on a total of 21.56 faults and the Swiss were second on 42.08. We had over five fences in hand.

We were to win the team gold medal at three consecutive European Championships on equally good form. In 1987 we won in St Gallen, where I won individual bronze. The team was the same except that John now had Milton. We beat the French by 25.11 faults with over six fences in hand. In Rotterdam in 1989 we won by four fences. That team was John and Milton, Michael on Monsanta, me on Apollo with Joe Turi riding Kruger. In those days the British were without doubt the best in Europe.

That show, Dinard, taught me you should never give up. I was well down the field, twelfth or thirteenth, going into the last day for the Individual and didn't think I had much of a chance, but Ronnie Massarella made me go. Ronnie was the Yorkshire-born son of an Italian immigrant family. At the age of ten, Ronnie would take a wooden wheelbarrow to the pithead and sell ice cream to the coal miners. He went on to take charge of his family firm and turn it into one Europe's largest ice cream producers and a massively successful catering company. You didn't argue with Ronnie, kind as he was.

I went in half-heartedly. All I wanted to do was jump round and get out, as I thought I had no chance at all. The third fence was a rustic oxer near the entrance and I let St James run into the fence. He knocked it with his front legs.

But there were no clear rounds, so four faults was good enough to move us quite a way up the placings. For the last round I was a lot more enthusiastic. We jumped the only clear, moving us up to fourth place. To think I could have ended up winning the gold if I hadn't been so stupid, and if I hadn't picked up a three-quarters time fault in the final round I'd have got the bronze. Instead, John got it on Hopscotch.

That I'd had a fist-fight with Ted Edgar was the scandal around all the shows and later on in August at the Hickstead Derby meeting I was interviewed by David Vine for the BBC. I announced that I was planning to leave the Edgars' stable at the end of the year.

Ted claimed that interview was the first he had heard of my plans to leave and that it was a shock to him, but that was bollocks. On 24 August 1985, Jenny MacArthur wrote in *The Times*: 'Mr Edgar said yesterday that things had not been the same between him and Skelton since Goteborg in April where the two had a fierce row over training procedures for the World Cup event in which Skelton was the eventual runner-up. 'I never forgive and I never forget,' Edgar said, adding, 'But it is time he was having to make his own way.'

On the same day Ted had given Jenny the story, I told Alan Smith of the *Daily Telegraph*, 'I'm twenty-eight and have decided it is time to make a life of my own. You wouldn't find a better trainer in the world than Ted Edgar and I think we have been a good team, but it couldn't last for ever.'

Jenny's report added: 'Despite his harsh words Edgar, when asked how he rated Skelton said: "He is the greatest in the world – you can't take that away from him."' So I guess Ted and I were square then.

10

Out on My Own

Sandall House Farm was taking shape nicely and I had to buckle down and concentrate on getting new owners and sponsors. I knew I had St James and Apollo, but I would need more horses. During Hickstead, I had been talking to a good friend of mine, David Bowen, and he had suggested that I should talk to Tony Elliott, who was David's main owner. Tony agreed to set me up with a string of horses and a horsebox to ferry them round in, which was great news for me and, as it was a private deal, not corporate sponsorship, it was especially generous of him.

Shortly afterwards I was approached by Raffles Cigarettes, who were already sponsoring Helena Dickinson, who later married the German rider Peter Weinberg and is now married to another German rider, Tim Stormanns. When they asked if I would be interested in any sponsorship the answer was YES!

I was thinking that it would come to about £50,000 a year. Back in 1985 that was a lot of money. A short time later I bumped into Paddy McMahon and his wife, Tricia, at a local show and when Tricia asked me if I had found a sponsor yet I told her about the Raffles deal. Tricia had done a very good job for Paddy with Toyota and she offered to get me double that figure if I gave her 10 per cent commission. I told her to go ahead and see what she could do. Sure enough, Tricia came up with the goods and Raffles sponsored me to the tune of £100,000 a year for three years. That helped to put me on my feet, and Sandall House Farm.

What I didn't realise until a few years later was that I had also signed up Tricia McMahon as my agent. It would cost me thousands of pounds to get out of. Tricia was unable to come up with a new sponsor when the Raffles deal ended but in the meantime I had found Burmah-Castrol for myself. Tricia insisted that I could not have them as a sponsor because I was contracted to her, even though she had not found me a new sponsor. In the end, I had to pay up. Tricia was sent to jail a few years later after a big scandal involving a drugs dealer.

Anyway, it was business as usual with the jumping and that September I flew to Spruce Meadows, Calgary, with St James and Apollo. It had rained a lot and although the ground wasn't bad, it was muddy, which Apollo didn't like but St James loved. Apollo won a class on the first day, I fell off him on the second day, then he won another class the day after. Saturday was the Nations Cup. It was the same team as Dinard and Ronnie Massarella wanted me to ride St James but I wanted to ride Apollo on the team and keep St James for the grand prix on the Sunday with a first prize of £38,000, which was vast in those days.

Ronnie and I had quite a squabble about this, but eventually I got my own way. Ronnie told me my neck was on the line and that I'd be up before the selectors when we got home unless Apollo went well in the Nations Cup. Apollo went very well, jumping two clear rounds, which got me off the hook. We won the Nations Cup and did Ronnie proud. Then on the Sunday Apollo came out and won the Speed Derby and St James jumped the only two clear rounds in the Du Maurier Grand Prix to win the big prize.

Back at Ted's, as I wasn't allowed in the house, I put a cheque for about $100,000 through the letterbox of Ted's back door. It was the most we'd ever won, but Ted still wasn't having anything to do with me.

It was painful to let go of the cheque and as it fell on to the mat I thought what a pity it hadn't happened a year later when I would be on my own. With hindsight, it would have been better to have left earlier, as St James was at his peak in 1985, it was his best year. The next couple of months went by in a complete haze as I worried about the future, going it alone with a wife and child to support, the whole thing. It was a big step into the unknown, but Sandall House Farm was ready and we moved in.

David Bowen had been to Paul Schockemöhle's PSI sale in November and bought two more good young horses for me to ride, Grand Slam and Duell, as well as a horse called Feiner Kerl that he had bought in Spain. So I had three horses to ride for Tony Elliot as well as Apollo and St James, who had settled down in their new home. Tony very generously provided me with a horsebox so I could get them to Olympia, where the three-year Raffles sponsorship was announced. Things were looking up.

Sally Mapleson, my teammate from junior days, was at Olympia and she told me she was giving up competing and wanted to send me her two best horses, Airborne and Rhapsody. True to her word, a few weeks later on 11 January they arrived and she even sent her own groom, Mark Beever, to help me out. Sally's words were, 'I'll send Mark with the horses to help for a while until you find somebody. But he won't put up with you, he'll never work for somebody like you, you are too bossy.' Those were famous last words since 'Beev' is still with me more than thirty years later! It's been one hell of a journey and Mark's been a major contributor to all the success I've had. I can't think how I would have managed without him, but then I've never had to, apart from a couple of weeks way back when he walked out and went free-lance for while. Utterly professional, supremely competent and with a thorough understanding of horses, Mark is one of the best grooms in showjumping.

Not long after Mark arrived with Sally's horses, I set off with Michael Mac and Tony Newbury for New Zealand, where we had been invited to compete on borrowed horses. Tony was married to commentator David Coleman's daughter, Ann, and her brother, Dean, kept a bar and restaurant in Auckland. So, our first task upon arrival was to find Dean. He turned out to be a very talented entertainer. He loved having a laugh and hadn't seen Tony for years, so he was determined to make up for lost time.

We rounded up a party of riders including Katie Monahan, Lynne Little, Mark Laskin and Trevor Graham, an Irish dealer who moved to America. Dean wisely put us on a table in the back of his restaurant next to a stairwell. He introduced us to a drink called a B52 Bomber. It's a layered shot cocktail, I think it was a mix of Kahlua, Baileys, Grenadine and Drambuie. The two American girls were a bit restrained but we lads were getting well stuck into these B52 Bombers, drinking like they were going out of fashion.

It ended up that every time we drank one down, we threw the glass over our shoulder, where it hit the wall, shattered and fell down the stairwell. The two girls didn't think much of our behaviour. Dean thought it was great fun, he didn't mind at all and just kept sending fresh glasses of B52s. Then the girls started to join in and they were slinging their empty glasses down the stairwell too. Whenever I see Katie I always remind her about the B52s.

The next night Dean took us to a nightclub. The place was full of stunningly beautiful women. But Dean, who didn't sing to the same hymn sheet as us, had told Tony and me that this was a transvestite's club. The 'women' were so glamorous, dressed up like dogs' dinners. Poor old Mackie fell for it. Except he sadly didn't live to be old as he died of cancer in 2014 aged just fifty-two.

We can't have behaved too badly because we were all invited back to New Zealand the next year. This time we took David Bowen with us. We flew from Gatwick but the flight was two or three hours late departing. Upon arrival in Houston we discovered that the connecting flight had left without us, so we had to stay overnight. This meant passing through Immigration control, but David didn't have a visa for entry into the United States. So we went off to a hotel for the night and David was taken away, along with a few other passengers, to be held overnight under a sort of house arrest in secure accommodation.

Next morning, we arrived at the airport to catch the plane to Los Angeles but couldn't find David Bowen. We asked around and Immigration had put him on the very first available flight to LA. I can understand why; anyone who knows David would! The authorities would have been desperate to get rid of him.

The connecting flight from LA to Honolulu was delayed as well, so while we waited we looked around for David. There he was, asleep on a bench. From Honolulu we flew on to Auckland, where we arrived absolutely shattered. An epic journey.

That year, 1986, was a World Championship year and I was selected for Aachen along with the same teammates as for Dinard and Calgary: Malcolm and Anglezarke, John and Hopscotch and Michael with Warren Point. This time I rode Apollo, who had started the year well, winning classes in Jerez, Madrid and Barcelona.

We went to a show in Wolfsburg about a week before, then stayed in Germany for a bit of team training. We got wind of it that at Aachen the German course-builder Arno Gego was planning to put a full-size water jump in the middle of the combination. This had never been tried before. Sure enough, on the first day at Aachen, there was the combination. A treble; a vertical, two strides to a 3.90m water jump and then two strides to an oxer going out. There was a lot of head-shaking going on. But we had practised this new combination in Wolfsburg.

The team competition – a two-round Nations Cup format – was a bit of a mixture for us. John and Hopscotch had a difficult round, hitting all three parts of the treble and stopping twice at the water ditch. They didn't go again. Warren Point wasn't up to his usual form, but Michael did a fantastic job on him to get round as best he could. Malcolm's Anglezarke cast a shoe at the double of ditches then, unbalanced, hit the second but went clear in the second round. Apollo jumped well for just a time fault in each round. The course caused a fair bit of trouble, especially that water combination, but we took the silver medal behind the US team of Michael Matz with Chef, Conrad Homfeld and Abdullah, Katie Monahan on Amadia, and Katherine Burdsall riding The Natural, who was the first million-dollar horse having been bought for that amount earlier in the year.

Going into the last day before the Final, Anglezarke and Malcolm were within striking distance, but Pierre Durand's Jappeloup and Conrad with Abdullah were well ahead. However, I had learned my lesson about never giving up and stayed optimistic. Malcolm's bad luck turned out to be my good luck. Just before the last round Anglezarke tipped up in the collecting ring and couldn't go on. In the final round I jumped into fourth, basically taking poor Malcolm's place. Pierre, Conrad and I were joined by the little-known young Canadian rider, Gail Greenhough and her horse Mr T.

Now I was in the final four. The Individual World Championship is a unique competition. The top four riders go through to a final in which they jump a round on each of the four horses. The rider with the least number of faults from all four horses is proclaimed World Champion. Unlike the Olympic Games or European Championships, the aim is to find the best rider, not the best horse-and-rider combination. However, that view is not necessarily shared by the riders.

The draw plays a big part in the competition as clear rounds depend very much on which rider you follow on each horse. If a horse has a bad time with a rider and you have to get on directly afterwards, an upset horse may not jump so well for you.

Saturday was a day off and all the riders were being interviewed on television. We were all asked which horse we feared riding the most. Everyone, including me, said Apollo. Pierre Durand actually looked quite ill at the prospect of riding him. Those in the know had their money on me or Conrad, the two most experienced riders, with either Pierre, who was a bankruptcy lawyer, or the little-known Art student Gail to take the bronze. How wrong they would be!

On Sunday morning Robert Smith, Harvey's son and a fellow rider, was there to support me and we walked the course together. Riders were allowed to take somebody into the arena to help them because the only chance you have to warm up on each different horse is over two fences in the main ring, right there in front of the audience.

We each jumped a round on our own horses; Pierre had two down on Jappeloup but Gail, Conrad and I were all clear. I felt a sense of relief, I had jumped clear on Apollo, the horse we all felt sure was the most difficult to ride. Or at least that's

On Oxo – I liked winning from an early age.

Me on Taffy with Dad.

With Mum on holiday in Bournemouth.

On Prince Tarquin, my style didn't change!

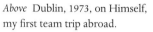
Above Dublin, 1973, on Himself, my first team trip abroad.

Above right High Jump Record 1978, that brave horse Lastic left the fence intact on his last try.

Right Receiving the trophy for breaking the High Jump Record 1978 from previous holder Don Beard.

Alternative Olympics, Rotterdam, 1980, on Maybe; by far the biggest track I'd jumped.

Left Dinard, 1985, celebrating the first of three consecutive European team golds: (*left to right*) John, Michael, Ronnie, me, Malcolm.

Middle left World Team Silver, Aachen, 1986: Malcolm, me, Ronnie, Michael, John.

Bottom left Riding Apollo, Seoul Olympics, 1988, where the Olympic bug really bit me.

Right Early days in our partnership: Barcelona, 1992, wasn't the best for Dollar Girl but she was on the up the year after.

Below Atlanta, 1996: Michael's serious reading matter.

Below right Harry and Dan, the jockey and trainer-to-be.

Above Showtime trying her best, Atlanta, 1996.

Left Guess who came over to talk to us: Muhammad Ali, Atlanta, 1996.

Below left After the accident in 2000, in the dreaded halo brace, with Harry and Dan.

Below right My fourth Calgary grand prix win, with Arko in 2008.

Arko, that amazing feat of jumping, Athens, 2004.

Beijing, 2008, on Russel.

I'd waited so long to get on an Olympic podium this was a bit premature!

2006	M. Ehning	GER	"Küchengirl"
2007	B. Madden	USA	"Authentic"
2008	A. Zoer	NED	"Sam"
•2009	D. Lynch	IRL	"Lantinus"
2010	E. Lamaze	CAN	"Hickstead"
2011	J.-F. Meyer	GER	""
2012	M. Whitaker	GBR	
2013	N. SKELTON	GBR.	

Writing our names on the Aachen Roll of Honour after the grand prix win, 2013.

what I thought. The atmosphere was great. The stands were packed, with a crowd of around 50,000. I jumped clear on Abdullah and again on Jappeloup, who gave me the most unbelievable feeling I have ever had on a horse. The more you held him, the more you squeezed him, the higher he jumped. But Gail Greenough was also going well, jumping clear on both horses.

Then I had to ride Gail's Mr T and she had to ride Apollo. I had to get on Mr T after Pierre had ridden him and he had struggled. The minute I hit Mr T's saddle he was ready to explode. He was really fired up. When I touched the reins and tried to hold him, he overreacted. He was very, very delicate to ride.

Then I made a serious error of judgement. I thought I'd try to ride him like Gail, who'd been the only one to ride him for three years until that day, and just sit very quiet. But Mr T was getting fairly strong and buzzy underneath me. He hit the second fence and going down to the final treble I didn't know whether to pull, push, or what, so I just sat very still. No hand, no leg, nothing. Two strides away, he broke into a trot so I gave him a big kick. That wasn't a good idea. He stopped, put his head on the fence and fell into it. He came round again and jumped it but we had three time faults as well. Goodbye World Champion! That was definitely one of the biggest disappointments of my life. I ought to have got on him and ridden him properly, kept him between hand and leg, like you should. I rode him like a complete fairy and threw the World Championship away.

I would have to have jumped clear on him, because Gail jumped clear on every horse, including Apollo. As we watched Gail get on Apollo, I turned to Robert and said, 'Don't worry, Apollo'll take care of her in a minute.' He did, but not in the way I had intended. Gail rode him very well and Apollo seemed to like the novelty of a lightweight girl on his back.

Gail admitted she had gone into that final thinking she would end up fourth, so she just set out to enjoy herself. She had no pressure on her at all and ended up doing a brilliant job.

On ten faults, I finished third. Conrad was second and Gail won. The system works well for some, but not for others. I felt sorry for Pierre because he and Jappeloup were such a brilliant combination, but they went on to win the individual gold medal at the Seoul Olympics and the European Championships.

Whether it was that he couldn't get over not winning or being beaten by Gail, I don't know, but I honestly think it finished Conrad Homfeld off. He didn't ride much after that. In his television interview before the competition he had said of the format: 'It's a lottery, it's in the lap of the gods now.' Clearly he hadn't been praying.

From the World Championships we moved on to Dublin, where Apollo jumped 7' 3" to win the puissance. Apollo was now taking over the top slot in the yard as St James was starting to feel his age. He was sixteen years old by then and had worked hard for me, but I was considering calling time on him because I like to retire my horses before the end, while they are still enjoying the job. Since he was getting a bit arthritic, keeping him sound was starting to become a problem and I didn't do so many shows with him.

Dublin is always a fantastic show and something momentous always happens – not necessarily in the showjumping ring. One year, when Ireland won the Nations Cup, Con Power was the hero of the team. I was there with Michael 'Mick' Saywell and we ended up having a few drinks with 'Captain Con' in the bar. We still had our boots and breeches on and were getting a bit on the rowdy side. After the Nations Cup, we always had to go to the British Embassy to meet the Ambassador and we would always have a few drinks there and a bit of a party. Ronnie reminded us not to be late as we only had ten minutes before the bus left for the Embassy.

Mick told his wife Vicky (my teammate from junior days) to go back to the hotel and get changed as he would take her out for dinner when he got back from the embassy. Off went Vicky. Still in our boots and breeches, we climbed into the minibus, along with the rest of the team. After a few more drinks at the embassy, Mick and I started to get even rowdier. When we left the embassy to go back to the hotel, Ronnie, for some reason, put his suit jacket in the minibus even though he was following us in a car driven by Orson Welles' daughter, who he knew quite well. We were driving on down through Dublin, Ronnie following us with the young lady, when Mick and I decided it would be a good idea to open the back door and throw Ronnie's jacket out in the road. As you do.

So we opened the door and flung it out, to a great round of applause from the other lads in the bus. We all watched with glee as Ronnie's car drove straight over it. The young lady had to pull up and stop so Ronnie could retrieve his jacket from the middle of the road. 'We're for it now, Mick,' I said.

It was even worse than we thought; somebody had given Ronnie a pot of strawberry jam, which for some reason he had put in his jacket pocket. Anyway, we didn't see any more of Ronnie that evening and when we got back to the show ground we met up with Con Power again. Con invited us back to a party at his army barracks. Off we went. Con was absolutely flying by this time. As we were driven through the centre of Dublin, Con was standing up in his cap and full army dress, head out of the sun roof, saluting all the passers-by. Of course we had a few more drinks at the barracks and around midnight I turned to Mick and asked did he think Vicky would be dressed and ready for dinner by then. Oh shit, we'd forgotten all about her. As the damage was already done and it was too late for dinner, Mick decided we might as well carry on.

Chainbridge had put a foot in the water in the Nations Cup earlier that day and we figured it was likely he'd do it again in the next day's grand prix. Training over the water in the main ring isn't allowed, but as we'd done with O.K. at Cock O'The North it seemed a sensible idea to get in some early practice. Still in our breeches and boots, we got a lift back to the stables. Unfortunately, by the time we made it to the showground it was starting to get light and everyone was getting up, so there was no way we could get the horse out, never mind use the main ring.

We left the show ground and wandered down the road looking for a taxi. Irish taxi drivers expect to find a fare at six in the morning, so we had no problem finding one.

Then we suddenly remembered Vicky again. Thank God I wasn't sharing a room with Mick, because he had to face up to her when he got back in.

Apparently, as Mick tells the story, he said to her, 'Now listen here, Vicky, they're all expecting you to be in a real foul mood with me this morning, but just play along as if there's nothing wrong at all.' Vicky came down in the morning and played the part to the hilt. She was perfectly cheerful. We were all envious that she was so tolerant.

However, when Mick and I arrived at the show later in the day, Ronnie said, 'I wanna see you two,' and sure enough we got a bollocking. He told us he was sick of our bad language and bad behaviour; any more of it, and we'd find ourselves in front of the stewards. It was a proper telling off. The strawberry jam incident had not gone down well.

Good old Ronnie. He never ever wanted us to get into trouble and he always tried to protect us. In 1986 we did him proud again by winning the Aga Khan Cup for the second successive year. That was the Aachen squad, with Malcolm replaced by Peter Charles riding April Sun and John on Ryan's Son. We beat the Americans! In all the years Ronnie was chef d'equipe he looked after us boys as best he could, which made us want to do our best for him.

11

My First Olympics

During the World Championships I had noticed a lad constantly following me around Aachen. If I went to the arena he followed me, he watched me warming up, taking pictures the whole time and in the end I was getting a bit worried. He was starting to get on my nerves, it was like being stalked.

One day towards the end of the year, I got a telephone call. In broken English the caller told me he was the person who'd been following me around at Aachen and asked would it be possible for him to come to England to train with me and help out. A Spanish lad, his name was Alfredo Fernandez Duran and he was twenty-two years old.

I thought yes, that's just the sort of person I need. I remembered him as a strong-looking lad, and we were starting to do a lot of farm work, fencing, railing, ditching. It was January and I told him to bring plenty of warm clothes as it was pretty bleak and not a bit like living in Madrid.

So Alfredo turned up and the whole time he stayed I had him carrying posts and rails all over the fields we were fencing. I didn't have a tractor and trailer, so he used to carry them on his shoulders. He was strong. Back and forth to the yard, fetching more rails, more posts. Alfredo nicknamed my farm 'The Killing Fields'!

He became a good friend and his instincts were right about coming to train and learn more about showjumping, as he went on to ride at the Seoul Olympics with Kaoua, a horse I helped him buy. Even though he only got to ride two horses during his stay, he rode very much in my style so he seemed to have learned a lot.

Sandall House Farm was starting to take shape. I'd converted the pig sties into four loose boxes attached to the side of the house, put up a block of nine wooden stables along the edge of the concrete yard and an outhouse on the other side of the house was converted into a stable. We were shoving horses in all over the place.

The indoor school, which wasn't big but a strong building, had a floor of dirt and shavings. I never changed it the whole time I was there. It did the job and I never felt the need for one of those expensive surfaces.

Coming into the New Year, I told Terry Clemence that I thought St James should be retired; he'd been a loyal servant and deserved a good rest and happy retirement.

Terry didn't agree. He was convinced the horse still had something left in him. He wanted me to take the horse down to Jeffrey Brain at Bourton-on-the-Water and get a complete veterinary report. Clearly, Terry didn't believe what I was telling him, but that is one of the problems you run up against with owners who are not horse people. I explained the situation to Jeffrey Brain, who agreed with me and reported that St James should be retired.

Despite Jeffrey's report, Terry Clemence sent the horse back to the Edgars for Marie, Ted and Liz's daughter, to ride. St James was retired later that year, along with Maybe, at Terry's home,

The Woodhouse, in Epping. When that house was eventually sold, Maybe was left there because Norma, who used to groom St James for me, was living there and stayed on when Rod Stewart moved in.

St James moved with the Clemences to their new house in Weybridge. Then Sarah-Jane rang me one day to say that St James had injured a tendon out in the field. They tried to operate and give him a carbon fibre implant so he could continue his retirement, but I understand poor St James died under anaesthetic.

David Bowen bought a horse, J Nick, which he had been riding himself. He decided to send it to me to try. It went well so David sold it to Tony Elliot for me to ride. J Nick was supposed to be by a horse called Wily Trout (an Irish thoroughbred stallion, not the famous dressage horse of the same name that Chris Bartle rode). Sure enough, he was a wily character. He arrived on the yard in the winter and was very hairy. It wasn't long before Mark Beever discovered you couldn't clip his legs. We even tried putting him on the lorry and jamming him between two partitions so Mark could clip his legs, but J Nick was having none of it. He had a lot of feather in his heels but he hated having them clipped. He couldn't bear having his legs touched – even putting tendon boots or bandages on him was a nightmare.

He was a strong-minded, strong-willed character and he was physically strong as well. But he was very talented horse and had a great jumping technique. He was quite hot to ride and his character wasn't easy, although with time and careful handling he got a lot better.

Like If Ever, J Nick didn't actually win many classes but the classes he did win were good ones. The week before the Hickstead Derby we were at a show in Gijon on the north coast of Spain. I had taken J Nick along with Airborne, who was well on his way to becoming a top-class horse. I was riding Airborne on the Nations

Cup team along with Janet Hunter and Lisnamarrow, Malcolm with Anglezarke and John on Hopscotch. Janet, Malcolm and I all jumped clear; as fourth team member, John didn't need to go because the score was zero. We all jumped clear in the next round as well, so, again, John didn't have to go in the ring. At the prize-giving John collected £2,000 and a Breitling watch and he hadn't even had to leave the stands!

But J Nick was less obliging and was proving a bit difficult. I rode him in a thick loose ring snaffle and he was pulling me around. When Gijon finished on the Monday we had three days to drive to Hickstead for the Derby meeting. John Whitaker and I were still sharing a lorry to travel to shows, and Clare Whitaker was driving. I was really annoyed with J Nick because he had not gone well and I said to Clare could she get him over to Hickstead as quick as she could. I think she drove day and night to get there in time, arriving at Hickstead in the early hours of Friday morning, the day of the Derby trial.

I virtually pulled J Nick straight off the lorry to jump in the Derby trial. He came out full of energy, bucking and kicking, not at all like a horse who had been travelling for three days. Yet he still mauled me all round the Derby trial. I think he had one fence down. On the Saturday he was still running away with me so I lunged him for an hour or so. I figured I had to wear him out or I'd never be able to hold him going round the Derby course.

I gave up with the loose ring snaffle and put a twisted wire bit in his mouth. I still couldn't hold one side of him; the Derby Bank felt like a speed bump in the road, he went up and down it so quick I barely noticed it. But he jumped the only clear round and won.

By now Tony Elliot had accumulated a lot of horses on my yard, all of them promising, talented animals including Serenade, who he bought from the American rider, Leslie Burr. The lorry he had loaned to me was painted in Raffles colours and the whole set-up had a very professional air to it. It was the year of the Seoul Olympics and life was looking up.

I've said it before about ups and downs, but I'll say it again: there's no substitute for horses when it comes to the fact that an up is always followed by a down. At a show in Bethune, a little French village, I was warming up J Nick to go in the ring. I got off to adjust my saddle and thought I'd just jump one more vertical.

J Nick was a very active jumper, when he came to take off at a fence he bounded off the floor. We went down to a vertical and took off; I heard this strange squelch noise. He landed on three legs and stopped dead, throwing his left foreleg around.

I leapt off to find blood everywhere. For a horse that you couldn't do anything to, he suddenly became a very sober, obliging animal. I looked down and saw that he had over-reached so badly that he had nearly pulled his foot off. It was held on by three inches around the front of the coronet band, the pedal bone was exposed. It was horrific.

Bethune was a little country show out in the middle of nowhere and there was no show vet. Andrew Saywell was grooming for me and coped with the trauma incredibly well. Everyone was running round looking for a vet. Poor J Nick was bleeding profusely and the nearest Equine Clinic was in Belgium. I just happened to have some plaster of Paris on the lorry so we filled him with painkillers, pushed the hoof back on as best we could and made a plaster cast to contain the injured foot.

We loaded J Nick on to the lorry and drove him to the clinic, having telephoned the leading German vet Dr Peter Cronau, who was in the south of Germany but drove up the through the night to meet us at the clinic. Sadly, Dr Cronau said there was no way he could repair the foot as all the arteries were broken. It was inoperable and they put J Nick down under the anaesthetic.

These things often go in threes and I wondered what the next serious incident would be, but after that dreadful event things improved. For the second consecutive year, I won the Hickstead Derby. Apollo took to the Derby course like a duck to water. He loved it. It suited his cross-country approach to life. I guess that is why he made such a good hunter when he retired.

Apollo was always forward going and strong. He was great for the big occasion and Apollo knew the Derby was one of them. He went on to win again the following year, giving me three consecutive wins, and he was also second three times. He was foot perfect over the Derby Bank, it didn't feel like a speed bump.

He wasn't always foot perfect, however. In New York one year the course-builder had included some very light, fragile, airy planks. Apollo had them down two days running and I felt sure that if they were used in the grand prix course he would kick them out again. I figured that the best way of guaranteeing he wouldn't knock the planks down was to eliminate them from the competition, which was of course not in the rulebook.

So that night I hung around until everybody had gone and then I went and found the planks, which were kept on a trailer in the collecting ring. I took all three and hid them on top of a pile of pallets stacked in the corner of the stable complex. Job done, I thought, they won't be in the grand prix tomorrow.

The next day when I went to walk the course, I couldn't believe my eyes. I must have missed one. Right there, going into the combination, was a single plank at about 1.50m with a brush fence underneath it. I was drawn near the end of the class and early on I thought my luck had changed. An American rider went in, had a stop at the plank, the horse put his head on it and smashed it clean in half. There was a five-minute delay while the course-builders went looking for the planks again and when they still couldn't find them, they came back with a piece of wood, a hammer and some nails and proceeded to repair the broken plank.

The class continued and about twenty minutes went by before a member of the arena party eventually found the hidden planks and came running in to replace the broken one. Well, after all that, Apollo jumped the single plank fine as the brush underneath set him off it a bit.

I was satisfied with how things were going. I was making it on my own. Sally Mapleson's Airborne and Tony Elliot's Grand Slam were developing into good horses and the rest of my string were going well. Apollo was definitely my top horse and he won the 1987 Aachen grand prix and was on the gold medal-winning team at the European Championships in St Gallen the same year. We finished third in the individual for bronze behind John Whitaker on Milton and Pierre Durand, who won the gold on Jappeloup. That put Apollo right up there with Milton and Jappeloup, undoubtedly two of the best horses in the world.

The rules for Olympic qualification had been relaxed and I was now eligible for selection for the 1988 Olympics in Seoul. My focus was all on that. I was having a successful season, Apollo won Aachen for the second successive year and he also won the Dublin grand prix. He was on form, and I was hopeful not just of selection but an Olympic medal.

Seoul would be the furthest I had ever travelled with a horse and my first full-blown Olympics. The team was named: David Broome with Countryman, Joe Turi with Kruger and Vital, Malcolm Pyrah with Anglezarke, and me with Apollo. Michael Whitaker was travelling reserve with Amanda.

We were a strong team, but not as strong as we should have been. We had to leave behind our best horse, Milton, whose owners, the late Caroline Bradley's parents, didn't want him to go to Seoul because they feared the journey would be too much for him, among other reasons. They wouldn't budge and I wasn't the only one to wonder whether their decision was in fact a bit of 'get your own back' for Caroline having been dropped from a previous team. It was a big shame for John, because Milton was at his very, very best and that was his chance of winning Olympic gold.

I was to find those Olympics highly entertaining. It was a laugh from start to finish.

We stayed in the Athletes Village, where Broomie was our fall guy. We took the piss out of him mercilessly. And Graham Fletcher came as our trainer, adding to the mayhem.

It all started at the airport. There we were, in our Olympic tracksuits; everyone looking exactly the same. The plane was full of Olympic athletes, and every single one of us had the same Olympic suitcase. Trying to find your own suitcase at Seoul airport was a complete farce, with hundreds of red suitcases all going round together on the carousel.

David Broome walked in wearing his tracksuit and baseball cap. He didn't look very athletic so I called to him, 'Shot-putters, that way!' Poor Broomie, we gave him a barrage of abuse on that trip. One night he even tried to throttle me out on the balcony of our apartment in the village.

Our apartment had four bedrooms and two bathrooms with a lounge and kitchen area. The bedrooms were pretty basic. The sheets and pillow cases appeared to be made of J-cloth, there was lino on the floor and the wardrobe looked like a metal gun case. A five-star hotel it was not.

You really have to be able to get on well with people in that situation, sharing those sorts of digs for three weeks. I shared a room with Michael, Malcolm shared with Joe Turi, David bunked down with Fletch, and Ronnie was honoured with a room to himself. Nobody wanted to share with Ronnie anyway because he could snore for England. He was the undisputed champion, the gold medallist at snoring.

Four of us shared one bathroom, three the other, and while cleaners came in twice a week, it often wasn't enough. Ronnie and David shared a bathroom and only allowed Fletch in under protest. They were very possessive about their bathroom.

David hated getting out of bed and having to put his feet on the cold lino, and he also hated getting out of the bath and putting his feet on the cold floor. So the first thing he did was to go and buy a bath mat and a bit of carpet so he could get out of bed in comfort. Michael and I used to nick his bath mat in the night and put it in our bathroom and put his bit of carpet between our beds. And we four all used to go and use his toilet before he got up. It kept our bathroom smelling sweet, which we thought was a bonus.

There was a communal launderette in the apartment building, where we had to do our own washing. We could tell that Fletch wasn't domesticated because he didn't know you had to put washing powder in an automatic washing machine. He thought an automatic washing machine was that automatic it would put powder in itself. And we turned heads one day when we walked into the village through the airport-type security scanners as Michael was carrying 200 Silk Cut and Fletch was toting a case of Carlsberg under each arm. Not exactly typical Olympic athletes!

You see some funny sights at the Olympics. Every morning at breakfast you could get any sort of food you wanted, from anywhere in the world. It must have been a catering nightmare. But my most vivid memory is of a Mongolian female basketball player. She must have been six foot seven with size 15 feet. She just put the food straight on to the tray, as much as she could stack on. Even Broomie couldn't eat as much as her.

The Athletes Village was very close to the Olympic Stadium and the horses were stabled about half an hour away. You couldn't have wished for a better, cleaner, more efficiently operated equestrian complex in the world than at Seoul. It would be the best Olympics I'd go to until 2012.

Our wives were staying at a dosshouse that called itself a hotel, out near the equestrian complex. We all used to go out together in the evening for meals in restaurants and then we lads would go back to the Athletes Village. Ronnie liked to keep the Olympic team atmosphere. He was absolutely right, and it was an experience I wouldn't have missed for the world.

We found a market where they sold all the fake designer gear: watches, T-shirts, suitcases, shoes, handbags, Louis Vuitton, Gucci – you name it, they had it. One day David bought himself a Rolex watch for about $20 and later that night we were out for dinner with Lord Harris, who owned Countryman. David was dead proud of his watch. He kept stretching his arm so his cuff came up to show his watch off. On cue, Lord Harris admired the watch and asked to have a look at it. David took it off and handed it to him. 'Is it real then, David?' asked Lord Harris. 'Of course it is!' said David. 'It will be waterproof then, won't it?' said Lord Harris as he duly dropped David's pride and joy into a pint of beer. Well, the look on David's face! That watch kept going for about a week then that was the end of it.

Every morning we got up at six o'clock and after breakfast we went to the stables and worked the horses. We had arrived ten days before the opening ceremony. That was an incredible experience, like nothing else on earth. We even managed to see some of the athletics. I sat trackside for the Men's 100 Metres Final featuring Ben Johnson and Carl Lewis. A few days later, one of the athletes was chatting to us and asked what we thought of Ben Johnson. 'Brilliant!' we replied. Nobody had told us that Johnson had been disqualified.

The day of the team competition dawned. We didn't exactly startle, we didn't move any mountains, in fact we didn't make much impression at all. By the time I jumped I was sick as a pig because I knew we wouldn't be getting a medal. Ronnie, the eternal optimist, told me not to worry, as if Jappeloup was to get eliminated we would get the bronze. Jappeloup, probably the best horse in the world then, was as likely to get eliminated as me to fly to the moon. We finished sixth, which wasn't a disgrace.

But now I was looking forward to the Individual, which was being held in the main Olympic Stadium, quite an honour. We had a very early start and had to walk the course at six in the morning. Ronnie came in to wake us up at five o'clock. He came out of his room shouting, 'Right then, come on, you lads, this is the day you've been waiting for!' To which Michael, our reserve rider, replied, 'Why? Are we going home?'

Michael sat through the whole of the Seoul Olympics, three long weeks, and he never got to jump. He was so good-natured, so helpful, he never let it get him down, he was brilliant and in his quiet way he contributed enormously to the fun we were having.

As we were rushing around to get dressed and ready to go, all David was worried about was where he could pick up his packed lunch at five in the morning! He wasn't worried about the course, or the fences, just his lunch. Ronnie having won the gold medal for snoring, the gold medal for eating would go to David.

It was still dark when we got down to the stadium. The floodlights were on, but they weren't daylight-bright, just a sort of twilight, so basically we walked the course in the dark. The course was huge, it was the biggest thing I had ever seen, and by then I had been to a lot of international competitions. Walking into the stadium gave you an eerie feeling.

In the first round, the last fence was a double; a triple bar with one stride to a vertical. Apollo had the back rail off the triple bar going in, which was very uncharacteristic of him. David was very unlucky: Countryman lost a shoe, slipped and had a plank down. David should have got a medal, he finished fourth. Apollo and I finished seventh. Not disgraced, I suppose.

12

A Run of Bad Luck

Paul Schockemöhle contacted me after the Olympics to tell me he had a fantastic horse for me. The horse was to be entered in his famous PSI auction but Paul thought I should look at him first.

I flew out to Paul's stables in Germany. He told me the horse was very, very careful but he needed a good rider, he was not an amateur ride. The horse was called Landsturm. I tried him in Paul's indoor school and the feeling he gave me over a fence was unbelievable. Like Paul said, he was very careful, although he didn't seem to have all the scope in the world.

Sarah went to the PSI auction with Sally Mapleson, my old teammate from junior days, and they bought him. When we got him home I sold a half share to a friend of mine, Gary Widdowson, another teammate from junior days.

That horse had such a good character. He had a lovely head on him and was a really kind horse. You couldn't hope to find a horse more careful over his fences. I am not exaggerating when I say that in the whole of his career he maybe had five fences down. He was a truly remarkable horse. We renamed him Major Wager.

The first show I took him to was Church Farm in Staffordshire.

He didn't clear the fences by inches, he cleared them by feet. But he didn't like water. In fact, he hated it. One day in Rotterdam he stopped dead and shot me over the brush straight into the water. From then on I didn't bother jumping Major outdoors where he'd always be looking for the water, his mind not on the job. I jumped him indoors instead, where there was no open water. He didn't mind water trays under poles, it was just open water jumps he loathed.

Gradually, Major Wager developed more scope and he would end up winning a World Cup qualifier in Paris in 1993 and the grand prix in Gothenburg. Returning to Paris in 1994, however, would turn out to be a disaster for Major Wager. He was still jumping much higher than necessary over his fences. He was a victim of his own ability when he jumped a triple bar so big and landed so steeply that one of his front tendons gave way.

Major Wager spent months in Germany in an Equine Clinic before coming home to convalesce, but he was never able to jump again and had to be retired. He lived near me for years with Alison and David Coleman, who used him as their hack. They loved him and he was very happy in his quieter life.

Back to 1988: the Horse of the Year Show came round and we headed off to Wembley. The stables were all outside with a sand working-in arena in the middle. That year we were allocated stables overlooking the sand arena, which meant the horses had lots to look at and as there was plenty going on they would never be bored. For Airborne, however, who was well on his way to becoming a top-class horse, it was a disaster. One of the feature classes at Wembley is the Police Horse of the Year competition where the horses are subjected to the type of scenes they will meet in the course of their duties. Each day, the police horses and their riders practised out in the sand arena, complete with a mini 'demonstration'. There were balloons, crowds shouting, firecrackers and, to top it all, a fiery burning hoop through which the horses had to jump. For police horses, this is regular, run-of-the-mill, everyday stuff, as they might experience far worse at a football match or in the violence of a genuine demonstration.

With all this going on a few yards from Airborne's stable door, he became very agitated. The show vet diagnosed a nervous colic and gave him an injection. Mark Beever walked Airborne in hand practically all day while the vet would come back every couple of hours to check the horse and, when necessary, give him another injection.

Towards the end of the day Airborne was in so much pain he was trying to lie down on the concrete path Mark was walking him on. There was only one thing for it, the vet decided. Airborne had to go to the Royal Veterinary College at Potters Bar for treatment. He got there in the late evening, Mark standing in the back to stop him lying down on the journey. Horses are not that well designed; their guts are long and in a body mounted on those thin legs supported only by tendons and ligaments they are vulnerable. The reason Mark walked Airborne to prevent him from lying down is that those complicated guts can twist. On arrival, Airborne was examined and the decision made to operate. Mark got back to Wembley in the early hours of the morning; Airborne came through the operation well.

While Airborne was still in the clinic at Potters Bar we arrived home from Wembley to find Full Cry, a good young horse of my own, suffering from colic. His condition deteriorated and he was sent for an operation. Full Cry recovered but I couldn't believe it was possible to have two horses operated on for colic inside a week, so I arranged to send all the hay, feed and shavings back to the manufacturers for checking in case there was some sort of contamination. That's what you do, look for anything that might have brought this on. In the end, we changed everything except the water. I wasn't going to take any risks.

Airborne seemed to have recovered, so he went to his owner Sally Mapleson to recuperate from his ordeal. It was not to be. About ten days later he had to go back to Potters Bar for a second operation. I was in 'sHertogenbosch when I got the news. Airborne had died in the operating theatre at the Veterinary College. It was devastating for all of us, but especially for Sally. Not only had she lost a lovely horse destined for a great future but a couple of months earlier she had turned down a lot of money for Airborne. Sally had never owned such a good horse before and she had decided that she would prefer to keep him and enjoy his success herself.

Looking back to the devastating time when we lost J Nick, I had wondered who the 'three' would be and now I thought I knew: J Nick, Airborne and very nearly Full Cry. Surely that was the end of my run of bad luck? Wrong again.

A couple of months later, Fred Harthill sent me a horse called Pennwood Fleetline. Mick Saywell's son, Andrew, was working for me and one day he was working the horse in the indoor school. Suddenly there was a loud crash. I went running in and the horse was dead on the floor. He had had a heart attack. Now I had lost three horses. These things always go in threes.

For the whole of that winter, Apollo had a good rest. I thought the Olympics might have taken a lot out of him, long journey and everything. He lived out in a warm rug and loved it; he much preferred being in the paddock to being in the stable, it suited his outdoor mentality. So he was fresh as a daisy for the start of the 1989 season. We kicked off in the sunshine at Rome and then won a third successive team gold medal at the European

Championships in Rotterdam, followed by my third Hickstead Derby victory.

Tony Elliot bought me three more young horses; there was Bluebird, bought from Mick Saywell, that later went on to win the Hickstead Derby with John Popely, then Governor and Destiny. My yard was almost full of Tony's horses; Apollo, Grand Slam, Serenade and Major Wager were the main contenders.

It gave me the opportunity to go on a spending spree of my own and build indoor stabling on the side of the indoor school to house more horses. The land at Sandall House Farm was mainly peat and very wet in the winter so it needed good drainage, but the advantage was that the ground was never hard in summer so I was able to use a small paddock on the other side of the stream for jumping. I built water ditches, dykes, banks – pretty much everything the horses could reasonably be expected to meet in competition.

We had seriously upgraded with the indoor stabling complex, which boasted a wash-box with hot running water and heat lamps for drying the horses, a feed room and an office. Hay and feed could be stored over the stables. The stables that were attached to the house were knocked down and the house extended. Now it felt like a house instead of a cottage.

Then I decided to try a spot of bartering instead of spending. I was riding one of my own horses, Attraction, around the collecting ring at Hickstead, chatting to John Whitaker who was on a mare called Florida. We were just walking around, talking, when I suddenly turned to him and said, 'I'm sick of this horse, it's just not doing what it should be doing.'

John replied, 'I'm sick of mine as well, I can't get her going, she's always stopping.'

'Do you fancy a swap then?' I asked him.

'Yeah, why not?' he said.

So we both got off and swapped horses then went on up to Ring 3 to jump. The word went round and lots of people rushed up to see what would happen.

John jumped a clear round on Attraction, then I went into the ring on Florida. I couldn't get through the start. It was like being back on Maybe. John was second in the class with my horse and he came up afterwards and said: 'Listen, I feel a bit guilty, that mare really can throw it in, I'll swap back if you like.' Like an idiot, I said no, I'd stand by the deal. I should have known better than to think I could take a horse that was stopping with John and expect it to go for me!

I didn't bother trying to jump Florida again that week, I simply put her on the lorry and took her home where I set about working her with the help of my brother Michael. We spent all afternoon trying to persuade her to cross the bridge over the stream at the bottom of the field so we could get to the jump paddock. Finally, we got her there and she jumped well. Afterwards, I put her on the lorry and took her to a little local show at the Offchurch polo grounds where there was a Small Open. I pulled her straight off the lorry with her tack on, jumped her in the Open and she won it.

At the end of the year, Florida was going well. I gave her to Sarah to ride and together they won the Grade C Final at the Horse of the Year Show in 1990. After that, I took the ride back and Florida went on to win the grand prix in Arnhem the following June, beating John into second place with Gammon. So after all I had got a good deal. Florida went on to win the grands prix in Zuidlaren and Leeuwarden.

Meanwhile the government changed the rules on cig- arette advertising, so the Raffles sponsorship ended early. Fortunately, Mick Saywell did me a big favour in introducing me to Steve Spouge, who arranged a three-year deal with

Burmah Castrol. The horsebox was re-sprayed in their corporate colours.

Throughout the turmoil of all the building work and the house extension Sarah was pregnant and on 20 September Harry was born. Sarah again surrendered herself to the mercies of Solihull Hospital and the birth went well, but Sarah wasn't very happy with me. I wasn't there. Mick Saywell had told me about a seven-year-old up in Yorkshire with Carl and Mark Fuller. Mick was convinced it was as good a horse as he had ever seen, so I phoned Tony Elliot, who said he thought the horse belonged to Paul Schockemöhle. I rang Paul, who told me the horse was returning to Germany so he could assess its potential; if I wanted to try it, I would have to go to his yard at Mühlen. Sarah was due to give birth any day and I was already committed to compete at Bremen. It made sense to combine the two trips but I didn't want to have to go to Germany any earlier than necessary. Mick insisted I had to go and buy that horse.

The horses were on their way to Bremen for 21–24 September so I drove over to Mühlen and tried the horse on Wednesday, 20 September. As soon as I sat on it I knew Mick Saywell was right: the horse was every bit as good as he'd said. That horse was Top Gun.

That very same day, Sarah went into labour. Harry was born while I was trying the horse. Even though I had been due to go abroad on the twenty-first anyway, Sarah never forgave me for going to buy a horse when she was due to give birth.

Gary Widdowson came with me to Paul's. He was looking for a young horse, but when he saw Top Gun jump he immediately wanted to buy the horse himself, for me to ride. Gary was a mate and already a good owner who had two horses with me. If I had known what was around the corner, I would have let Gary buy Top Gun, but instead I insisted Tony Elliot had first grabs. I phoned Tony and told him this was probably the best horse I had ever seen. He bought Top Gun for me to ride.

Johnny Wrathall, my friend and musketeer from the old days, was driving the horsebox for me and he collected Top Gun on the way home from the show at Bremen while I flew home to a new son, a new horse and a load of grief from Sarah.

Of the two important arrivals, I couldn't do much with the baby, although I was thrilled he'd arrived, but I could with the horse so the first thing I wanted to do was to get my new equine star out. The following weekend was a Talent Spotters Final at Stoneleigh. I took Top Gun, who jumped three clear rounds and won the final. At seven years of age he was capable of jumping big tracks, but personally I don't think jumping too big a track at a young age is good for the mind of a horse. Maybe they can do it, but they shouldn't be asked to. If you try to do too much with a seven-year-old you pay for it later. When horses get past eight or nine years old, so long as you can keep them sound, then you can keep them going until they are sixteen or so, because their mind stays confident. It's all in the mind and it's all about confidence.

So Top Gun competed in the smaller classes as third horse at international shows. He was an amazing horse, he had tremendous scope. When you jumped him, it didn't matter if you were six inches too close, or six inches too far off; as long as you were somewhere within the vicinity of the fence, he could jump it.

Jet black, he stood 16.2 hands and was by Grannus of the famous 'G' line. Top Gun was a character. He was a bit spooky when I first got him; sometimes he would spot a gremlin, turn and run the other way. The first day I rode him I had a job to get him up the field, just like Florida. Top Gun saw something in the hedge, reared up and whipped round. We had a bit of a disagreement but after that there was never a problem.

GOLD

Apollo rested after Bremen. After winning the gold at the Europeans, he'd done his bit and deserved a break. Grand Slam and Serenade were numbers one and two, and Top Gun was third horse.

Grand Slam was a lovely, easy horse. Not over big at 16 hands, he was also by Grannus but looked more thoroughbred in type. A beautiful model of a horse, he had a very kind temperament. When Daniel was only five he would ride Grand Slam around the yard and could even trot and canter him around the indoor school. That horse was very balanced and had beautiful manners; he just wanted to please. He may not have shown all the ability in the world when Tony Elliot first bought him for me, but he improved over the years.

One year at Amsterdam – and I can't for the life of me remember which year but I just remember the story – I had qualified for the Masters with Grand Slam. It was a real power-jumping class and that sort of pure power didn't suit him. Careful as he was, he didn't have the most scope. There were seven of us in the competition and we had to draw the order. I thought there was no way I would win it and by the time my name came out of the hat the worst draw I could get was fourth; so I simply chose to go fourth in each round.

The Masters was a unique class in that the winner took all. There was no prize money for second or third. It was fault and out, and each rider who jumped clear nominated a fence to be raised, or widened, immediately before they jumped their next round. Obviously, each rider raised the fence he thought his horse would be able to jump, but hoped it would catch out the opposition when it came to their round.

Grand Slam jumped clear in the first two rounds as a couple of riders dropped out. I kept putting up the planks, the last fence. I was going for careful jumping, not scope. As the rounds progressed, the other riders all faulted. There was just me, with Grand Slam trying his heart out, against Frenchman Hervé Godignon on the brilliant breeding stallion Quidam de Revel. There was no way I was going to beat him, so I figured the only way I'd get any money out of that class was to try and do a deal with Hervé. I offered to pull out if he split the prize money with me. No way, he said.

So Grand Slam went in again and jumped clear; then Hervé and Quidam jumped clear. I went back to Hervé and said, Come on, the lights are flashing on the dashboard and I'm in the red, I'm at my wits' end, let's do a deal. 'Non.'

Back in the ring, I put the plank up again, it was about six feet high. Grand Slam was incredible and tried his heart out and went round clear. It was the oxer coming out of the double that Hervé put up each time. He was going for scope. Up it went again and as Hervé and Quidam landed over the oxer they had so much pace they had the plank down! Grand Slam and I had won. Whether I was more pleased at winning the £11,000 or seeing Hervé lose, having twice offered him a deal for me to retire, I don't know, but Grand Slam was a hero! How he jumped that oxer coming out of the double I don't know. He practically walked up the front rail, scrambled across it and climbed down the other side, all without dislodging a single pole. Amazing.

The Dutch rider Jan Tops was one of the biggest horse dealers in the world at that time and went on to found the Global Champions Tour in 2006. He came to stay at Sandall House Farm before catching a flight from Birmingham Airport the next morning. At about nine o'clock that night the phone rang. It was Tony Elliot and he dropped a bombshell. He would be selling all nine of his horses. This included Grand Slam, Top Gun and Serenade. Apollo would be my only good horse left, apart from Fiorella, a speed horse owned by Gary Widdowson.

Tony needed a vast sum of money quickly, and wanted them sold within a week. He named his price for the lot, and offered me a small percentage commission. Big of him, I thought, considering I had just built them up into one of the top strings in the world. He was taking my livelihood from me, after all the work I had done. I wouldn't be left with much.

I was utterly devastated, absolutely shell-shocked. I didn't stay on the phone to him for very long. I couldn't believe what I was hearing and bitterly regretted not letting my mate Gary Widdowson buy Top Gun. When I told Jan Tops what had transpired, he wanted the details. Tony's price would ensure he made a healthy profit over what he had paid for them. I convinced Jan that in Top Gun I had possibly the best horse in the world on my yard, so the next morning Jan tried him. We went back into the house and talked it over.

Jan offered to buy all nine horses, and the horsebox, and gave me three months to find another buyer for them who would let me keep the rides. This was very generous of him. With me as go-between, he and Tony then haggled about the price and finally struck a deal. In order for Jan to get the lowest possible price, I had thrown in my commission as a sweetener. Now I had just three months to find buyers for the horses in order to keep the rides, otherwise all I would have left would be the ageing Apollo, Fiorella, Major Wager and young Florida, my swap-shop horse.

I rang round everybody I could think of in England who might buy a horse for me. I contacted David Broome in case Lord Harris wanted to buy them, or some of them, or even just one of them. The one I was desperate to keep was Top Gun, who I knew would be one of the best horses in the world. I called all the leading lights at the BSJA: Michael Bates, Michael Bullman, Ronnie Massarella. I even tried to get a syndicate together, but nothing came of it. No one would, or could, buy them.

A Run of Bad Luck

Ludger Beerbaum had become a good friend in the days when we were buying horses through Paul Schockemöhle. I called Ludger, who offered to speak to Alexander Moksel, his sponsor at that time, but sadly nothing came of it. Jan, being a dealer, needed profit on these horses and Mr Moksel wasn't interested.

Then Jan suggested that if I couldn't find a buyer within the three months we could sell the horses individually for as much money as possible and split the profit. I decided that wasn't too bad, at least I would earn some money out of it all.

The season was just starting, so I set off to the World Cup shows with the horses, all of them owned now by Jan Tops. In 'sHertogenbosch Top Gun won the grand prix; people on the circuit knew the situation and there was a lot of interest in the horses but I wasn't doing very well finding a buyer for myself, I'd virtually given up. Now my main efforts were aimed at trying to sell them for as much as possible so I could split the profit with Jan.

On the way to the 1990 World Cup final in Dortmund we were stabled with Axel Wöckener in Germany, where the American rider Debbie Dolan tried Top Gun. She didn't buy him and I expect she regretted it.

At the World Cup final, Top Gun won the grand prix, he was definitely realising his potential. Then, unbelievably, Grand Slam won the second leg of the World Cup final, beating Milton! Although Milton went on to win the final and Jappeloup was second, Grand Slam and I finished sixth overall.

The whole sorry saga came to an end when Jan Tops arranged to sell Top Gun to his own sponsor, Alfonso Romo, and kept the ride for himself. Jan also arranged to sell Governor to Belgium's Philippe Le Jeune; the horse went on to win two Mercedes Masters in Stuttgart. Bluebird was sold to John Popely and went on to win the Hickstead Derby, while Serenade was sold to Martin

Lucas and became his best horse. That really was a true top string of horses. The remaining horses all went to Holland to Jan's dealing yard and I came home from Dortmund with an empty horsebox.

Jan told me that the horses had been sold for no more than he had paid for them. I found that hard to believe. At least I had the horsebox.

Back home, the situation was very tough. I had hardly any horses and no money as everything was invested in the property. I wasn't the easiest person to be living with and this put a strain on my marriage.

In May, Jan told me that Grand Slam had not yet been sold. I talked it over with Sarah and then had a meeting with our bank manager at Barclays. We arranged to mortgage the farm to raise the money to buy Grand Slam. Maybe not a very wise thing to do, but my back was against the wall and I had to do something. I needed another good horse on the yard. We insured Grand Slam for the price we paid, and also took out a Life Assurance Policy on my life so that the mortgage would be paid off if anything should happen to me.

But Grand Slam turned out to be an excellent buy. At the World Championships in Stockholm that year, the first ever World Equestrian Games, he was on the British team with Milton, Monsanta and Countryman. Between the four of them, those horses carried John, Michael, David and myself to a bronze medal. Grand Slam was improving with age and that year he won £60,000; that helped towards the mortgage.

Johnny Wrathall, one of the three musketeers, had been driving my horsebox whenever he had the chance. He enjoyed coming to shows, and I enjoyed having him there, he was good company. Johnny had driven the horses out to Lucerne, Rome, all over Europe. About two weeks before we were due to leave for the World Championships in Stockholm, Johnny called me to say he wasn't busy so could he drive my horses. I had to tell him they were booked to go with John Whitaker and he already had a driver. So Johnny got a job driving for David Rogers' Northampton-based transport company, which was looking after Madonna's Wembley concert. David Rogers is a staunch supporter of showjumping and nearly always comes to the World Cup final and the Championships.

Johnny was hired to drive all Madonna's equipment from Wembley to Paris the night after the concert, together with another driver. Johnny drove to the ferry and then they swapped over in Calais. The other driver fell asleep at the wheel while Johnny was taking a nap in the bunk at the rear of the cab. Tragically, the lorry hit a bridge and they were both killed. If only I had let Johnny drive my horses in my own lorry, he would still be with us today. Like our other musketeer, Stuart Crutchlow, Johnny is remembered with a trophy. The Johnny Wrathall Memorial Trophy is presented annually by the Midlands Area Point-to-Point circuit to the Leading Gentleman Rider.

13

Rising Thanks to Phoenix

My luck took a turn for the better when, in June 1990, David Broome offered me his horse Phoenix Park to ride. Phoenix Park had been plagued by injury throughout his career and by the time he came to me he only had one lung, as a result of a nasty bout of pleurisy and pneumonia, and he had a carbon fibre implant in one of his front tendons. Caring for him was a real challenge and Mark Beever rose to that challenge. Phoenix Park was fourteen by then, a big grey Irish Sports horse. He'd had two years off with his lung problems and hadn't jumped much. With only one lung and three good legs, you'd have thought he would have had enough traumas in his life, but there were more to come.

Phoenix Park was an odd horse. He'd never lie down and when he went to sleep standing up he would fall over – there must have been something wrong with his balance mechanism. We'd hear a big crash in the stable and there he would be, down on the floor. But he had a nice soft landing as he was always bedded down on paper because of his delicate respiratory system.

I struck up a good relationship with him from the start. If he hadn't been plagued with injury, he could have been one of the great horses. He had an enormous jump, was very careful, but he was difficult to sit on over a fence. When he landed he would often anticipate the next turn and make a left or a right before you were ready. And sometimes he would guess wrong and go the wrong way.

He nearly unshipped me once at Wembley but he actually did get David on the floor in Paris during the World Cup. It was at a combination; he jumped in and unshipped David as he landed. David came off and was sitting with his back to the second element, an oxer. Phoenix Park kept going, all on his own, and jumped straight over the top of David, and the fence, and then jumped the third element!

I rode him in one show at Franconville north-west of Paris then took him straight to Dublin where he won the grand prix. And he won it again the following year. Just from June through to Olympia that December, Phoenix Park won close on £100,000. At the end of the year, David Broome and I couldn't agree on the prize money split. Sometimes owners have disagreements with their riders about the prize money split. The late Malcolm Barr, John Whitaker's father-in-law, once suggested to John that they should have a different arrangement the next year. 'Why?' asked John. 'Do you wanna ride the horse?' Apparently, Mr Barr never raised the subject again.

I told David that I wasn't prepared to go on riding Phoenix Park under his terms so the next season the horse was sent to the Edgars' and Marie had a go at riding him, but it wasn't a success. Sure enough, David knew which side his bread was buttered and Phoenix Park arrived back in my yard in July.

He immediately started winning again. We won the Kerrygold Grand Prix in Dublin, were fourth in the grand prix in Rotterdam, had a good show at Spruce Meadows in Calgary and took a Team

Silver in La Baule at the European Championships. To finish off, he won the Masters at the Horse of the Year Show.

And then he finished himself off. After returning home on the Sunday morning he was turned out in the paddock when I heard an almighty crash on the outside wall of the indoor school. I ran to have a look and found Phoenix Park standing there with his hind leg swinging. The metal sheeting of the school was bent a foot inwards, he had hit it with such force.

He was led in on three legs, his one hind leg swinging round and round. I rang David to warn him that we would probably have to put the horse down, as he appeared to have broken his leg.

My then vet, John Williams, lived in the village and he rushed over. He diagnosed a broken tendon down the front of the hock. Phoenix Park was taken to John's Avonvale Equine Clinic where the injury was judged to be inoperable. I wanted the horse to have a chance though, so I telephoned Dr Peter Cronau. He flew over from Germany and successfully inserted a carbon fibre tendon.

Phoenix Park came home to recover but within a week he developed colic. Watching him trying to get down to roll but unable to because of his newly repaired hind leg was one of the worst sights of my life. Back at Avonvale he had another operation. I called him the Bionic Horse after that. Amazingly, he made a full recovery and finished his days happily jumping with local Warwickshire rider David Austin.

When the Burmah-Castrol arrangement came to an end I was again without a sponsor. I feared lean times ahead but in the summer of 1990 Mike Rowland from Alan Paul Hairdressing offered to sponsor Geoff Billington and me. The Alan Paul colours were very pretty – pink, white and grey! The saddle cloths were white with pink writing and the bandages were pink. Jackets were grey with pink and white writing. Not very macho but I got used to it, eventually.

The horsebox, painted up in that Alan Paul livery, looked startling. It's surprising to me but pink horseboxes seem to have become quite popular these days. Maybe we started a trend.

Mike Rowland rode at a lower level so he understood horses – he was a laugh was Mike. Alan Paul were great sponsors but unfortunately Mike and his partner Alan Moss got into a bit of trouble and had to wind the company up. Mike was very good about it, he told us what had happened and the sponsorship ceased after about eighteen months.

There were no hard feelings, we didn't fall out over it, and Geoff and I took Mike Rowland to Kössen skiing later on in January 1992. Every year we competed at the snow show in Kössen and combined it with a spot of skiing. Mike had never skied before but Geoff and I told him that the best way to learn was to go up to the top of the mountain, put your skis on and just come down nice and gently.

Mike obediently put his skis on and straight away he fell over. Geoff started laughing and I told Mike, 'Come on, we'll ski down a bit and then you follow us.' He looked at us doubtfully. I assured Mike we'd wait for him and when he'd caught up we'd go on. I could see him thinking, 'Yeah, right,' but Geoff and I set off down the slope. We stopped after a couple of hundred yards and we could see Mike coming down; he was doing pretty well, considering. But there was a group of beginners all stood in a line and as Mike skied towards them, seemingly in control but actually not, he shouted, 'Watch out!' and promptly wiped out about six of them like skittles.

Geoff and I laughed our socks off. I said to Geoff we should get on as Mike was going to be all day. We left him lying in the middle of the ski class and shot off down the slopes. Two hours later we were in a bar drinking Glühwein. In the distance we could see this figure, skis on his shoulder, slipping over every ten yards. It was Mike. When he finally arrived he complained how nice it was of us to leave him there like that. Well, now he knew what it felt like when he left us as he had without sponsorship! It was all in good humour.

Not long afterwards, Mike and Alan's 'bit of trouble' escalated and they both spent some time in one of Her Majesty's hostelries. Tragically, Alan died very soon after he was released. It was terribly sad. He was a lovely man, despite his creative accounting. I think the stress was all too much for him.

It's a wild place, Kössen. I went there three or four years running, so I must have liked it. Hannes Stern was running the snow show. His family owned the Gasthof Post hotel in those days. One year I took Richard Dunwoody with me. He needed a holiday as he was fed up and bored, having been banned for three weeks for pushing Adrian Maguire off the track at Nottingham. We shared a room and had some wild nights. He thought the jockeys knew how to have a good time, but we showjumpers definitely held our own.

Another time, Geoff Billington, Michael Whitaker and I ended up in the same bed. I have no idea why. It's a good job I only went there once a year as I needed a rest when I got home. One year I was sharing a room with Chris Goosen, father of Guy and Mandy, who both went on to be successful international showjumpers. I woke up in the morning, and on opening my suitcase found that Chris had been sick in it. Charming!

Chris's son, Guy, was a useful young rider back then. He had come up through pony ranks and it was time for him to move on to horses. Despite his having thrown up in my suitcase, when Chris asked would I have Guy come to me for a winter's work,

I said yes. Guy was a lovely lad and some of the best times at Sandall House Farm were had while Guy was there.

We didn't have a proper bedroom for him – we were short of staff accommodation – so Guy had to sleep on a bed shoved in a corner somewhere. I think he had been pampered a bit, growing up. I often grounded him for minor misdemeanours. If he did something wrong, or if the tack wasn't clean enough, he would either be grounded or he would have to clean the toilets. Perhaps some of Ted's treatment had not been showered off me.

Guy certainly wasn't an easy man to get out of bed in the morning. Every day he'd turn up late on the yard, so in the end, five minutes after he was supposed to be on the yard, I opened his door and slung a bucket of water over him. Apparently, it took days for his mattress to dry out. I always have been very frugal with the central heating!

His habit of getting up late meant he was always in such a rush to get ready that he'd often turn up on the yard unshaven. I used to tell him to get a shave. Sometimes he did, sometimes he didn't. One night we had been to a show at Stoneleigh and got back quite late. We did the horses then five minutes later Guy came over and said: 'See you later, I'm just going out.' I assumed he was going to see his girlfriend so questioned why he wasn't going to have a shower and a shave. He said he'd do it when he got back – poor girlfriend! I tried to persuade him but Guy was insistent, he'd shower when he got back. Chris had told me to be quite hard on Guy as the lad wasn't spoiled just very laid-back. So I laid the law down: 'You're not going out unless you get showered and shaved. Otherwise you are stopping in.'

Guy caved. 'All right then, I'll go and do it.' But I had a bright idea that could cure him permanently of going out unwashed. I told him that if he wanted to go out that night, he'd take a shower in the horse washroom, where the water wasn't heated, so he'd remember in future to get cleaned up properly before he went out. Guy had no choice but to comply even though it was the middle of winter. He went off down the yard to the horses' wash box and I threw him a bar of soap and a towel and shut the door on him. Ten minutes later, Simon Gatward, who was also working for us, went down to the stables and opened the wash box door to see how Guy was getting on. He had switched on all the solarium lights used to dry the horses and was having a nice cosy, warm shower. Simon promptly took a photograph of him. I wish I had a copy of that!

At least after that Guy never forgot to take a shower while he was with me. Heaven knows what happened to his shower habits after that, but Guy had a lot of success with Gary Widdowson's horse, Fiorella, who he eventually bought. He went to work for Paul Schockemöhle in Germany with his sister, Mandy, another good rider. In 2014 Guy and his wife Zhanna set up their own place near Munster; Mandy and her husband Oliver are based in Bavaria. Their mother, Tina, is still based in Warwickshire and is an accredited coach and involved with the World Class Development Programme.

Driving home from another Kössen skiing holiday in January 1991, we were waiting for the ferry when the phone rang. It was Freddie Welch, giving me the heads up that I should expect a call from his wife, Sue, about a horse of hers called Glint of Gold: 'Sue's got a big chestnut horse she wants you to have. It's not very careful but, whatever you do, don't be horrible about it because she thinks the world of it, it's a pet. But if you take that one and get on with it for a while you're sure to get another one.'

A bit later on, Sue called and asked whether I would like to have Glint of Gold. My head was thinking, Er, not really, but my voice said I would be absolutely delighted. Thanks for warning me, Freddie! That phone call produced one of the best owners

Rising Thanks to Phoenix

I could ever have wished for. Sue understood that horses aren't machines but have to be carefully nurtured. Of course she would, having been a successful rider herself. As Sue Cohen, before she married Fred, she was Ladies European Champion in 1960. Fred had also been a very successful rider and was regularly on teams with Harvey and Broomie. He was the first British rider to win the puissance at Olympia, on Rossmore II, in 1977, the year before my high-jump record. When he stopped riding he concentrated on breeding racehorses and showjumpers, which he did until he died aged eighty-one in March 2010.

I don't know what I would have done without Sue in those days. Not only did she supply me with some very good horses, she was like a second mother to me. I wouldn't be where I am today without her support; I knew I could call her at any time of the day and rely on her. It wasn't only with showjumping, as Sue also had a few good racehorses and in the wintertime we'd go racing a lot together.

When Glint of Gold arrived I found he could kick poles better than Kevin Keegan kicked footballs. I had the horse for a few months before finally Freddie and I persuaded Sue to pass him on and buy something better.

We went to Paul Schockemöhle and bought a horse called Just Blackie, the first of many horses Sue bought for me. In later years, Sue bought Werra and Limited Edition, and then at the 1991 PSI Sale she acquired Showtime, who competed in the Olympics at Atlanta in 1996. How I wished Sue had been around as an owner when I'd had the chance of buying Top Gun.

Werra arrived at the yard in September 1991. She was quite a difficult character, very strong to ride but an excellent jumper, so careful. She wasn't super sound; she was was an older, more experienced horse, already twelve when Sue sent her to me. Werra was bought as a backstop to keep me going and she did exactly that, winning a couple of grands prix before retiring and going back to Schockemöhle's to breed.

Limited Edition won a lot of good classes for me but was plagued with unsoundness. He won thirty-three classes from 1992 through to 1995, and prize money adding up to nearly a quarter of a million pounds. Like Apollo, Limited Edition was very versatile; he won puissance, speed classes, grands prix and the King's Cup at Hickstead.

Showtime, by Pilot, was only six years old and had already had a foal by embryo transfer before she came to me. I took it easy with her to start with.

They didn't have equine college courses in my day and all my staff have learned and got experience on the job. The only satisfactory college student I ever had on a work placement was Charlotte Scott. She really could ride well, she was a natural. She was riding the older horses, Phoenix Park and Apollo. It was funny but although she was a real redhead I never saw a flash of temper from her. I asked her to get Apollo 'Grand National fit' for his last assault on the Hickstead Derby. I was planning to retire him from top-class competition later that year.

Charlotte took me at my word and gave him lots of long, slow canter work and walked him up and down the hills for hours, making him tremendously fit and strong. As an older horse, Apollo needed to be super-fit to cope with the gruelling Derby track. He looked terrific when he was loaded up to go down to Hickstead and, sure enough, he was super-fit.

He leapt over the open water at a gallop and then I tried to check him for the upright of rails straight after. I was expecting him to be a bit tired and to come back to me easily, but he wasn't remotely worn out and took the rails too fast, just clipping the top pole off. He was second but because it was his last Derby he was decked out in a garland of leaves and a fuss was made of him. He probably thought he had won! I hope so. I wanted him to go out at the top.

We moved on to Dublin later in August where I became even more convinced that Apollo, now sixteen years old, should retire. Every time Apollo had been to Dublin he had always won a class, but after his exertions in the Derby he was struggling. His last indoor show was Copenhagen that October, then I kept him in work over the winter, we didn't turn him away for a rest, before I took him to Kössen to jump on the snow. This was much lower key for him and he enjoyed himself, he thought it was fun, but after he came home I told his owner, Linda Jones, it was time to retire him; he had done enough. I was absolutely staggered when Linda suggested we sell him as a Young Riders horse! How could she even consider letting the horse go on working hard after he'd been such a good servant?

I knew Apollo wouldn't want to languish in the field, so I asked my father if he thought my stepmother, Janette, would like to have him to hunt. Janette was delighted and Apollo went to live at Odnaull End Farm, grazing in the fields where I had started riding with Oxo. When I told Linda Jones that I had given him to my stepmother to hunt, she wanted to know how much Dad would pay for Apollo as a hunter. I told her that there was no way she was going to have the last penny out of him. I told her the horse didn't owe her a thing; she should be honoured to have owned a horse like Apollo and now she should just leave him be and let him retire doing something he enjoyed.

Linda put the phone down on me and I never heard from her again.

A couple of years later, I borrowed Apollo to hunt and went out with my vet friend, John Williams, who was riding West Tip, winner of the 1986 Grand National with Richard Dunwoody. I couldn't hold one side of him and after half an hour I gave up.

He was beautifully behaved for Janette and did everything she wanted from him. But as soon as I got back on him he was off again, he must have been re-living old memories! Apollo lived to the grand old age of thirty-one. After four seasons hunting, he retired completely to roam around Odnaull End Farm.

Having lost the Alan Paul Hairdressing sponsorship, I was once again without a sponsor. In November I was in the collecting ring at the Maastricht show in November when the last person in the world I expected to help me marched straight up and asked, 'Do you want Everest back?' It was Ted Edgar. Those were the first words he had spoken to me since I had left back in 1985. I was surprised he'd spoken to me at all, let alone offered me a good sponsorship deal.

A contract was thrashed out with the Managing Director, Kevin Mahoney, and Gerry Cregeen who was in charge of PR for Everest. It was a generous sponsorship. Back on with Everest? Déjà vu!

The horsebox was repainted in the blue and green Everest colours and all the pink jackets, shirts and umbrellas were given away to friends. Smart new Everest ones took their place. All the horses had their prefixes changed yet again, but in those days horses' names changed almost annually!

Everest was a fantastic sponsor and we had some good times with Kevin Mahoney and his deputy Wayne Money. They had a real interest in the sport and were always on the riders' side. After taking me on they also pulled John and Michael Whitaker on board. During the company's twenty-eight-year involvement with showjumping they were probably the biggest contributor to our sport in this country, sponsoring classes as well as riders.

We always went to their Christmas parties at the Royal

Lancaster Hotel. Over seven hundred people would attend. In February they would have a meeting of the 'Millionaires Club', a men-only night, for the members of their workforce who had done more than a million pounds' worth of business that year. That was always a good night out, but I don't know what happened to the women who had done more than a million pounds' worth of business.

One night in particular springs to mind; John, Michael and I went down to London for a night out with Wayne and Kevin, together with a few other guys from Everest. We were in a bar and restaurant called Soho Soho, in Soho funnily enough. We finished up very late and I took a taxi to the station and got on the train to Coventry. But I fell asleep, missed my stop and had to turn round and come back from Birmingham in the early hours of the morning.

I thought that was a rough deal, but John and Michael didn't get home until two days later. They had both had far too much to drink and couldn't possibly drive home. So Kevin and Wayne ordered a car transporter to take Michael's car home. Then they sent John and Michael home in a taxi, all the way to Nottinghamshire where Michael lived. That's the sort of sponsors they were: generous, good-hearted and great fun.

I'll never forget teaching Kevin Mahoney to ride. He wanted to learn and get the experience on video so he could show off at the annual Everest awards. At that time the quietest horse in the yard was Dollar Girl, who would be one of my great horses, so I taught him on her. The first day was quite good, the second day was a bit better, but then Kevin became ambitious and wanted to canter. He was in the school as she went from trot to canter and Dollar Girl could tell that Kevin wasn't competent. She gradually built up speed and went round the corner of the school like a motorbike, at which point Kevin fell off, bounced off the wooden kicking boards at the side of the school and got splinters in his bum!

Kevin was very determined. He was adamant that he was going to be filmed jumping Dollar Girl. I couldn't see any way this was going to happen. In the end, I filmed Kevin cantering around the corner to the fence, then I stopped filming, Kevin got off the horse and took the video camera from me, I got on, Kevin started filming, Dollar Girl jumped the fence with me and then I put Kevin back on board to continue around the school. We wore matching clothes and used very poor lighting. We showed the video at their promotional meeting and I think we got away with it.

I haven't seen Kevin for years but I still see Wayne at the races.

14

Olympics and Racing

I rarely used to sell horses but in 1992 I was approached by Canadian Terrance 'Torchy' Millar. He asked if I would consider selling Grand Slam, who was then twelve years old and still a complete gentleman; he was ideal for a Young Rider. Fifteen-year-old Skye Eurilo came over from Canada to try him and loved him. He went beautifully for her so I sold him and he went to live in Canada. Grand Slam had definitely proved a good buy; he had more than paid back the mortgage on the house. He jumped well with Skye for several years before very sadly dying of a burst artery in his stomach.

When my marriage to Sarah ended it was messy. The press raked it all up when I came back after breaking my neck and even after we won team gold in London, but it was our business and I'm not raking it up again apart from to say the final straw was my affair with Bettina Melliger. Every Monday was set aside to drive up to Shropshire to see Daniel and Harry. I used to collect them from school, bring them home for the night and then take them back the next morning. For seven years I religiously visited them, driving up to Shropshire like the old days when I was dating Sarah.

The children would stay with me for school holidays, sometimes turning up complete with ponies.

Daniel had a chicken house at my farm. It was his hobby, he loved his chickens. He had all sorts of exotic breeds and in his holidays he would go to market with Janette's father. David Southall used to pick Daniel up and take him to Henley market every Wednesday. Daniel would set off with an empty crate and come back with a full one every time. He didn't rear chickens for eating like I used to, he just bought them, bought some more, hatched a few and then sold a few. David said that Daniel drove a hard bargain at market, even though he was only about twelve years old.

One Christmas I bought Daniel and Harry a pair of reindeer. They were cute fawns but they soon grew and after a while they became so big we had to build deer fencing around their paddock. We kept them for a few years but eventually sold them to a deer farm when they became much too big to handle.

Remember the lad who bundled me up in my sleeping bag and threw me out of the Edgars' horsebox many years back? Well, it was an Olympic year and Tim Grubb came over from America for an attack at getting on the British team. And guess where he based himself? Yep, at my house. I was his nanny.

He brought three horses: Denizen, Two Plus Two and another whose name escapes me. I seem to recall his groom, the long-suffering Fiona Scott, had to sleep in the feed room as we had run out of accommodation. I was on my own and Tim's wife, the American showjumper Michelle McEvoy, was not happy with him and had stayed over in America. The warning went out locally: 'Lock up your daughters!'

Tim treated the place like a hotel and lived as if we had a maid coming in every day. Every morning I'd come down to find all the lights on, the television still on and Johnny Walker lying dead on the floor! He'd use six towels when one would do and then leave them lying wet all over the bathroom floor. But he was so good-natured and had an excellent sense of humour – something I had to acquire, living with him!

He used to get up at noon, go outside and ask Fiona to tack up his horses. She would refuse, telling him she'd already worked them and that I had ridden Denizen for him. So he would go back in and get some lunch. It's poignant to remember those days now as Tim sadly died in 2010 from congestive heart failure. He was only fifty-five.

Dollar Girl originally came into this country for John Whitaker to ride. Her owner, Joe Haller, always hung around John and could often be seen having a drink with him in the evening. Joe was not the easiest of owners. He wasn't a horseman and apparently had worked as a TV repair man before marrying well.

I'd been to Joe's birthday party many years before – I can't remember how many – at the Argentinian restaurant opposite the Martinez Hotel in Cannes. Joe had invited me along with John and Michael Whitaker and my Australian pal, Jeff McVean. Swiss rider Thomas Fuchs was there with his great mate Willi Melliger, who was still married to Bettina then.

Joe wanted Dollar Girl to go to the Barcelona Olympics but he wasn't getting on too well with the present rider, Thomas Fuchs. Obviously, to compete at Barcelona the horse would have to make the Swiss team. At the Geneva show late in 1991, there was a bonus prize of 50,000 Swiss francs on offer for the horse that went through the show with no faults. By the end of the show, Dollar Girl was the only horse left that could win the bonus prize; she hadn't had a single fence down the whole time. Thomas Fuchs was in the jump-off for the grand prix but instead of playing safe with a steady clear, he tried to win the class as well as the bonus prize. Going fast against the clock, Dollar Girl had the last fence down and consequently didn't win the grand prix or the bonus prize. Joe Haller threw his toys out of the pram and promptly took the horse away from Thomas Fuchs and gave her to John to ride early in 1992. John was his first choice of rider because it was assumed that Milton wouldn't be going to the Olympics after what happened before Seoul in 1988.

John rode her in some of the World Cup qualifiers but she didn't suit his way of riding. In the meantime, it was confirmed that Mr and Mrs Bradley would let Milton go to Barcelona and that he would be John's intended mount. Dollar Girl was still without a jockey for Barcelona and as the horse was registered to the British team, it was too late to change nationality. I did not have an Olympic horse, so John suggested that Joe gave Dollar Girl to me to try. She had been off for a while with an abscess in her foot, which I think she'd probably had for a long time, and that would explain why she didn't go so well for John.

I first rode Dollar Girl at the Hickstead May meeting where they put on a special Olympic qualifier class at the end of the show after the grand prix. I had to go in never having sat on the mare; she had not arrived down at the ring soon enough and I only had about five minutes to warm up. I had to get round with 8 faults or less. Added to all this, Dollar Girl had never before been in the unique Hickstead arena. It was quite an ordeal for both of us, but we managed to scrape through with only two fences down. At least I was qualified for Barcelona, although maybe qualifying was the worst thing I could have done, bearing in mind what was to come later that year.

I campaigned Dollar Girl at Wolfsburg, Arnhem and Aachen. I had to try and get as much experience with her as I could. At Aachen we finished second in the grand prix to Jos Lansink on Egano. We then went on to Royan in France along with John,

Olympics and Racing

Tim, Michael and David as the five selected for the team at the Barcelona Olympics. David fell heavily at Royan and hurt his back, leaving him lame for a few days. Ronnie had five top horses and riders, but would only need four in the team. Who would he drop? The tension in the camp was palpable.

We arrived at the Barcelona Olympics still not knowing which one of us would be dropped from the team. There was a bit of bad feeling when David found himself on the substitute's bench. I think David felt that Tim Grubb, who had been living in America for years, should have been dropped, even though Tim's horse Denizen was on very good form. But David had hurt his back and wasn't 100 per cent; I am sure that was the reason Ronnie left him out of the team.

In the Olympic Village I shared a room with John, and Michael and Tim shared with Ronnie – they both snore for England so I doubt they kept each other awake. The dressage riders and the event riders were in our apartment as well; we were all jammed in together, although we did make sure we got the biggest rooms, seeing as the dressage riders were new boys. Carl Hester's never forgotten it!

Barcelona wasn't the *craic* that Seoul had been. It was humid, there was no air conditioning and Spain in August can be very hot. The jumping was held at the Real Club de Polo, venue of the Barcelona Show. The lovely grass arena had been ripped up and replaced with sand and a new stabling complex had been built.

The horses travelled out on Chris Goosen's lorry; he came along as our 'entertainments manager' and drove us from Royan to Barcelona. We didn't participate in the whole Olympic spirit as much at Barcelona as we had at Seoul. We didn't make it to the Opening or Closing Ceremony but we managed to go and support the Eventers out on the golf course in the mountains. We enjoyed ourselves but we were taking the job seriously. With

Milton, Monsanta, Dollar Girl and Denizen we had four of the world's top horses. We thought we had a strong team; this was going to be our Games.

Throughout my jumping career, I was always first to go for the team. Ronnie always said he put me there because I was organised and he knew I would be ready on time. The team competition was an early start: eight in the morning. When I walked the course, I remember thinking it was pretty big, but I wasn't worried because Dollar Girl was on good form.

Starting off on the course she was jumping fantastic, she never put a toe on a pole, but it was a very long course, sixteen jumping efforts. She was jumping so well, putting in such a lot of effort. Then I turned away from the entrance towards the final fence. With hindsight, I don't think it was anything to do with the water, although it was a big, full-size water jump with two spooky curly planks over it, but the sun hadn't got up fully, the ring was very bright in one part and in the shade it was very dark. It cast a bad light on the water.

That was the excuse everyone made for Dollar Girl but maybe she just thought, sod it – I've put in so much effort, do I really have to turn away from the entrance and keep going? Whatever the reason, when she got to the water she stuck her head down and said no. We were clear until then, the last fence. I turned her away and tried again but she dug her toes in three times and was eliminated. I couldn't believe it. For a horse that had been jumping so well to throw the towel in and get eliminated, well, it was odd.

I felt bad for the other team members because it put them under intense pressure. When they went in the ring they knew their round would have to count, there was no discard score to fall back on. I know *if* is a little word with a big meaning, but if I had gone clear in that round I think it would have built the lads' confidence up.

Olympics and Racing

I went out and got off. I didn't bother to school Dollar Girl or build a fence outside which was like the water, I just left her alone with Mark. I was sick as a Blackpool donkey. In the second round, she jumped the water with no problem but had two down. The Olympics were over for me.

In the individual competition I ended up biting the dust at the triple bar. Tim Grubb and Denizen also bit the dust; then John and Milton had an unlucky peck in the double of oxers and had to pull out of the second part, having jumped in too big. And Monsanta gave up going down the combination. The combination was big; vertical, oxer, oxer. Monsanta knew he couldn't make the back rail so he simply jumped the front rail, diving down between the front and back rails. Nothing dangerous, the horse just knew he couldn't make the spread. It was quite smart of him really.

It wasn't our year. All in all, it was a miserable Olympics. I got home still in shock over our elimination. Apollo had been rested after the Seoul Olympics, but that wasn't going to happen to Dollar Girl. After all, she'd hardly done anything and the journey to Spain was not arduous. I went to Rotterdam where we finished sixth in the grand prix. No repeat of the refusal so that was, just as I thought, a one-off. But Dollar Girl didn't seem to be enjoying her jumping.

I jumped her indoors throughout the rest of the year without winning much, so after Berlin in December I decided to give her a complete break to see if I could freshen her up, much to Joe Haller's disgust. He couldn't understand why a horse has to be rested for four months in the field. He was one of those owners who thought horses were money machines, not animals.

Her preparation for the Barcelona Olympics was not normally how I would do it. I had rushed around trying to get as much mileage on the clock as possible because I only had a couple of months to get used to her. I decided to put her in the field and start afresh next year.

That was the right decision; 1993 was a good year for Dollar Girl and she went on an up after that. She won a good class in Rome, the grand prix in St Gallen, Ascona and then Calgary where the Du Maurier was worth $250,000. It was my second win in that prestigious event. She then went on and jumped indoors all that winter, winning consistently. In the course of her career, Dollar Girl won over a million pounds.

She was 16.1 hands and Hanoverian bred by Dynamo. She was so very kind and could be ridden by almost anybody, which is why Kevin Mahoney had learned to ride on her, the most expensive riding school horse ever!! The grooms all loved her and if ever there was a 'human' horse it was Dollar Girl.

She wasn't the soundest horse in the world. She had very delicate feet and it was essential to keep the balance of her feet correct in order to keep her sound. I once sent her down to David Nicholson's at Jackdaw Castle because she was a bit lame on the turn but sound on a straight line. She had to be kept fairly fit so I asked David to have her so she could canter on the perfect surface of his gallop. But I never thought to send her own feed with her and David was pumping high protein racehorse feed into her, it wasn't doing wonders for her blood.

When I got her back she was sound and fit, but incredibly fresh. I took her to Rotterdam where she tied up very badly with Azoturia and we had to put her in a trailer to take her back to the stables. She had protein poisoning and it took a week or ten days to get her blood right again.

Driving a lorry for six horses plus living accommodation requires an HGV licence, which Mark Beever didn't have, so whenever the horses went to a show I had to employ a driver to go with him. Towards the end of the year, Julie Leonard, aka Cilla, who did have an HGV licence left Paul Schockemöhle and came to work for me. She now works for Dan at Lodge Hill. I had met Cilla a few years earlier when she worked for Freddie Welch. I knew she could be relied on to take care of my horses, and she had driven all over Germany for Schockemöhle so I felt confident she could handle a large horsebox. Showjumpers are very valuable – a careful driver is essential.

It had never really gone away, but liaising with David Nicholson about Dollar Girl gave me the racing bug again. I'd told David I fancied having a couple of point-to-pointers that I could train myself and he suggested that I call David Minton, who used to work for the British Bloodstock Agency. Through David I bought Jolly Roger, who had run under rules and had a bit of form, to-gether with a young horse called Mystic Mickey, a five-year-old. My brother Michael was riding in point-to-points so I set about getting my new horses fit. A lad called Tony Brown, who had pre-viously worked for Martin Pipe, was based with me and I decided he was the best person to look after the pointers. Tony took them over and developed a real interest in them, instigating a fitness regime and taking charge of their feeding.

We had Jolly and Mickey ready to run at the first meeting of the season in January. and on Christmas Eve I thought I would take them over to Jackdaws Castle to have a good blow out. My brother Michael rode Jolly and I was on Mystic Mickey. Halfway up the long gallop, Mickey started to cough. I immediately pulled up, jumped off and within seconds the horse dropped down dead. He'd burst an artery in his lung. I had been incredibly lucky be-cause if I hadn't jumped off I could have been trapped underneath him. Everyone at the yard was very upset but it was no one's fault and sadly could not have been avoided.

Jolly Roger turned out to be quite useful. He placed second in two point-to-points and in two hunter chases at Nottingham and Bangor, all with Michael riding him. Sadly, he then broke down in front at a hunter chase meeting at Cheltenham.

Many years before, I had been hunting in Ireland with Eddie Macken; we were out one day with the Meath and we needed to cross a river. We had to jump in, wade across and then jump out the other side. There was a plucky grey pony in front of me who leapt straight into the river, unseating his jockey. The pony clambered out the other side and I fished the little kid out. He was absolutely drenched; he could only have been about ten. I got him up, put him back on the pony and asked him his name. 'Adrian Maguire,' he replied.

I met up with Adrian again at David Nicholson's and he reminded me that I had rescued him from the river in Ireland. We became firm friends.

A block of land had come up for sale at the back of the farm; it ran from the edge of my fields to the motorway and the price was right. I haggled with the agents and bought about 36 acres. I built a sand gallop for the racehorses; it was on a curve and had a nice pull up the hill to give the horses something to work at. Sheep grazed the fields and would wander on to the sand, scattering as the horses cantered along. The showjumpers used it as well and I am sure it helped a lot with their fitness. Part of the land fronted the lane and there was a big barn and planning permission for a farm cottage. The whole deal had a lot of potential.

After the success with Jolly Roger I got another nice horse for hunter chasing which had won two point-to-points, one by a distance. He was called Carrots and was owned by a dear old lady, Betty Sykes. Carrots did actually win for me. He was second the first time out in a point-to-point and he won his second race for me, only to break down afterwards and never run again.

That was the end of me as a trainer, but I was still suffering badly from the bug.

When a mare by Strong Gale called Certainly Strong came up for sale, I bought her even though she had never run, and sent her to David Nicholson to train. This was serious stuff. Certainly Strong won her first race, a bumper at Ludlow, and was second on her second outing at Uttoxeter in a National Hunt flat race. David's claimer Robert Massey rode her in those races.

Adrian Maguire took over the ride on Certainly Strong and she ran her first race over hurdles at Haydock Park and won. It was Adrian's 500th winner and David's 1,000th winner. She was now moving into the bigger leagues and went on to win again and be placed second over hurdles. In her novice chasing year she won two Grade One Novice Chases. Every time out, she was always first or second. The showjumpers were having a lean time of it that winter and Certainly Strong helped to keep the yard going with her winnings. After Adrian was injured in a fall, Richard Dunwoody rode her. They were both friends of mine and I always liked her to be ridden by one of them.

With Richard Dunwoody, Certainly Strong won her second Grade One Novice Chase and he kept the ride on her until Adrian was back in the saddle. At the end of the season at Newbury in the Mares Novice Hurdle Final she was sixth.

Part way through the season Certainly Strong didn't have a race lined up for a few weeks so I asked if she could come home for a break and go in the paddock. David Nicholson wasn't very happy about it, but he finally agreed. I sent Mark down to fetch her in the horsebox and Certainly Strong came back with enough feed to last her through the break and exact, detailed instructions from David on how she was to be exercised!

The next season she went Novice Chasing. She was doing well that year and was one of the favourites for the Arkle Novice Chase at the Cheltenham Festival. But misfortune struck and two weeks before the race she sustained a hairline fracture of her pedal bone. She couldn't run; she was finished for that year.

The bone was operated on and two screws inserted into the

pedal bone. She healed up well and came back as strongly as her name the following season to win another Handicap Chase.

Adrian was often injured in falls. The time he broke his arm I took him off to a show at Jerez in the south of Spain. We were down there with Malcolm Pyrah, Peter Murphy and a few other riders. One night we went out and found an Irish bar. Straight away, Adrian was at home. We were in the bar and on the Guinness. Adrian, being a jockey, is quite slight and didn't take as much filling up as we did. At the end of the night, Peter Murphy and I literally carried him for about a mile back to the hotel. Adrian was sharing a room with me and we had great difficulty easing him through the doorway, comatose, horizontal and with a broken arm.

Malcolm's room was just across the corridor and at breakfast the next morning he asked us, 'Did you two steal a piano last night?' We were flummoxed. 'No,' we replied. 'Well,' said Malcolm, 'all I could hear was, "Left a bit, right a bit" . . . it sounded like you two were trying to get a piano into the room!' That was no piano, we explained, just the wounded Maguire.

Another time when Adrian was grounded he and his girlfriend, Sabrina, came on holiday to Bermuda with Bettina and me. Like Richard Dunwoody, Adrian got very bored when he couldn't ride – we all had that in common. We were the guests of Robert and Rosemary Ockendon-Day, whose daughter Rebecca had trained with me for a season and bought a good horse called Correzienne.

Robert and Rosemary used to live in Bermuda and they had some friends there called the Haycocks. They let us have the use of their pool house, in the grounds of the main house. It was tremendous fun. We hired mopeds and drove around the island, two of us on each moped. The girls were very trusting, I must admit!

Later on, Adrian married Sabrina and they had a baby, Shannon. Their wedding in Killarney was a party not to be missed. I had to take a flight the next day to Calgary; I woke up in Killarney, got on a plane and the next thing I knew I was waking up in Calgary. I am godfather to their second child, Finny, who became a jockey and won his first race on a horse trained by Adrian, who had to give up riding after a serious fall. We could not have known at that stage how much more in common we were to have.

15

Atlanta and a Bit of a Con

The World Equestrian Games, the second time all the equestrian disciplines would contest their world championships in the same place, was to be held in The Hague, Holland in 1994 and everyone thought it was going to be a fabulous show. Wrong. It wasn't.

That was all to do with the organisation, or lack thereof, but the sport side didn't go well for us either. After the first day we were in a good position with less than a fence between us, the Germans, French and Swiss. The weather next day was searing hot and the course was long with some tricky distances. Dollar Girl went in the water and lowered two poles so we didn't make the cut for the individual. The team was sixth but Ronnie was devastated. Only Germany's Franke Sloothaak jumped a double clear on the amazing mare Weihaiwej. They went on to win individual gold. We went home. The only positive thing that happened that August was that Bettina finally moved in with me. I was very happy to be looked after properly again! I had been relying on takeaways for too long and Bettina is an excellent cook.

Dollar Girl had won the World Cup qualifier in Millstreet, Ireland, so I set about qualifying for the 1995 Volvo World Cup final in Gothenburg, where Volvo had their headquarters. That was memorable for the kerfuffle over the television rights. The FEI had made a cock-up in selling sole TV rights to the final to German TV company DSF and Volvo were poised to pull out of the sponsorship. Winning a top-of-the-range Volvo car was one of the highlights of the World Cup and the loss of Volvo would have been a big blow to the sport. When Volvo finally pulled out in 1998, after twenty years, their contribution had established the World Cup as one of the most prestigious events on the showjumping calendar.

Throughout that winter season Dollar Girl had qualified for the final by winning at a variety of shows. Even though riders are allowed to compete two horses in the final, I only took Dollar Girl to Gothenburg. She had benefited from her racehorse training and was very fit and strong. She would need to be. Without a stable companion to share the load, the World Cup is a tough competition. But it meant I was able to focus completely on Dollar Girl.

We got off to a fairly good start on the first day, finishing fifth in the speed leg – a Table C competition over a more-or-less Table A course (that means it was big!). Eddie Macken won with Miss FAN, a horse he had only been riding for two months. On the second day we were seventh. Michael Whitaker and Two Step came in third but were leading overall, with Dollar Girl and me just three faults behind. Franke Sloothaak was half a fault behind in third place. Eddie and Miss FAN disappeared down the ratings to fifteenth.

I am sure that having only Dollar Girl to focus on helped me. I worked her every day then, on the day off, I wandered over to the show but didn't work her. Dollar Girl rested and slept most of the day. I went to bed early that night as well. That was a first! I had a dream that night. When I woke up on the Sunday I told Bettina, 'I'm going to win this final.'

I went down to the stables to work Dollar Girl. Less than one fence covered the top three placings and there was a bunch of other good combinations just behind us. In the first of the final two rounds, Michael and Two Step picked up twelve faults to drop them well down the grid. I made a mistake at the first part of the second last and Franke with Weihaiwej had a single fence down as well. But Lars Neiberg and For Pleasure went clear to take the lead.

I was starting to feel less psychic. Maybe it had been just a dream, not a vision.

Going into the second round, Lars was leading on five faults and I was lying second with seven. We were jumping in reverse order and I was able to put pressure on Lars by jumping clear. Dollar Girl tried her heart out. There was a triple bar two from the end and she turned herself inside out to clear it. She really tried for me.

When Lars went into the ring I couldn't bear to watch. For Pleasure was jumping fantastic and when he cleared the huge triple bar I thought it was all over. But Lars had had to push hard for the triple bar and he couldn't get the nine-year-old stallion back for the next fence. He brought it down to finish on nine faults, leaving Dollar Girl the winner. I was ecstatic. Ten years earlier I had been the understudy with St James so I knew how Lars felt. But Dollar Girl had been brilliant, she deserved that win. One of Harry's earliest memories was watching our win on the TV. He was six. When I got home to Warwickshire a raucous party was already going in the Durham Ox, my local pub.

That year I had quite a few young horses at home and I needed a stable jockey to bring them on and take them to local shows. We'd been out in St Gallen for the Europeans and won team silver, not a bad day. But that was a strange show. It had poured with rain for weeks and the football stadium grass was peeling off. The Germans left and it was touch and go whether the whole show would be cancelled. At the end of September in that part of Switzerland rain is almost guaranteed. The team was me on Dollar Girl, Michael on Two Step, John on Keeley Durham's Welham and young Alison Bradley on a horse called Endeavour, who jumped double clear in the two-round Nations Cup and pushed us up to get the silver medal behind the home team. I asked Alison if she would like to come and base her horses with us. She liked the idea and came with her groom, Debbie Brooks, to live in Warwickshire, bringing her horses, Endeavour and Tinka's Boy, both owned by Charles and Dorothy Sibcy.

One day at the Aldershot Show, the Sibcys told me, out of the blue, that they wanted to sell both of Alison's horses. This was a disaster for a young rider like Alison, but it happens, it is just part of showjumping. Bettina had always liked Tinka's Boy and she bought him. Endeavour was sold to American rider Debbie Dolan.

Alison is still bringing on young horses, and now lives with my brother Michael; they have a son called Charlie who is my youngest nephew. My sister, Sally, has a son Nicholas, who was born back in 1990. We have all had sons, not a daughter between the three of us. It took until Dan married Grace and they produced Florence, my granddaughter, to get a female offspring in the family. Flo is the apple of my eye!

Tinka's Boy was only six when we bought him and I started riding him in 1997. He took part in his first Nations Cup in La Baule and then competed in Gijon where Swiss rider Marcus Fuchs expressed interest on behalf of one of his owners. Basically, we were made an offer we couldn't refuse and sadly he was sold.

I thought a lot of Tinka's Boy, he was always destined for the top and he proved me right with Marcus Fuchs. He was probably the best horse in the world in his time; easy to ride and uncomplicated, he had a great mind. I bred three foals by him out of Florida, the good mare I'd acquired in the swap with John Whitaker.

At about the same time, I had been sent a horse called Zalza by Joop Aaldering, a Dutch horse dealer whose wife, Kyra, had been riding him. Zalza was a very talented, pretty little chestnut horse but he could be quite difficult. Bettina liked him and she bought him for me to ride. He won a couple of grands prix and the Masters at Olympia before being sold to Robert Smith. He was subsequently sold to America.

My sister, Sally, had a friend who had been paralysed in a swimming accident. The lad badly needed an electric wheelchair and Sally hit upon the idea of holding a horse show to raise the funds to buy the wheelchair. She enlisted my help, my fields and most of my staff!

Sally had never run a horse show before, but she set to work like a sergeant major, drafting in her friends Jackie Hobday and Gaye Williams to help her. Not content with helping to run the show, Jackie and Gaye organised a ball at the same time, raising funds for the British Equestrian Olympic Fund and the BSJA. A huge marquee was erected, dance floor installed, lighting, the lot. We held the balls for years and had some tremendous fun. In the autumn we would host the Injured Jockeys Fund Ball, held the night before the Hatton Team Chase.

The show ran successfully for two years before it grew so large that we needed more land. A good friend of mine, Melvyn Barraclough, who trained a few racehorses, agreed to let us use his land at Arden Park Farm for the next three years. A lovely man, he'd do anything for me and I don't know anyone who would say a bad word about him.

Oxo was there for Dan and Harry when they started riding. That little pony started off so many riders. When Ted and Liz's daughter, Marie, was about four years old, I loaned Oxo to her and she competed him in lead rein classes and benefited from the same grounding as I had. I would never, ever have sold Oxo, but I loaned him to several child riders. Anne Backhouse's children had him and Althea Barclay's children used to hunt him. The last person to have him on loan was Jeff McVean's daughter, Emily. I was glad to have Oxo back for my boys. Whenever Daniel and Harry were staying with me, every morning, first thing, they would run down to the yard and give Oxo his feed.

One day we were all up especially early to go to the New Forest Show and they were down at Oxo's stable before the grooms were up. They found Oxo lying dead in his stable. He had died in his sleep. It was a nice way for him to go, but the boys were very upset. So was I. He was a good old soldier was Oxo, the best, and thirty-nine was a great age.

I rang Dad to tell him and he arranged for Carey Sage to bring a JCB over and bury Oxo next to my old dog, Dora, in the field. It was a pretty dismal day at the show, but we arrived home to a story that lightened the atmosphere. By the time Carey arrived with the JCB to dig the hole it was raining. Dad was directing operations but he had an umbrella up. As Carey lowered Oxo into the hole, Dad stepped back and the metal of the umbrella touched the electric fence – it was a mains electric fence, not battery operated, and Dad got an awful shock and nearly fell in the hole with Oxo.

Again the beginning of the New Year was dominated by the World Cup final and 1996 was no different. It was in Geneva and Hugo Simon and ET beat Willi Melliger and Calvaro in the jump-off for first place, leaving Dollar Girl just one fault behind in third place. She was having a good 1996 despite being sixteen years old; I had no plans to retire her, I felt she still had plenty of life in her and she was enjoying her jumping.

Meanwhile Sue Welch's mare Showtime was eleven years old. She was in the prime of her life and started off Olympic year by winning the grand prix in Madrid, then taking second place at both Lisbon and Barcelona. For three consecutive weeks, she had top places at major shows and it was Showtime who was selected for the British team to go to Atlanta.

Tim Grubb had taken US nationality and was now riding for the Americans, leaving the fourth slot in the team vacant. John Whitaker was selected with Keeley Durham's Welham, Michael Whitaker was taking Two Step, I had Showtime and the new recruit was Geoff Billington and It's Otto. Robert Smith and Tees Hanauer were non-travelling reserves; it was arranged that they could be flown out as late as 25 July if they were needed. Malcolm Pyrah came with us as team trainer.

The horses were flown out to Atlanta three weeks before the competition so they could acclimatise to the hot, humid, Georgia weather. Showjumpers are used to arriving at a show and then competing, almost immediately. The horses were all jumping well in training but they were there for such a long time that psychologically it must have been a strain for them. After all, they don't know the schedule, they never know which day you will be asking them to perform their best. The horses went for weeks, wondering when the show would be.

As far as we lads were concerned, we were all going to be together for a long time and at times like that you need a good team to be with, otherwise boredom sets in. We were used to being very busy all day and to suddenly be dropped in a strange place and only have one horse to ride was alien. We had a lot of time on our hands and nothing to do. We went to watch the eventing, we walked their course, but it was generally pretty boring.

Atlanta and a Bit of a Con

We stayed in the village for the first couple of weeks. Atlanta isn't exactly the biggest tourist trap in the world and we were at a loose end most of the time. One memorable exception was when Michael and I headed to the restaurant to get a cup of tea. We sat down at a table and who should walk over and start talking to us but 'The Greatest' himself, Muhammad Ali.

The facilities were good in the village. Ronnie and Malcolm shared a room, Michael was with Geoff and John bunked down with me. We had our own apartment in Atlanta, it wasn't like Barcelona where we were crammed in with the eventers and dressage riders. Our team vet, Marc Suls, shared the apartment as well.

After a while, the boredom developed into a routine. Every evening we used to go to a lap-top bar. We assumed it would be a sort of cyber café, but it wasn't. We never spotted a lap-top computer, but we spotted a few fast bits of work. The place was called Cheetah's but we spent so much time in there that we renamed it the Office.

One night we were coming back from the Office quite late, about eleven o'clock and somehow Ronnie and I became split up from the others. We wandered into the village through the nearest entrance, which was actually the furthest point from our apartment, about a mile's walk away. Michael, John, Geoff and Malcolm went in through a different gate.

Ronnie didn't fancy walking all the way across the village. Frankly, he didn't look as if he would handle the walk. The normal bus service had wound down for the evening. Instead of running every five minutes as a shuttle, it was now once an hour. There was nobody about. If you've ever been to Disney World you will have seen the bus service they have there; a little tractor engine with half a dozen carriages, like a train. We went in through the gate and saw one of these little bus trains parked up nearby. There was no one with it.

I turned to Ronnie. 'Hey,' I said, 'there's a bus here, I'll drive it and you get on the back.' The keys were in it and the CB radio was switched on. I don't know where the driver was, he must have nipped to the loo. I started it and Ronnie sat in the far back corner, about thirty yards behind me.

I set off driving through the village and I could hear a guy calling out on the CB radio: 'Bus gone missing, bus gone missing, look out for the number 37, it's been stolen.'

I was trundling this thing along back to our apartment when I drove around a corner and saw about fifteen or twenty athletes at the bus stop. I turned and shouted back to Ronnie, 'What shall we do?' He advised, 'Stop and pick them up.' As he would.

As I drove towards them, they surged forwards. I stopped and let them on. I set off again and around the next corner there was another bunch of athletes stood at the bus stop. By the time I was halfway to our apartment, my bus was full. Every now and then the CB radio would crackle into life: 'The number 37 bus has been stolen, look out for the number 37,' but I just ignored it. I thought it best not to reply. No one on the bus seemed worried, I guess they didn't understand English. Ronnie was still sitting in the far back right-hand corner and every time I turned around, he gave me the thumbs up; he was the conductor, he was in charge, as usual.

I pulled up at the food halls and luckily everybody got off, that's where they were all going. We drove on with another half a mile to go and then, just as we were nearing our apartment, as we were going down the hill past the Olympic pool, there were two big black guys standing at the bus stop. I pulled up and let them on and when we got to our stop I switched the engine off and got out. The two big black guys said, 'Hey, man, we wanna go to the restaurant,' to which I replied, 'Sorry, mate, this is where my shift ends. You'll have to wait for the next driver.' God knows how long they waited before they realised no one was going to turn up. And the whole time the CB radio kept shouting, 'Bus 37, has anybody seen the 37?'

Ronnie and I beat the other lads back to the apartment; we were sitting with our feet up watching television by the time they arrived.

We wanted to be closer to the horse park during the competitions so we moved out to the White Columns Inn, owned by Epp Wilson, Master of the Belle Meade Hunt. Epp's father, the late James Wilson, owned Pine Top Farm, the top US eventing centre, so he was quite used to the foibles of horsey folk.

Although we missed our usual fall guy, Broomie, we had a replacement, Geoff Billington. Every day we did something to Geoff. When you arrive at the Games, you are given lots of little gifts: hair shampoo, sunblock, aftershave, all sorts of things. One day, when Geoff was in the shower, John got hold of some haemorrhoid cream. We emptied Geoff's sunblock out of its tube and replaced it with aforesaid haemorrhoid cream. Ronnie was clued up to what we were doing, so when Geoff came out of the shower Ronnie said, 'Now lads, make sure you've got your sunblock on, or you'll get burnt today.'

We all started putting sunblock on our faces, arms, legs, everywhere, and Geoff was plastering it all over his face, his arms, his legs; we were having trouble keeping straight faces, Geoff was covered in haemorrhoid cream!

Next day, while Geoff was in the shower, we emptied all the haemorrhoid cream out and filled the tube with liquid shoe cream. Sure enough, on Ronnie's orders, we all smothered ourselves in sunblock and Geoff was plastered in shoe cream, all rubbed in, everywhere. Off we went, down to the stables.

The next day, we got caught out. Geoff's horse It's Otto gave the game away. John had emptied out the shoe cream and filled the tube with toothpaste. Again, Geoff plastered himself with it, face, legs, arms, everywhere. But when we arrived at the stables, Otto started licking Geoff. He said, 'There's something the matter with this horse, he keeps licking me. He's never done that before.' We all burst out laughing, whereupon Geoff smelled his arms and realised that he was all pepperminty. Otto loved his mints and would burrow down to the bottom of his tack trunk to find them. Geoff knew something was amiss so we confessed. But he hadn't been sun burnt! Just shows you don't need all that fancy expensive sunblock; shoe polish or haemorrhoid cream will do nicely.

Our performance in the team competition was startling in that we had gone to the Games as one of the favourites and we came out eleventh. The conditions had been appalling and the arena had flooded in the downpour but Showtime tried her hardest and jumped well to finish with eight faults and four; in the first round she put a foot in the water, which was unfortunate.

The whole team was hauled over the coals by the press and some said we had taken the horses out there too early, but if we had taken them out later and they had suffered with the heat it would have been worse. Some of the press had asked after the World Games in The Hague whether it was even worth sending a team to Atlanta with all the worry over the heat, so we were between the devil and the deep blue there.

The fences for the team competition are built so that they don't bury the lesser nations who are sometimes riding horses who are not up to Olympic competition. But horses and riders have to qualify for the individual, which allows the course-builder to test the best. With hindsight, I should not have gone, even though Showtime had qualified. She had coped with the team competition, but the individual was a different story.

It was like driving a lorry in the red, she was always under pressure in the first round. She actually went round for four, which is good, although she went in the water again. But the second round was very big and difficult and she had had enough by then, she had come to the end of her tether. There was a double of walls and she took one look and ran at them. She just wanted to get it over and done with as quick as possible and get out of there. She had three down.

After Atlanta, Showtime continued to win consistently until she was retired in 2000. She was sixteen when she went home to Sue and Freddie Welch's farm. She had a foal by Tinka's Boy. Of course it was called Tinka's Showtime.

At the beginning of December Joe Haller rang up and asked me to bring a cheque for his share of Dollar Girl's prize money to Olympia. That was unusual as I normally took his cheque to Zurich in the spring after I'd done my annual audit – there was no electronic transfer in those days!

I took the cheque to Olympia and gave it to him on the first day, which was a mistake. Dollar Girl was sixth on the first day and then I rode her in the World Cup qualifier where she finished fifth. I had an unlucky fence down but the time was quite quick. As I came out of the ring, Joe Haller was standing there and he looked up and said to me, 'That's the last time you're riding her, she's going to Mexico to be retired.'

I couldn't believe my ears. I was gobsmacked. That was the first I had heard of it. My immediate thought was that Mexico was a long way to go to be retired. Joe had previously agreed that when she retired she would stay with me in England and we would try to breed from her. I wanted her to finish her days with me, she was the pet of the yard and everyone adored her, including me.

I asked him where she was going and he said he had given her to Alfonso Romo, who had sponsored Jan Tops. I am sure I remember him saying he had *given* her to Romo. Joe Haller said

Alfonso Romo had agreed to let him have the first foal from her and that Jan Tops would take Dollar Girl home from Olympia with him.

I immediately went to find Jan and ask him what the hell was going on and he denied knowing anything about it. But I was having none of it. I insisted; he must have known what Alfonso Romo was doing, so he might as well tell me the truth. Jan replied that Mr Romo had paid for Dollar Girl a week or so before at the show in Geneva. So Joe had not *given* Dollar Girl to Alfonso Romo, he had sold her.

I was absolutely appalled. How could someone sell a horse into retirement after all she had done for him over the years? Joe Haller wasn't anywhere to be found, I didn't see him for a day or two, I thought maybe he had gone home.

But he hadn't. The next time I clapped eyes on him he was outside the Royal Box upstairs at Olympia. I confronted him and told him exactly what I thought of him. At one point, I nearly had my finger down his throat, I was shaking my finger at him, so close to his face. The late Ann Martin, who wrote for *Horse & Hound* and the *Evening Standard*, was there, trying to get the story from him. She certainly got her story. I remember telling him the only good thing that would come out of it would be that I wouldn't have to see his fucking face around the shows any more.

It was getting quite heated and then Haller just walked away. As he left, a policeman who was on duty outside the Royal Box came up to me and asked if I had a problem. I told him, 'Yes, that's the bastard that's just sold my horse from underneath me.' To which the policeman replied, 'You should have hit him then!'

On the last night of Olympia, the organisers, the Brooks-Wards, held an impromptu retirement ceremony for Dollar Girl. I jumped a fence and then took her saddle off. She got a standing ovation whilst the commentator outlined her glittering career, telling the crowd how much she had won. I swear Dollar Girl knew something was going on. All throughout Sunday she wouldn't eat, she was restless. She knew something was wrong and she really had the sulks on. The children, Daniel, Harry, Bettina's daughter Michelle, the grooms, we all went to her stable to say our last goodbye to her. She knew she was going and we desperately didn't want to lose her.

Of all the horses I'd had at that point, and I'd been lucky enough to have some very good horses, I think Dollar Girl had everything. She had character, manners, ability – she was the sweetest too and everyone loved her so much. A tear was never far from my eye throughout the whole of Olympia.

Dollar Girl went to Monterrey in Mexico and had several foals. Every now and then we would hear from someone who had seen her and they'd tell us she seemed happy enough, but we missed her and she should have stayed with us.

Back in the mid-nineties I had been riding a horse of Sue Welch's called Sublime that we had bought out in California from Larry and Hilary Mayfield. One day Freddie Welch rang me to tell me he had come across two Australian women who were looking to buy a couple of top horses and that he would like to bring them to have a look at Sublime.

The two Australians, Evelyn Burton and Lyla Andre, were in London looking for domestic staff and they had contacted Frances Hutchinson who runs an exclusive staff agency. Frances also owned Arabs and show hunters, so when Burton and Andre expressed an interest in buying a showjumper, she introduced them to a friend of hers, the Showing producer Marjorie Ramsay, who in turn introduced them to Sue and Freddie Welch.

The Australians wanted to get into horse sport in a big way. They were real high rollers and lived a very wealthy lifestyle.

Evelyn Burton arrived at my yard in a chauffeured Bentley, Freddie was in his own car. I showed her Sublime and she then asked if I had anything else. I thought she might as well take a look at Tinka's Boy; after all, if she was interested in buying a horse for me to ride, then that is the horse I would like to keep. She liked the look of Tinka's Boy and agreed to buy him and Sublime.

As we walked back towards the house, Burton took me to one side and quietly told me that she was looking to contract a rider to ride for her through to the Sydney Olympics in 2000. She would be willing to give them a contract to ride her horses for five years.

I asked her what sort of money she was thinking of paying. 'A million pounds a year for five years,' she replied. Well, it didn't take me long to agree that I would do it! We had a cup of tea in the house and then she kept us entertained for about an hour talking about all the different things she had done in the world. She told us she was an investment banker and that she could double an investor's money in a short period of time. She wasn't very discreet and went on to tell us how much she was earning and how much money she was worth. I'm not much into investment banking and it all went whoosh, straight over my head.

On leaving, she invited me down to London for tea the following week at her hotel in Maida Vale. I arrived there to be met by the doorman; I asked for Miss Burton and he took me up to the top floor where she had the whole top floor, the penthouse. The butler took me into the drawing room where Evelyn was waiting for me. There was a silver tea service, the works. I sat down and she produced a contract, which we both signed; a million pounds a year for five years to ride her horses. Burton told me the money would be deposited in my bank account the following week during Olympia.

All the time, she talked about what she wanted to do for horse sport; she planned to sponsor Olympia the following year and

Simon Brooks-Ward gave her a hospitality box at the show. At Olympia I won the Masters with Zalza and when I went back up to her box after the class, Burton told me she liked the look of Zalza, how much was he to buy? I told her the price and she agreed to buy him as well as the other two.

What Burton maintained she would do for the horse sport in this country was nobody's business. She also offered to buy a horse for a girl called Lisa Murphy and back her financially with horses and lorries. Two horseboxes were ordered from Oakley's, one for Lisa and one for me. At this point, Bettina and I thought we had died and gone to heaven, it was too good to be true.

By now, word was getting round that Evelyn Burton was a big spender and that things were going to happen. I kept asking her when I would receive payment for the horses and she kept telling me it was on its way. She then moved from the hotel in Maida Vale to Knightsbridge and invited us to dinner. We were met at the front door by a butler and then we all went to Scott's Restaurant for dinner. She had her whole family with her, mother, sister, auntie, granny, everybody was there. As time wore on, it became apparent that Evelyn Burton and Lyla Andre were more than just friends; they were lovers.

During dinner she told us she was buying a prestigious Stud in Newmarket. There seemed to be no limit to her spending. Part way through the evening, a big fellow walked in carrying a brown envelope and gave it her. She opened it in front of us all and produced a big wad of £50 notes. You could have choked a donkey with it. She proceeded to shove it down her bra. Mind you, there was enough room in there for it.

Every time I asked Burton when I would receive payment for the horses, she stalled; the money was on its way, the money was held up in China, then in Russia, then in Hong Kong. That money was held up in practically every country in the world. She sponsored an Arab Show at Haydock Park and agreed vast prize money, which had never been heard of before in Arab showing classes, but no one ever received their prize money. One day she turned up at Windsor and promised to sponsor Windsor the following year. Simon Brooks-Ward arranged for her to have a hospitality table but she never paid for it. It went on.

Burton was eventually investigated for fraud and subsequently sent to jail for five years, along with Lyla Andre who was sent down for three years. All the time they had been in England they had been conning money out of wealthy, sophisticated people by offering to invest it, promising to 'double your money' and then spending it on their own hedonistic lifestyle instead. During the investigation it came to light that they owned and ran a brothel in Melbourne called Magic Moments. Lyla's leather-clad alias was 'Madame Xavier'!

16

Hopes Springs

Early in 1995 Everest had decided to pull out of showjumping. Kevin Mahoney had moved on, the new management had decided on a change of approach so at the end of 1996 our contracts were not renewed and John, Michael, me as well as Liz and Marie Edgar and Geoff Luckett were without sponsors.

John and Michael had always come as a package deal because they are brothers, but we thought we would try to keep the three of us together and see if we could attract a joint sponsor. John managed to come up with a sponsor for himself and Michael: Virtual Village, owned by David Heap. Sue Heap, David's wife, knew John many years ago in Yorkshire. He met up with her again at the Windsor Horse Show and, when she heard he had not yet found a new sponsor, stepped in and said her husband would sponsor John.

What nobody realised was that the person working as their stud manager was Greg Parsons, my old friend the chicken plucker from my days at Odnaull End Farm. Apparently, when David Heap told Greg that he was thinking of sponsoring John and Michael, Greg piped up: 'If you do that, you must sponsor Nick as well.' And very generously, they did.

Geoff Billington got wind of what we were up to and muscled in on the act. Virtual Village was now sponsoring the four of us and we were all decked out in the company's purple and yellow colours.

One evening, Sue and David Heap invited us all down to their house in Montpelier Square for dinner. It was quite a big party including the two Whitakers, Geoff Billington and me. I had to get back to Warwickshire that night, I couldn't stay over, so I offered to drive. Consequently, I wasn't drinking.

It was just after Calgary and Michael's horse Touchdown, owned by James Kernan, had had colic out there and was left behind to be operated on; Michael wasn't happy, he was stressed and worried waiting for news.

When we arrived the lads started drinking beer, then it was on to dinner and red wine. The evening was going well, everyone was getting well stuck into the wine and I was on water. We were trying to amuse and impress the Heaps with our stories and outdo each other. The lads had started out on their best behaviour, but it was starting to deteriorate; Michael kept making lewd offers to Sue Heap but she was fending him off nicely.

At about midnight Michael got a call from a fellow in the equine clinic in Canada. The line was poor and Michael thought the guy had said Touchdown was dead. Michael was devastated, he's very emotional at the best of times but the alcohol took over. He started crying.

Michael said, 'I'm sorry about this, I just feel so sorry for James.' Next to me, John was crying as well, because he felt sorry for Michael. I thought, I don't believe this.

I'm reaching for my Perrier and they are on their twenty-fifth bottle of red wine. I glanced to the other end of the table and Sue and David Heap, and Annie, were all crying. I looked around the whole table. Everyone was in tears, they were all so upset that Touchdown was dead.

After a while everyone got over their emotion and I said, 'Come on, Geoff, it's about time we went home.' Geoff was dallying. I told him, 'If you're not there in two minutes, I'm leaving you,' and went outside and got in the car. Geoff leapt in the car as I pulled away from the kerb and was asleep before we had gone a hundred yards.

The next day, I was on the tractor driving across the field when my phone rang. It was Geoff. 'Guess what?' he said. 'Touchdown's not dead at all.' All that weeping was for nothing. The Heaps must have thought we were a right lot.

As I've said, I like building; the whole process of planning, construction, change. I had built everything I could think of at Sandall House Farm, indoor stabling and outdoor stabling, indoor school, horse walker, winter stabling barns – you name it, I'd built it. I even tried to build a swimming pool in the garden of the house but the neighbours objected so I had to abandon the plan.

I had loads of stables but not many horses; the place took a lot of maintenance and maintenance just isn't as much fun as building. I decided I needed a new challenge so I put Sandall House Farm on the market. The land I had bought years earlier when I was training point-to-pointers had planning permission for a farm cottage, so I applied for permission to convert the barn into stabling and my idea was to move the horses and the staff to the new yard, just a field or two away, and to buy a completely separate house for Bettina, the children and myself.

As soon as I let it be known that Sandall House was for sale, Julia Tooth was on the phone to me. Julia and her husband, an

Irish rider called Brian Smith, lived at Brook Furlong Farm, a short distance up the lane. They later divorced but Brian was very obliging and used to ride a couple of horses for me.

Julia's father Raymond Tooth, the well known celebrity divorce lawyer, owned quite a number of useful thoroughbreds and she needed more space. They promptly made me an offer for Sandall House and sold Brook Furlong to Robert Smith. Julia operated Raymond Tooth Racing that owned Lear Spear, a Group Two winner, as well as a number of other useful flat horses. Sadly, Julia, who went on to train in Lambourn, died of cancer in 2010.

Carey Sage had retired so I needed a new builder and Robin Hobday, aka Dobbin, came to my rescue. Along with his sidekick, Dickie Dover, he built stables, tack room, feed room and wash room inside the barn and I renamed the place Sanbrook Farm. The horses were moved into Sanbrook Farm, we moved out of Sandall House Farm and Bettina and I found ourselves with nowhere to live. We rented a small cottage at Shrewley House up in the village and Julia let my grooms stay on at Sandall House until Dobbin had built the new farm cottage.

In the meantime I went house-hunting. There was a large Victorian house in Rowington for sale which needed a lot of renovations. It seemed an ideal outlet for my creative building obsession and we moved into Finwood Lawn in November 1997. We spent a long time renovating that place!

Finwood Lawn had a large staff flat on one side so the grooms were able to leave Julia's and come to live with me. All winter we waited for the farm cottage to be finished – it was April before they were able to move in.

After moving house I actually started to think about retirement. I was only forty years old but I hadn't got the horsepower any more. Showtime was in her twilight years, was winding down and would soon call it a day. I felt that maybe I should call it a day too.

I took Showtime on the Sunshine Tour to Barcelona, Lisbon and Madrid, where she won the grand prix, proving she still had what it took. I was pleased as Sue and I both wanted her to go out at the top. But I was short of an up-and-coming top horse.

One day, on the Tour, I was chatting to Mike Bullman who was our Chairman of Selectors, bemoaning the fact that I needed another top horse. Mike, who knew pretty much everything that was going on, mentioned that he had heard a whisper that I would be offered a top horse. He told me, 'I think you're going to be getting Hopes Are High.' He had heard it in passing, just in conversation, nothing definite.

I didn't get my hopes up because Hopes Are High was a nice horse and he was going well for his rider, Andrew Davies, but he looked a bit difficult to ride. Andrew had jumped Hopes in the Nations Cup in Lisbon but it didn't look like an especially top horse at the time.

After I got home, David Broome called me. 'Hopes needs a stronger rider. I don't think Andrew will manage him at a bigger level,' he told me. I said I'd try him but wondered what Andrew would think of all this, whether he knew about it. I didn't want Andrew jocked off the horse without him knowing what was going on. It's happened to me and it's not very nice. Contrary to what Andrew's mother maintained at the time, I didn't call David and ask for the horse, it was offered to me.

Hopes Are High came to me in time for the Royal Show at Stoneleigh, the same show where I started with Phoenix Park for David, all those years back. I jumped in the big class on the all-weather surface. Hopes had just the last fence down but felt very scopey. I could see what David meant when he said the horse needed a stronger rider. Sometimes Hopes trotted behind while still cantering in front; I call it cross-cantering. He was actually quite difficult.

The following week we went to Hickstead for the Royal International and jumped in the King's Cup. It poured with rain and it was very deep ground. We were second, beaten by Robert Smith on Mighty Blue. From then on the horse improved in leaps and bounds. At the New Forest the next week he finished second in the Team Trials and third in the Daewoo Championship.

Next stop was Dublin. Hopes jumped a double clear in the Nations Cup and won the Kerrygold Grand Prix to take home £25,000. It was my fifth win at Dublin. The horse was starting to show some real form and David sold Hopes Are High to Lord and Lady Harris, owners of a lot of good showjumpers and racehorses.

We had a short break and, now under new ownership, went to Gijon in the north of Spain, a Nations Cup show. Hopes won the grand prix. By now, this was an unbelievable run of success. We came home, had a week off and Hopes flew out to Calgary along with Showtime. But in the Nations Cup at Spruce Meadows, the peg fell out, it all went wrong.

There was a line of fences down the centre of the ring and a related distance from the water jump to a set of curved planks. I jumped the water and tried to contain him but he started to trot behind. I don't know how many strides he had, or should have had, but he ended up with his head on the top of the planks, his knees on the floor and me on his ears. I pulled up. I thought it was a stop because he never actually reached the other side of the fence and I walked around thinking they would ring the bell and rebuild the fence.

Nothing was happening and I wasn't very happy. I walked around and turned a few circles and then I threw my dolly out the pram and walked out of the ring, much to Ronnie's horror.

Hopes Springs

Technically I was eliminated. They were now a team of three.

It seemed the judges thought that I had made a jump at the fence; they said I had left the floor and therefore should have carried on.

I telephoned Lord Harris to tell him what had happened; he always wanted me to call him whenever his horse jumped and would want to know what had happened, good or bad. He was a very keen follower of his horses, as he still is. I told him that maybe I shouldn't bother going in the second round, perhaps Hopes should jump a few smaller classes, come home and regroup.

Lord Harris said that I might as well jump in the second round, it wouldn't do Hopes any harm. He instilled a bit of confidence in me and we jumped round in the second for only four faults, just one down.

I walked the course for the Du Maurier the next day and it was big and difficult. That is nothing out of character for the Du Maurier; it is usually a very tricky course. After all, you are jumping for $250,000 to the winner!

There were only five or six clears and Hopes was one of them. We were last but one to go and the second course was huge, in fact it was massive . . . There were no clears before me and Hopes jumped clear but had half a time fault. I was happy with that. If the last horse jumped clear I would be second. It would be a good result. The last horse was It's Otto with Geoff Billington. The Du Maurier is famous for being won with only one double clear and when I came out with half a time fault I rushed back in to watch Geoff. I think he had the third fence, an oxer over a water ditch, Otto had it down behind.

That was it. I was the winner with a clear and half a time fault. My third Du Maurier, as the Masters was known then. I equalled John Whitaker as the only other rider to have won it three times, with Milton, Gammon and Grannusch. It was Hopes Are High's third consecutive CSIO Grand Prix win.

We came home from Calgary and went on to Rome in October for the World Equestrian Games. We joined Geoff with It's Otto, John Whitaker on Heyman and team debutante Di Lampard with Abbervail Dream and managed to come home with the team bronze behind the Germans, who again took gold, and the French. Hopes ended the year at Olympia and finished third in the grand prix. From our start together in July to December he had won a total of £230,000.

Despite a dismal start 1998 ended on a good note thanks to Hopes Are High, then just before Christmas things got even better when Daniel and Harry came to live with me at the new house. Sarah was not coping. She had her own problems, sadly, and although the boys knew she tried her best, at thirteen and nine, boys being boys, they needed a bit more discipline and a more settled environment. They brought all their ponies with them and Dan brought his chickens. Dan was enrolled at Princethorpe College near Rugby and Harry at school at Arden Lawn in Henley-in-Arden. Some years later Sarah died in a hospice, it was when the boys were working at Paul Nicholls'. What happened made us all stronger as people and closer as a family and that's why I won't rake up the past again but let Sarah rest in peace.

I was told that Virtual Village were cutting down their sponsorships, so while they continued to sponsor John, Michael and Geoff until the company folded in 2001, I went my own way. No more team colours. Two companies came to the rescue. Equiline sent me jackets, caps, show jackets, shirts, ties, bandages, bandage wraps and saddle pads, and Horseware of Ireland sent rugs, all embroidered with my name. Both companies have supported me ever since, they've been great partners.

Hopes Springs

I reckoned I had a chance of making the team for the European Championships with Hopes Are High. It was to be at Hickstead that year and it's always special to take part in a championship on home territory. The campaign trail was Modena, Cannes and Aachen and while Hopes hadn't reached top form, he was going well. Then at the Royal International he won the King George V Gold Cup, beating Ludger Beerbaum, and was third in the grand prix at Dublin. But there was something bothering him, he didn't feel the same as he had the previous year. He was more difficult, something wasn't quite right. We went to Calgary and he definitely wasn't sparking there.

In the Europeans at Hickstead we finished fourth in the first leg, a speed competition. In the Nations Cup he was clear until the last two fences when he ran off with me down a line of fences on related distances and he ended up like in Calgary, he pulled up. As he stopped, I think he landed on the foot of one of the big, oak Derby Rails. We circled around, jumped it and finished the course, and we jumped in the second round, but when he came out for the trot up the next day, he was lame. Hopes was taken to the Veterinary College where they scanned his hoof and found a hairline fracture of his pedal bone. I think it had been bothering him for a long time and landing on the foot of that rail at Hickstead aggravated it.

Hopes went home to David Broome at Mount Ballan. In addition to the fracture, the horse had developed an infection in his foot which went up into the hoof causing more problems. He was off the road for a long time but he did come sound again, and David's son Matthew took over the reins. They were on the team which won gold at the European Young Riders Championships in 2002.

With Hopes sidelined, Lord and Lady Harris bought another horse for me to ride, from Joop Aaldering. Lalique was eight years old but she'd taken time out to have a couple of foals so she was quite inexperienced. I felt she had real potential. Then another four horses arrived for me to ride. The Italian rider Guido Dominici had tragically died young from a brain tumour and one day I had a call from Gary Widdowson's brother-in-law asking me if I was interested in taking over the ride on Guido's horses. He was friendly with the owner, Arianna Gilardoni, who lived in the Italian part of Switzerland.

It was terribly sad about Guido, who I had met all those years ago at the Junior European Championships in Dornbirn, but I was short of horses. None of them had been in work for a few months so the first job was to get them fit, which took a while. Then we went to a little indoor show at Solihull, just to give them a warm up. It was 27 October. The first horse I jumped was Frisco, the horse Guido had considered the best of the bunch; Frisco jumped the first fence, went on to the second, a small oxer, and picked up a stride too early. He jumped into the middle of it, turned a somersault and I hit the floor. I was in a lot of pain and realised I had broken something. I was airlifted to hospital where they diagnosed a broken collarbone. This isn't a very serious injury so I was hopeful of being back in the saddle before the end of the year. I competed at Olympia but it was obvious something was wrong. I couldn't hold the reins properly, I had no strength in my shoulder and the pain indicated a problem.

I went for more X-rays which showed that the original diagnosis had not been correct; the collarbone had been shattered, not just broken. No wonder I was in pain – I was laid up for another couple of months; now I wanted to be competing again in February, in time for the Sunshine Tour in Spain.

By the time February arrived, two of Guido's horses were lame and had to be sent back to Italy to be retired and another was sold, but I was left with the black stallion, Jalisco. He won the grand prix at Royal Windsor, three area international trials and good classes at Barcelona and Madrid. He was the leading national horse in 2000 and was then sold to Mike Dawson for Scott Smith to ride.

After I first injured my collarbone I made my regular trip to the Fairyhouse Foal Sales in Ireland where I bought five National Hunt foals. Whilst I was there I met up with John and Pat Hales, who were also buying foals. John was the owner of the racehorse One Man, and had just bought the last relative of One Man at Fairyhouse. He was in a genial mood as we shared a taxi to the airport and flew back to Birmingham together. The Hales' daughter, Lisa, rides and while I always spoke to John and Pat when I met them around the shows it was nothing more than general conversation.

Then a couple of weeks later Lisa Hales called me. She asked if I would be interested in riding a young stallion owned by her mother, Pat. I certainly was interested, and immediately agreed. The six-year-old stallion, Magic Darco, arrived at Sanbrook Farm shortly afterwards, at the end of December. I was laid up until February but it was lucky that Andrew Saywell, who had worked for me some years before, had come to live at Sanbrook Farm. He was renting a yard across the lane and rode all my horses while I was grounded. He was a great help to me.

Over the winter, Joop Aaldering called to tell me he had seen a nice horse and I should go and look at it. I told David Broome about it and suggested we bought it for Lord Harris. David and I went to Hamburg to see the horse and it was lovely, a six-year-old. We came back all excited but we couldn't persuade Lord Harris to buy it. He thought it was too young.

I got back in the saddle in time to take Pat Hales' Magic Darco and a few other horses to the Sunshine Tour at Vejer in southern

Spain. It starts in the second week of February and runs for six weeks, which is great for getting horses going outside early in the year. I tended to fly back and forth as a rule but unusually stayed over in Spain the whole time that year. That horse I had seen in Hamburg was constantly on my mind. I really wanted it and I had a good feeling about it. One day I was talking casually to Lisa Hales and told her I had seen a promising stallion but couldn't find anybody to buy it. I showed Lisa a video of the horse. 'Send this to my dad,' she said.

Daniel and Harry were going home to go back to school after half term, so I sent the video home with them, telling them to send it on to John Hales. A few days later, Lisa came to find me. Her father liked the look of the horse in the video and wanted to go and see it.

This was getting exciting. I flew home mid-week then flew on to Hamburg with John Hales and his vet, David Jagger. I rode it. John Hales liked it, David Jagger vetted it. We arranged for it to be brought home. The horse's name? Arko.

Arko reminded me so much of Tinka's Boy, I saw the same qualities in him. Standing 16.1, Arko was, well he still is, a compact horse and beautiful looking, a real mover and a great character. I was getting keen again, my enthusiasm was fired up and there was no more talk of retirement. I could see a good string of horses coming along – they were all at early stages but I felt sure Arko would be a top horse a few years later. In John Hales I had a new owner I was very happy with. I was keen to build up a team of horses, and in John and Pat and Sue Welch I had owners who were horse people. I had prospects again; two owners I could rely on. Yes, I could get back to the top again.

Arko really progressed that year, qualifying for the Foxhunter, Grade C, and the Six- and Seven-year-old Finals at the Horse of the Year Show. As John Hales drove me the length and breadth of the country to get those qualifications what he always had was enthusiasm. Lots of it, especially after a few hard nights!

Arko's success fired John's enthusiasm as much as mine and when he wanted to buy another horse I went shopping in Holland again with Joop Aaldering.

17

One Fall Too Many

Lord and Lady Harris's mare, Lalique, was coming along well. After the Spanish Sunshine Tour she jumped on the Lisbon Nations Cup team but I concentrated on the county show circuit, which was ideal for her. She was showing some form. She travelled alongside her new stable companion Arko, who was always the gentleman. Lalique was never a problem either, never had been since she first arrived on the yard. I was just taking her slowly and building up her experience.

That September we went off to the Parkgate Show near Chester. The sun was shining, the ground was good and we were enjoying the day. I had jumped in one class and got a feel for the ring, which was a bit uneven, a bit hilly. The ring was on a bank so it wasn't level.

We got ready for the International Trial and in I went on Lalique. We jumped the wall then turned back to a triple bar going uphill. It was fence six or seven I think and Lalique was jumping clear. The triple bar was quite wide and on approach I placed her a bit too close. As she took off I couldn't push or help her, I had to sit still. I wasn't worried as Lalique didn't have a stop in her. She would usually go.

She took off in front but obviously thought she couldn't make the back rail, so she stopped and put back down again. Her front feet were over the front rail, she was in the middle of the fence. As I had expected her to jump the fence I had gone forward, that's always been my style, helped by Ted hitching my tie to a martingale all those years ago. That old hunting saying 'throw your heart over the fence and your horse will follow' is pretty much what I have always done.

But as Lalique stopped I went up her neck and she put her head down. My hands were trapped underneath me, on the top of her head. At one point I suppose I was only eighteen inches off the floor. If she'd kept her head down I would have slid off safely. But she didn't. She ran backwards and threw her head up, catapulting me into the air. All I can remember is landing right on the top of my head, with my full body weight following me down. There was no angle to the fall; I dropped vertically from about five feet in the air.

As I landed I heard a loud crack, literally inside my head. A lady standing nearby heard it as well. And as my head hit the floor I dropped to one side, lying on my back, facing the sky, a few feet back from the fence. Whenever I fall, the first thing I do is to try and get up. But I just couldn't move. All I could think of was the tremendous pain in the back of my head. I lay there motionless.

People dashed into the ring; John and Pat Hales, my son Daniel, Robert Smith, Peter Charles. I was scared, really scared. I couldn't move my arms and my legs, they were completely numb. The first aid team and the show doctor got to me and kept telling me to lie still because I kept trying to move, but I couldn't move, not at all.

I didn't lose consciousness but oh that pain in the back of my head. After a few minutes I could feel a tingling sensation in my fingers and my toes. A couple more minutes and I could actually move them. The feeling was coming back. After what felt like another few minutes, I could pick my arm up. Then I could move my legs. The fright ebbed away. What a relief. I wasn't paralysed. I was going to be OK. But oh that pain in my head.

The only thing I couldn't move was my head. I could not lift my head from the floor. I kept trying but it wouldn't move.

An ambulance had been called and when the paramedics arrived they wanted to take my hat off. I can still remember shouting, 'Don't take my hat off!' That couldn't happen, the sensation in my head felt so weird I thought my head would fall off if they took my hat off. I told the paramedics that I thought I had broken my neck, or my back.

But there was humour even in the midst of that entire trauma. Robert Smith asked them which hospital they would be taking me to. Liverpool was the answer. Peter Charles said, 'If he's going to Liverpool we'd better take anything valuable off him else he'll come out without it.' So he and Robert took my gold Breitling watch off my wrist!

When we arrived at the show I had noticed that the long rough track we drove down to enter the show ground was bumpy and pitted with potholes. What you don't need with a neck injury is to be jolted around, so the air ambulance was called in. The new team of paramedics arrived and they wanted to take my hat off so they could put a neck brace on. I argued against it but the air ambulance doctor insisted on it. So they took my hat off.

And it felt as if my head had fallen off. What had happened was that the area of internal bleeding in my head was directly beneath the back edge of my hat and as my hat came off the blood was released down into my neck. It was a horrible sensation.

They gave me gas and air, fitted a neck brace and put me on a stretcher and then it was time for my helicopter ride. I knew what to expect, I had been in an air ambulance before. The stretcher is pushed in at the back of the helicopter, beneath the rear rotor – the gap where you go through is only about eighteen inches high. If you were claustrophobic you could panic at that stage. But I had learned that the best thing is to just close your eyes and wait until you come out the other side in the cabin.

They flew me to the Countess of Chester Hospital. John and Pat Hales followed, while Daniel had phoned Bettina when I was lying on the ground. He said I'd had another fall and had been taken off in the air ambulance, just like at Solihull. This time, he warned, I didn't look so good. I was rushed in for X-rays. At that stage, no one knew what damage had been done, but I was in great pain. They gave me morphine.

That made me talk gobbledegook and I was feeling quite morbid. Bettina called my mobile. I told her I thought I was going to die.

John and Pat were there when the doctor came in with my X-ray results. My boots were off but I still had my riding jacket on. When the doctor announced they couldn't find anything wrong, I wasn't too high on the morphine to snap back: 'Well, try something else. I'm telling you, I can't move my head, it won't come off the pillow.'

They took me off for a scan. Sure enough, it revealed I had broken my top vertebra, the C1, in two places. That explained why I couldn't move. It was the same type of injury suffered by Christopher Reeve five years earlier. The *Superman* actor had also fallen forward when his horse stopped at a fence. It left him paralysed.

While the medics went off to consult, I remember seeing this figure at the end of the bed, playing with my feet. It was Pat Hales, but she was out of focus. I could see John but couldn't think of his name. I don't like morphine, it makes me feel completely out of it; if I can stand the pain, I would rather do without.

Then the specialist, Mr Braithwaite, came and told me I had a pretty serious injury. They would have to put a halo brace on me. I didn't know what the hell a halo brace was, but he explained it to me. I didn't like the sound of it.

The nurses cut off my riding jacket and my shirt, literally chopped them up to get them off me. I was taken to a private room. They couldn't get a halo brace immediately as each one has to be made to measure. It was Saturday and one would be ready by Wednesday. They laid me on a board with a thin mattress over it, and strapped my head to the board. Blocks were placed each side of my head to keep my neck in place. For the next four days I lay there, strapped to that board.

I couldn't move my torso at all. I could only move my arms up and down. My friend Melvyn Barraclough had driven Bettina to the hospital. Obviously she was shocked when she saw me. At first I said I didn't want to eat but then Bettina spoon-fed me some ice cream. But that made me feel sick and frightened of vomiting while lying flat on my back.

I just lay there for four days. I could hear the television but I couldn't see it.

I remember counting the tiles on the ceiling. Every day I counted the tiles, trying to figure out different ways to lay them out. I was so bored. Every couple of hours the nurses came to roll me so I wouldn't get pressure sores. Two of them held my shoulders and head down and another would gently roll the rest of my body side to side to release the pressure for a few seconds.

The boredom was relieved by visitors; my parents, Aunty Delma. Some of the lads came in: Peter Murphy, David Bowen, I can't remember clearly who else. Mike Florence brought me a fan – it was September and it was hot, so that was a relief. And Pat or John Hales visited every day; they were both so good to do that. John told me he had bought the horse we had seen on our second shopping trip to Holland. 'I've bought Leidi for you. She'll be waiting for you when you get better,' he said.

The Parkgate Show organisers were very helpful and arranged a hotel room for Bettina. Then on the Wednesday morning Dad was with me when Mr Braithwaite and his team came in to fix the halo on my head.

It was a team, six of them to sit me up, with two or three people holding my head while the others dressed me in a rigid vest with a sheepskin lining. The sheepskin was to stop me getting sore. Then they produced this hoop made of titanium and told me what they were going to do next. They were going to screw it into my skull.

They placed the hoop on my head, all the while holding me firmly, and gave me a shot of local anaesthetic to freeze the skin where the screws went in. Then Mr Braithwaite just screwed the bolts in place. The bolts were Allen keys, each with a sharp needle point. As Mr Braithwaite turned the bolts I could feel blood running down my face. He screwed two in my forehead and two in the back of my skull, right into the bone. As a form of torture, I think it would work.

They then inserted four rods, two down the front and two down the back, which went from chest level on the vest right up through the halo and out the top. The rods were tightened up until the whole thing was solid and they were happy with it. All the time they were telling me I would make a complete recovery.

Then they gradually moved me up to a sitting position using the electric controls on the bed. The halo was quite painful and to start with I felt a bit claustrophobic. Another patient who had a halo fitted was meant to come and reassure me that I would soon get used to it, but I don't remember seeing him. I felt top-heavy, as if I would fall over if I stood up. It was a funny sensation, sitting up after lying down for four days. The following day I was allowed to get up and sit in a chair.

Now more visitors started to turn up: Alison Booth, the secretary from Parkgate Show, came in every day and would bring anything I needed, newspapers, food. I was very grateful to her. All the staff at the hospital were exceptional. I had a laugh with them and gave the nurses the runaround. Breakfast in the morning wasn't up to much so one of the nurses used bring me back sausage sandwiches from the staff canteen.

The next step was walking. A couple of nurses held me up and got me walking around the corridors. They took me for a few trips in a wheelchair at first to get me used to the extra weight on my head. My balance soon improved.

The Olympics were about to start so I watched the opening ceremony with Pat Hales and Bettina. I saw John and Michael Whitaker walk past on the television and I rang John. He had his mobile with him and I spoke to them both while the ceremony was on.

And then it was time to go home. The nurses came to see me off and helped to get me into the car, which was quite difficult because the rods protruded a few inches above my head. My escort party decided we would not take the motorway but the A roads as it would be quieter. This turned out to be the worst thing we could have done. At least the motorway would have been a smooth surface. Those A roads were so unlevel and every time I went over a bump I felt pain in my neck and in my head where the bolts were screwed into my skull.

Back at home my secretary, Mary, had arranged for me to borrow her mother's electric bed so that I could be propped up in a sitting position. By all accounts, it was desperately heavy. Martin Charles, Dobbin, Steve Green and John Botlo all struggled to get the bed into a horsebox and into the drawing room at Finwood

Lawn. That was where I slept for three and a half months.

Robert Smith, my neighbour, was one of my first visitors and I remember telling him that when I was lying on my back I had decided that it no longer mattered whether the poles stayed up or fell down. What was important was getting round without injury, clear or not.

I have always been able to sleep, I could sleep on a washing line, but sitting up wearing the halo, sleep wouldn't come. The Olympic Games, taking place in Sydney on the other side of the world, were on TV throughout the night. They were my saviour. I would stay awake and watch the Olympics until I became quite an expert on obscure sports.

I was referred to the Royal Orthopaedic in Birmingham and made a couple of visits to the specialist, Mr Alistair Stirling, to make sure that everything was going OK. Every time I had a consultation, they told me I would make a full recovery, I would ride again.

I soon got bored of sitting in bed and decided it was time to go down to the yard. One day I managed to climb into the Discovery we had at the time, ideal as it had plenty of head room. I drove myself over to the yard. That, of course, was a stupid thing to do. I only had half a mile to go but if anyone had seen me driving through the village they would have thought there was a monster on the loose. I got a lot of bollockings for driving, from everybody.

Gradually, I started to go out. There weren't many clothes I could wear on top of the brace; I was pretty much limited to track suits. The sheepskin was itchy and I used to shove tea towels up inside to protect my skin. I went to the Horse of the Year Show where people were extremely kind. I didn't look very pretty.

Even though I couldn't sleep at night I'd still get tired a lot and would suddenly fall asleep in the daytime. It turned out the halo was great for falling asleep in as my head never wobbled; that was its job, to keep my head and neck still.

About ten weeks into the programme, around five o'clock one Saturday morning, I woke up with an intense pain in my head. It was worse than the pain of the actual fall and I didn't think pain could get any worse than that, but it did. The site of the pain was the bolt in the left side of my forehead. The rod attached to it had somehow come loose and was pushing up against my skull. The only way I could relieve the pain was to pull the rod down, releasing the pressure on my skull.

Bettina rang the hospital and Melvyn Barraclough offered to drive us to Birmingham. We only reached the end of the drive before I climbed out of the car in agony, tears running down my face, but somehow Melvyn got me to the hospital. Mr Stirling was away and the specialist on duty didn't want to touch the halo, but eventually he took an X-ray to see what was going on, then made the decision to take the halo off and replace it with a hard neck collar. It felt very weird, my neck felt very weak and vulnerable without the halo brace supporting it. I knew it had come off too early so I was very careful. I still slept downstairs on the electric bed but I could lie flat, which was a huge relief.

I went for another scan between Christmas and New Year and then went on holiday to Goa with Bettina, the children, Shaun O'Brien and Keeley Durham. I would get the results of the scan when I returned.

In Goa, I was swimming every day and my neck started to feel strong. I took the brace off to swim and it was moving quite well, it felt good. After two weeks' holiday I was looking forward to going home and riding again, getting the horses ready for the Sunshine Tour.

But when I arrived home there was a message from Mr Stirling: 'Whatever you do, don't ride a horse until you've been to see me.'

Superb Story – Dan and Harry's first Cheltenham Winner: Vincent O'Brien County Handicap Hurdle, 2016.

Above Training for the Injured Jockeys Fund Challenge at Olympia, with A.P. McCoy, Victoria Pendleton, Frankie Dettori and Harry.

Left With Laura, walking the course for the individual.

Above The last fence, Rio, 2016.

Left Gold.

Top right With Eric Lamaze in Rio. He told me, 'It couldn't happen to a nicer guy.'

Top far right The celebrations begin – Rio, 2016.

Right Gary, me and Terry Spraggett in Rio.

Above left Gary, Beverley and me in Rio – what a journey.

Far left Beverley at the One Love Bar – the challenge was set.

Left Mission Accomplished. At the One Love Bar.

Above Michael, the morning after the night before, Rio.

Above right Celebrations at the pub: me and Dad.

Right Florence in her Olympic outfit with Dan at Lapworth Show.

Above Lovely present from the Bunn family commemorating my 12 Hickstead wins: (left to right) Chloe Breen, Laura, me, Lizzie Bunn and Edward Bunn.

Below A new role presenting the trophy for the Ascot Stakes at Royal Ascot to Thomas Hobson's jockey, Ryan Moore, 2017. With trainer Willie Mullins and owners Susannah and Rich Ricci.

Above Dan, Harry and me at Stratford Races, 2017.

Right A real family day at our local course, Stratford: (left to right) Dan, Grace, Harry, me holding Flo, Dad and Janette.

Big Star, last day at Royal Windsor, 2017. What he thinks of the photographer!

Big Star starring at our retirement ceremony, Royal Windsor Horse Show, 2017.

One Fall Too Many

I was puzzled and wondered what the problem was, but I got up to see him as soon as I could. He dropped the bombshell; in his opinion, I shouldn't jump again, ever. The vertebra had healed but the ligament between the bone and the spinal cord had snapped and fallen away, allowing movement. There was no support there, so if I were to have another fall, or a whiplash injury, the bone could touch the spinal cord and that could be fatal.

I was speechless, in total shock. The doctors had always told me I would make a full recovery. They suggested I had the top two vertebrae fused to help stabilise it, but that would mean the loss of half the turning ability in my neck. It would make it impossible to jump.

I came home in shock and delivered the news to Bettina. Then I called Lord Harris, who was expecting me to make a comeback with Hopes Are High. Lord Harris kindly arranged for me see another specialist in London. I went to the Blackheath Hospital to see Richard Gullen for a second opinion, but he arrived at the same prognosis. My career was finished. I was finished. I had to call it a day after one fall too many.

18

Back into the Saddle

When the initial shock had worn off a bit I had to decide what to do. Riding, jumping, competing and winning were my life, and that was all gone. I tried hard to concentrate on coaching and teaching but I didn't enjoy it. How could I, when I couldn't show people how to do things right? And if people didn't put the work or effort in, well, it was frustrating. I'm a positive person and I was trying to figure out what I should do, what I could do, what I was going to do. I didn't feel very positive right then. I didn't know what was going to happen but I know I was hell to live with.

One night I met this guy at a dinner. He told me he bought and ran a lot of pubs and clubs. I said I'd be interested in going part ownership in a pub. As it happened, our then local pub at Shrewley, the Durham Ox, came up for lease which I was quite excited about. I went into it wholeheartedly and we got it refurbished and for the first couple of years it was successful. With the amount of people I knew, we managed to pull the crowds in and it was certainly popular. The opening night was a great success with all the locals and various people from the racing world such

as Richard Dunwoody, A.P. McCoy, Jonjo O'Neil, Richard Johnson and his then girlfriend Zara Phillips. Paul Young, the singer,
was there too. Former Footballer Andy Gray used to come to
the pub and Suzanne Dando, the former gymnast, as they were
all locals.

My friend Tony 'Tommy' Iommi from Black Sabbath used to
bring lots of friends in on a Thursday night when we had a steak
night. You just used to cut your meat however you wanted it and
pay by the weight. Those steak nights became quite famous. With
Tommi and his pals we'd end up with a table of twelve to fifteen
and it was great fun. Tommi and his wife Maria were neighbours
at the time and I still see them quite regularly.

Fun times went sour when I asked how much profit the place
made, only to be told we hadn't made any. I felt that was very
odd when it was constantly full. The pubs my partners owned
on their own were going well and the one that I had a share in
was going downhill. It served excellent food and drink and people
used to come from quite a way away. I was shocked that it didn't
make any money. In the end it went into liquidation and I lost
my money and that was that. It all goes back to a saying Harvey
Smith told me years ago: 'You never earn owt out of nowt
you know nowt about.' I remembered it when the pub went
pear-shaped and I have always thought about it since when I've
been about to go off and do other things. Basically I stick to the
horses now!

One saving grace, although I couldn't ride him, was that the
Hales had left Arko with me, they hadn't taken him away. It
was really nice of them and I said I would try to find someone
to ride him. Andrew Saywell had kept him ticking over and
brought him on slowly and after a year I thought John Whitaker's
son Robert, an up-and-coming young rider then aged eighteen,
might be the one to take Arko on if I couldn't. Robert came to

base with me, with John's blessing, to see things from a different angle.

Robert rode him from around July 2001 and took him round some Young Rider tracks, six- and seven-year-old classes, that sort of thing, then they went to the Spanish Sunshine Tour where Arko didn't go so well. I was keeping an eye on them and in the end I didn't think he was quite Robert's ride. Arko needed a lot of leg and he just didn't click with Robert.

During that time I had been looking for a way back. I simply could not let it go. The press may have reported at the time that I had been forced into retirement but I have only retired once. I had done the rounds of specialists and consultants. Bettina's uncle happened to be the head of Neurology at a hospital in Nuremberg so she suggested I send my latest scans – I was getting scans all the time – over to him. He took a look and reported back.

He said he couldn't see a problem with me riding as the ligament around the spinal cord had healed and grown back on to the bone. He said if I had another bad fall and landed on my head again I might break my neck again but I wouldn't break in the same place. Bone heals and although there was no guarantee the whole thing would never happen again in the same situation, he did say there was no reason at that point why I shouldn't ride.

Well, that was good enough for me. It was just what I wanted to hear. I went down to the stables, told everyone the news, and got Arko tacked up. I got on him and worked him a bit. It felt great, all was fine, I was confident and I couldn't wait to start jumping. I put up a little cross rail.

As I rode Arko down to that rail he spooked and ran past it. I came off but luckily landed on my feet. When I looked up there were people running around shouting and swearing at me. I got back on and carried on. I was determined to keep going.

Back into the Saddle

On 13 May 2002, a year and eight months after that devastating fall, I took Arko to Gorse Farm arena where I rode him in a 1.25m class. We came second and won £35. I thought I'd take it easy and see how I went on with him that year. Me and Arko got on. A week later we went to the Wales and West show at David Broome's place. We won the 1.40m class. We stayed on the county show circuit and Arko was winning. I was happy with that.

I was riding another horse for the Hales, called Flambeau. I took both him and Arko to the City of Chester show in July 2002. Arko picked up a second place and Flambeau had a win in the 1.20m class and a place in the Grades B and C. Then in the last class on the Sunday afternoon I was riding Flambeau and we had a horrendous fall. I can't remember what happened, maybe I got too close to a fence, but I fell forward and the horse fell too. Then, as he got up, he trod right in the middle of my back, just above the base of my spine. That took the wind right out of me.

I was just lying there on the ground, and as this happened so soon after I had started riding again there was a bit of a panic on. I remember thinking 'this hurts'. Pat Hales was there watching and she came running into the ring to see if I was all right, along with Geoff Billington. They got me up. I insisted I didn't want to go to hospital but I was in so much pain I couldn't bend. I somehow managed to get into the car but there was no way I could drive. Fortunately, Suzanne Dando was commentating at the show. A good friend, Suzanne lived round the corner from me at the time. While I was waiting for her in the car, Geoff came over and I said thanks very much for coming into the ring with Pat to see if I was OK. He said he'd thought if I was knackered he'd try and get the ride on Arko!

Suzanne drove me home. When I got in, all I could do was lie on the carpet with an ice pack on the big haematoma which had developed on my back. With hindsight, I'm surprised I didn't go to hospital. I suppose I'd seen enough of hospitals at that stage, but I did go the next day and got my back X-rayed. There was nothing broken, fortunately, but over the next few days the bruising came out. What a sight that was! Complete bruising the whole way round my body; black at the front, black at the sides and black at the backside, aside from a big white patch where the hoof had landed. A week later I went to Hickstead. I looked as if I was wearing a pair of black shorts. I dropped my trousers for one of the photographers, who snapped the shot and put it in *Horse & Hound*. It had to be done. What I didn't know at the time was the consequences that fall would have, but the bruising subsided and I got on with steadily bringing Arko on.

Our first trip abroad was to the southern coast of Portugal. Two shows in beautiful settings, Lezirias and Vilamoura. Arko won big classes at both shows. I was happy with that. We went on to the Horse of the Year Show, which that year moved from Wembley to the NEC at Birmingham. As we hadn't won enough money and I was way down the rankings we had to qualify for the big money classes. We did, and Arko took me to third place in the grand prix with a double clear. Arko was being talked about as the next future star horse.

In 2003 we stepped it up. With things starting to go well, the Hales had decided they would like to get some more horses. I said I'd stick with three nice horses, not go flat out every day and keep myself a bit selective. We'd bought a nice horse to bring on, a seven-year-old called Pandur, and Lisa Hales had given me a horse of hers to ride, Russel.

We went to Rome on the Nations Cup team via a couple of smaller Italian shows. That was my first team call-up since my accident. After St Gallen, where we were fourth, the team was second at both Dublin and Calgary, then Arko and I were picked again for the Nations Cup team at Hickstead, the Royal

Back into the Saddle

International Horse Show. I cricked my back the day before the class and was dosed up on painkillers, but Arko was brilliant and jumped a double clear. That Nations Cup, my first since breaking my neck, was won. The European Championships were to be held in Donaueschingen, Germany, a couple of weeks later. We were chosen for the team.

There had been some major changes to team life since I'd been away, not least our beloved chef d'equipe Ronnie Massarella had retired after the Sydney Olympics. He'd done the job for thirty-two years. Derek Ricketts had taken over and as he'd been World Champion in 1978 he had the background.

Off we went to Donaueschingen; me and Michael Whitaker, Robert Smith and Richard Davenport. That show was a disaster. Our performance there was crucial to qualifying for the Athens Olympics. We didn't.

But I did end up going to Athens. I was selected to go as an individual along with Robert Smith. Arko was ten then. After watching Sydney 2000 with a torture device screwed to my head it was a big deal for me to be going to the Olympics. Arko won the British Open Championship in Sheffield at the beginning of that year. Hickstead, in July, was interesting. Arko'd had a slight cough and with the Olympics coming up as well as Dublin it was better he had a few days off. I rode Russel in the Nations Cup.

Russel was a funny horse. Going to the same shows, Arko and Russel used to stable next to each other but they hated each other. Arko was OK but Russel just didn't like Arko. He was probably jealous because he knew Arko was better than him! Arko, well everybody loved Arko as he was so pretty, so neat with his legs and such a great jumper, but Russel, he was awkward, there was no horse more awkward than him. He was a classic jumper but on the flat he never had four legs going in the same direction. If he was cantering on the right leg going round a corner he'd switch leads. He'd be what I call cross-cantering or others call disunited. I tried and tried to work him to get him to stay on the right leads but no, he always used to switch. He was a talented horse, he had scope, any amount of jump and he was careful. The only reason he'd have a fence down was when he ran himself into trouble with his cross-cantering. He would never listen to what I was trying to tell him and I just had to make the best of it.

So back to Hickstead: we had a bad start. Russel was being Russel and at the eighth fence in the first round of the Nations Cup he stopped, sending me straight over his head. Robert Smith went clear but Robert Whitaker and Richard Davenport had eight faults each. I was praying I wouldn't have to go again in the second round. I was sore. But when Robert retired Qualité after she banged her leg I had to jump and I had to jump clear. We hadn't won a Nations Cup all year so things were a bit desperate. Russel for once knew how important it was and he jumped clear. We won. Then he came out the next day and won the grand prix, my sixtieth international grand prix win, then the day after he was second in the King George on a double clear. He was awkward but he was good!

I'm talking about very, very good horses but I still hadn't met a perfect one. Being totally critical, Arko didn't have the best mouth, but I found a bit that worked for him. We got along together and if his rideability was 7 out of 10, I accepted that was the way he went and I worked through and found the best way we could come to terms with each other. And it did work, really well. Arko was very careful, brave and had the scope. Arko is in my all-time top three – and what a lovely character he was, and is.

In Athens, Arko jumped amazingly, but with hindsight I think he was probably a little bit inexperienced for the last day. He jumped clear all the way through and we were only one of two clears in the first round of the individual, the other was Ireland's Jessica Kuerten on Castle Forbes Maike.

The first day they had this triple bar in the course, it was like three triple bars in a fan and you could choose which side to jump. The wings were like big walls in the middle and I remember coming round to it on that first day. Arko took a look at it, cocked his jaw and then he went to run out. I think it took him by surprise, so I hung on to him and he jumped, not over the triple bar but over the wing wall in the middle, straight over the lot. There was a tree behind the wall and he jumped that as well. It threw me to the wrong side to jump the double and I had to jump the bigger part of the double not the smaller one. But anyway he finished clear.

I went back afterwards and asked the course designer Olaf Petersen if he would measure it. I wanted to know how high and wide Arko had jumped. Olaf got out his measure. Well, the top of that wall was 1.90m and the width of it was 2.20m, and with the tree behind it Arko jumped even wider than that. I seem to remember that photo was on the back page of one of the newspapers the next day.

Things were looking promising going into the second round. Jessica had a few down and dropped out of contention. There were no clears so when I rode into the ring, last to go on Arko, I knew a clear would win us the gold, four would mean a jump-off for gold. We jumped clear until we had to turn away from the gate. What was next? That triple bar, on its own this time but the same wall, the same rails. With hindsight, I think it spooked him a bit after that massive jump in the first round. It was sickening to hear a rail fall. Arko clipped it and I think it scared him a bit as he ran off to the combination. When a rail fell going in and another going out, that medal I'd set my heart on was gone.

John Hales missed the whole thing. He'd gone to hide in a

hut behind the grandstand. He couldn't watch, he never could, he always relied on Lisa to tell him what had happened. So we finished thirteenth but considering that four years earlier any thoughts of being able to ride at any show, let alone an Olympic Games, had been well and truly squashed, I was happy with that. It was a great experience and Arko had gone well; we'd had a close call and it didn't work out, but that's showjumping.

19

The Find of a Lifetime

Arko put Athens behind him, as did I. We finished the year at Olympia where Arko came second in the grand prix – Marcus Ehning beat me by a fraction of a second. Russel won the six bar; he was brilliant in those classes and won thirteen consecutive six bar competitions. In fact I think he was unbeaten in them. At Olympia the last in the straight line of four fences stood at 6' 4". He didn't have a chance to cross-canter going down a straight line of fences!

We won a tough World Cup qualifier in Leipzig on the way to the final in Las Vegas. Arko jumped brilliantly. On the final day in Vegas Arko jumped clear but it went belly-up in the second round as we got it all wrong going into the double and I came off in the middle of it.

In May we went to the Nations Cup in Rome. That was a great show as it was the first British win at the Piazza di Sienna arena since 1991 and I'd been part of that with Apollo. Michael Whitaker riding Portofino and me on Arko jumped double clears to clinch it over the all-female US team of Beezie Madden, Anne Kursinski, Schuyler Riley and Laura Kraut, who was to become very important in my life.

The same team – that is Michael, me, Ellen Whitaker (John's niece, who was only nineteen then) on Locarno and Will Funnell on Mondriaan – went to the European Championships at San Patrignano, Italy. When we got there we didn't know exactly who was going to ride on the team as Derek Ricketts hadn't decided. When he did, John was fifth man and he wasn't happy. We jumped a round and it was all looking hopeful after the first day. We were in fourth place after the speed leg. Arko had jumped clean and was fourth overall.

We tried to pacify John with a meal out and a few drinks but he wasn't having any of it. We got back and that was that, John wasn't going to ride any more. He threw his boots out of the window. The hotel, in the old Italian seaside city of Rimini, was surrounded by sloping roofs and those boots fell on to one of the neighbouring roofs. Then Ellen's horse suffered a bout of colic. They were out and the next morning John had to ride, but first of all he had to go climbing over those old Italian roofs to get his boots back.

The wheels fell off for all of us after that and we came home empty-handed. We got criticised in the press, especially me for having Arko in Spruce Meadows, Calgary, so close to the Europeans. But we won the grand prix there.

Redemption came in Dublin. John, Michael, Will and I took our team horses for the Nations Cup. Arko jumped a double clear, then John's difficult ride Exploit du Roulard had four down. Will's Mondriaan didn't like the going and had three down, but Portofino got round on five faults with Michael so we held off the Germans by a single point. It was John's fiftieth birthday as well and we kicked off the celebrations at the British Embassy.

Dan had gone to work for trainer Paul Nicholls in Somerset the previous year. Both the boys started out showjumping, doing well in ponies then juniors. While I'd be away at shows, so would they, starting off just as I had. That was our lifestyle. Dan got very interested in point-to-pointing when he was at Leicester University studying design. John Hales had sent him a horse called Be My Friend that he was getting fit and training for the season. He'd get up at silly o'clock to ride, then drive to his lectures four days a week, then drive back to spend two hours in the gym to get himself lean and fit enough to race. That was something I could sympathise with; I like my food but it tends to leave an impression if I'm not careful.

John Hales had horses in training with Paul and said to Dan if he was going to train one for him he'd better go down to Paul's and see how it was done. Paul had suggested Dan go down there for a week during his holidays to ride out. We went down to Paul's owners' day and Dan stayed on for the week.

I got a nice text from Paul to say if Dan ever wants a job, there would always be one there for him. I asked what kind of job and Paul replied he'd make one for him. Dan decided straight away. He was fed up and knackered with driving to Leicester, so on Paul's offer, off he went.

Harry was never going to do anything other than horses. Mick Fitzgerald reminded us all recently that he's never seen anyone hit a couch as many times as Harry did. When he was little he used to sit on the arm of the couch or on a stool, whip in hand, and ride out finishes. One day I'd taken him to ride out at Reg Hollinshead's. Old Reg was a legend (he died in 2013 aged eighty-nine) as a trainer of flat horses but also of riders; he produced Walter Swinburn and champion jockey Kevin Darley, among many others. He brought on so many jockeys and apprentices his place was an unofficial jockey school. The first day Harry rode out he got run off with, loved it and that was that. After they'd all ridden, Reg used to sit down with Harry, as he did with all his lads, and talk through everything. Harry learnt so much from him. When

Harry was fifteen I got the inevitable phone call from his school. I could hardly argue with it, I'd done exactly the same. In 2005 he left school without sitting an exam.

Harry was light enough at the time to be riding on the flat so he went to Richard Hannon near Marlborough. He was breaking in yearlings and he thought it was brilliant. Oxo had done a great job starting off my boys.

Once the boys left home we were rattling around at Finwood Lawn, so when I found out what the market value was for the place I decided to start looking for a property with a view to putting Finwood on the market and moving.

Arko was added to the BHS Hall of Fame that year and he had earned the highest prize money of any British horse, mainly thanks to the Spruce Meadows grand prix and £101,000 from his second place in the Las Vegas Invitational in October. It was a huge deal back then but pretty insignificant now, thanks to Scott Brash winning a million euro bonus for the Rolex Grand Slam. There were some very big money shows, for the day, starting to crop up and in early 2006 Arko picked up about half his annual sum at one show, the Al Maktoum Memorial Challenge in Dubai. Over his career he won over £1.2 million.

The following year's championship was the World Equestrian Games in Aachen. Arko started the year well and he won the grand prix in Lucerne, then he seemed to lose his form so I took him to a few smaller shows before the Royal International at Hickstead. The team was due to be announced on the final day of the show after the King George V Gold Cup. As we approached the fifth fence, a double of gates, Arko stopped dead. I went over his head. I wasn't hurt but it shook me up, not just the fall but that Arko had stopped like that. He wouldn't be going to the Games but he would be getting checked over.

I was reserve for Aachen with Russel, that talented crosscanterer. We were there but we weren't going to be jumping. I did the warm-up on the first day there then, on the first competition day, I was in the hotel lazing about. Everyone had gone down to work their horses. The phone rang, it was Laura. She said I'd better bring my breeches as she'd just seen Robert Smith's horse go by and she thought I'd be jumping. So I had to get my gear on and get ready. We had a time fault in the first round of the Nations Cup and five in the second, so the team finished in eighth place. Russel wasn't the ideal championship horse; he could win classes and he was talented, but it was very difficult with his cross-cantering and legs everywhere. I decided then I'd never go to a championship or an Olympic Games again unless I'd got a horse that was actually going to win. It takes a long time to get there, then to get there and do no good? I'd had enough of that.

I'd looked at the place we're in now a couple of times. It was very different then, very run-down and dilapidated. I could see there was a lot of work to be done but I liked the setting, the location and the views, which are amazing. It was sold in three lots: the fifteen acres here at what is now the jumping yard, eighty-five at what is now the racing yard, where there was just a sheep building, and a further couple of acres over the road. One day I was talking to a farmer friend of mine, Gabe Mahon – we've been friends for years – and he said I ought to buy the place as I could make it into something. At the time, however, I thought it was just too much work. I kept looking and looking, and in the end I came back and looked at it again. I made the decision, made an offer and ended up getting it. One of the main reasons for taking it on was that I was thinking of Dan one day in the future. The big hill might be a great place to put a gallop, when and if he wanted to train on his own.

The house was tiny and all the outbuildings were on what is now the front lawn. I just loved the views, especially from the top of the hill at the racing yard. It's panoramic and you can see for miles. That the potential racing yard was separate was another point in its favour. So, I bought the place in November 2006 and we moved in in September 2007. We did a lot during those ten months, including putting in the essential arena. It was a lot of work, but I love building and there is nothing I like better than driving building machinery.

The terrible shock of 2007 was the sudden death of my mum. She needed a hip replacement operation, which was always going to be difficult as she had an almost irrational fear of hospitals. It took us all forever to persuade her to go for the operation and she finally agreed. Then the night before she was due to go in she just didn't wake up. It was a complete shock; I remember the feeling of disbelief even now. At least dear Mum never had to put herself through the experience of a stay in hospital. I think about her every day. Just when we had finished the barn here she came for a visit to see the place. It was the week before she died. As she was leaving, she reversed her car and made a dent in the barn doors. It's still there to this day.

Arko had ten months off in the end; he had torn a ligament near his navicular bone. When he came back to work I needed to build his confidence up. He wasn't on form in St Gallen and when we went on to Aachen, the selection trial for the European Championships in Mannheim, he started well, winning a class on the first day. Then it went wrong. The rain was torrential and Arko wasn't happy. Neither was I. Feeling he wasn't ready to take on the Nations Cup course I withdrew him so I pretty much withdrew him from selection with that decision. But then we went on to the Global Champions Tour in Estoril, which is a beautiful show right on the beach at Cascais. Arko won the grand prix, he was brilliant, and he was second in the grands prix at Athens and Valkenswaard.

The Find of a Lifetime

After having said I wouldn't go to another championship without the right horse, where should I end up in 2008 but at the Beijing Olympics with Russel! I was the reserve and I think at that point there weren't many people with the right horses, but anyway I agreed to go as fifth man. Just as I had been in 2006 I was in the hotel lazing around while everyone else was working the horses, and again I got the phone call from Laura to bring my breeches as she thought I was going to be riding.

This time it was Michael Whitaker's horse Portofino that went lame, so I joined John, Tim Stockdale and Ben Maher, thinking to myself, Oh God, I don't want to be doing this. Anyway, we got stuck in, and then when John's horse Peppermill couldn't jump on the first day due to muscle stiffness we were down to three. There was a bit of a controversy over that, but in the end we came fifth as a team. Laura ended up winning the team gold medal with Beezie Madden, McLain Ward and Will Simpson, which was great. Her little horse Cedric jumped his heart out and only had a pole down on the first day. He was retired in Florida in 2017 and then came home to us in Warwickshire.

We had a wonderful time in Hong Kong, which is where the all the equestrian events were held for quarantine reasons. The racing history and facilities up at Sha Tin made for an ideal venue and they did a great job with the courses. It's an amazing city, we had an excellent team hotel and we had a lot of fun eating out at great restaurants and shopping. It was still a very Olympic atmosphere, as it was all at the same time the other events were taking place on mainland China. We were down the road, albeit rather a long way down the road and over some water! Yes, it was a good Games.

Back in 2007, I'd had a call from my old friend Gary Widdowson. Since the Major Wager days, Gary had been busy with the family business and I hadn't heard from him for a few years until that call. He was thinking of buying a stud – I seem to recall it was Eddie Stibbe's place in Cambridgeshire – and he asked would I come and run it for him and look after it. I remember saying straight out that it would be the biggest waste of time I've ever heard of! What? Trying to breed showjumpers, just like that? I asked Gary how many mares he was thinking of getting and he said five or six. I pointed out that Paul Schockemöhle has around six hundred mares and he breeds six hundred foals a year and the result percentage-wise is not brilliant. I told Gary not to bother doing it.

I put the phone down and Laura said that was *not* the right answer, that I'd upset him. I disagreed; I don't believe in trying to breed showjumpers with that few mares. I didn't hear anything else until I was in Cannes for the show and I bumped into Gary one day, walking down the street. He was on holiday at his house down there so I suggested he came to the show that night for the grand prix. He said he would, so we got a table and we sat there having some dinner and wine and watching, talking about old times and this, that and the other.

Gregory Wathelet was riding a horse called Lantinus in the grand prix. They won and Gary got all excited and said he was going to buy that horse for me. Great, I said. He urged me to go and find out how much they'd want for Lantinus. Gary had been away from showjumping for a while and over the years the price of horses had shot up dramatically, as it continued to do, so when I went back and told Gary, I think he got a bit of a shock. When I told him the prize money was also growing, he was keen and wanted to get a deal done, but to cut a long story short it didn't happen and the horse was eventually sold to Thomas Straumann for Denis Lynch to ride.

Since Gary was clearly interested in buying a horse, I thought,

The Find of a Lifetime

Let's see what we can do. So a couple of days later I called him and was about to tell him about another horse when he stopped me and told me no, no, he didn't want another horse, he'd just got excited in the atmosphere of being at the show. No problem, never mind, I thought and put the phone down. I think I might have rung him again about another horse but the answer was still no, he'd just been excited at the time; he didn't want another horse.

A couple of months later I was in Germany looking at horses and I saw these two or three horses that were for sale as a package and they weren't super expensive. I rang Gary and I said, 'Listen, I've found these three horses and don't say no, just send me half the money and I'll go halves with you – just don't say no.' And he didn't. The plan was that I would get them going, then we'd sell them at a profit. We bought them and did exactly that, which made Gary happy as he does like a profit.

The lucky thing about that year, 2008, was that the US team had to go training in Holland. Laura went a day earlier than the others as she was based in Holland then so was driving up to the north of the country. There was a little show on and she thought she'd have a look. As she drove up to the ring there was a bay stallion jumping. What she saw caused Laura to jump out of the car – she can't see very well at a distance – and go running round to the exit as the horse came out. She saw the rider, Alan Waldman, an American from California who lives in Holland and deals in horses. Laura knows him well. She told him she loved his horse and asked about him. The horse was five years old. Laura asked Alan how much and he replied, 'Really expensive and I want him to go to a really good rider.' Laura got the price and told Alan she didn't have anyone to buy but asked if he would mind if I had the horse. Alan said he'd love me to have him.

Laura called me. She was very excited and said you'd better call

Gary and you'd better come and see this horse and don't hang about! After we'd sold those 'package deal' horses, Gary had said, 'Listen, if you see a nice horse, I'll buy you one. Just one, but it's got to be a nice one.' I had already organised for us to go to Germany, up to Jorge Naeve's near Hamburg, to see three or four horses.

I called Gary and told him Laura had seen this five-year-old stallion in Holland, that she thought it the best thing she'd ever seen and that we'd better go and see it. But we'd already organised to go to Germany and we didn't want to let Jorge down. Gary had chartered a private plane, so we flew to Hamburg and met Laura there.

I thought we were only going to buy one horse, since that was Gary's stipulation, but he remembers it differently. No matter. We saw the horse we liked, which Laura had already ridden in the ring and considered would be a nice horse for me. That was Nemo, who was eight or nine years old at the time. We bought him and while we were there, two others. I think we might even have bought three others, but my memories are a bit overshadowed by what happened afterwards. Anyway, we bought those in partnership together, so I thought, Well, that's it, we've done the cash so there's no point going down to see this five-year-old. But Laura insisted we had to go.

So we're flying down from Hamburg to Eindhoven, myself, Gary, Laura and Albert, Gary's dad, who was eighty-odd then. We're sitting there on this little plane and Albert decided he wanted to go to the toilet. So up he gets up, goes in there, shuts the door, and we run into a bit of turbulence. There was quite a bit of bumping around. Then, all of a sudden, the doors fly open and there's Albert sat on the toilet with his trousers round his ankles.

When we landed at Eindhoven we picked up a rental car and

drove to Alan Waldman's. It was five or six in the evening by the time we got there. We walked into the yard and this five-year-old stallion was stood in the cross ties. I'll never forget it; he was fat and he had the longest forelock I'd ever seen, it was down to the end of his nose. No joke, he looked like a drum horse.

He started neighing as we took him out of the yard where I was going to ride him in a big grass field. There were mares and foals either side of this paddock, so we thought that was why he was neighing. We didn't know then how famous that horse would be for it. Well, after a warm-up, I started to jump this horse. It was incredible. I thought it too good to be true, that no five-year-old could jump like that. We put the fences up; Albert in particular wanted to see him jump big and I thought, let's see if this horse is as good as Laura thought. I rode this five-year-old down to a fence about the same height in feet as he was in years and he gave that fence a foot to spare! To be honest, I was in two minds about having this horse. I thought it could not be true; no horse could be that brave and that careful at that age. I was coming up with excuses almost, saying it was a lot of money for a young horse, that Quick Stars can be difficult. 'Don't listen to him,' Laura told Gary.

And of course I thought we were only buying the one horse and we'd outdone that already. There was no more money to spend. But before we even got to the stage of trying to do any quiet negotiations, Albert burst out: 'Right, I'm buying him!' Just like that, Big Star was bought. Gary did try to negotiate but they weren't having any of it! What Gary had in mind was not just buying one, but buying the best – and that day they bought me the best horse in the world.

In October the decision was made to retire Arko. Lisa was very keen for him to go to stud and what a great job he has made of that, siring top horses like John Whitaker's Argento and several other graded stallions who ensure his lines go on. He was jumping better than ever, so he would retire at the very top just as Lisa wanted. He'd been crowned Showjumper of the Year for the fourth year running at the start of the year and he went out on a total high when I took him to Spruce Meadows. Arko went and won the grand prix!

20

A Big Star Emerges

The chubby stallion with the longest forelock arrived at his new home in Warwickshire while I was still in Beijing. Young Amanda Derbyshire, who was working for me at the time, took on Big Star until she moved to the USA where she now works for the Gochman family at Baxter Hill in Florida. She trains with Laura and me, has some good horses and rides at grand prix level, still for GB. Amanda took him to the Scope Festival and Gary rang me to say he looked amazing. I got back in time for the final and Amanda was warming up. That was the first time I had seen him jump. All I could mouth to Gary was 'wow'.

Amanda took him steady in five-year-old classes and had a couple of wins, but winning wasn't the endgame at that point. Nor would it be for a while, despite it being my basic instinct that the game is all about winning. This was far too important. The winter Big Star turned six I was away in Florida, so I gave him to my half-brother Michael Jones to ride down at the Sunshine Tour in Spain, which is always great for giving young horses experience and mileage. Michael rode Big Star in the six-year-old classes.

The worst thing for me back then was knowing how good Big Star was but having to get the experience into him. It was a matter of waiting, but time was going so slowly for me because he was just incredible. Time? I kept wishing it would hurry up! With any young horse you've got to be careful not to speed them too much when they're developing – i.e. don't go fast against the clock – but there were two championships, the Horse of the Year Show six-year-old final and the six-year-old championship at the Scope Festival, which both carried decent prize money. I set myself the goal of trying to win both with Big Star. Going twice against the clock was not going to hurt him. He won both and Big Star became the horse everyone was talking about in 2009.

Harry, meanwhile, had nailed a win in the Irish Grand National on Niche Market, a horse trained by Bob Buckler. Aged nineteen, he was a rising star in the jump racing world and I was one proud dad. After a year at Richard Hannon's, Harry had got a bit heavier so had to make the move over to jump racing and to Ditcheat to join Dan at Paul Nicholls' yard. Everything was going well.

The accident had put a huge strain on the relationship with Bettina. I was a pain in the arse to live with. When you go through something so life-changing, you don't think straight, you don't think logically. By the time I got back to competing, which meant I was away at the shows while Bettina was at home, things had changed, I'd changed.

The thorny issue after Beijing was personal, complicated and it was my fault and only mine. All good things come to an end, although it didn't feel very good at the time for anyone involved. Whether I'd thought I could have the best of both worlds or just hadn't faced the situation as I didn't want to upset anyone, I don't know. The outcome was that my relationship with Bettina ended. I am forever grateful to her for doing a brilliant job bringing up the boys. She's a great person and will do anything to help anyone.

I will always think of her as a good-hearted friend. Bettina now lives in Spain.

Circumstances were different with Laura to both my previous relationships. We were doing the same thing; riding, training, competing. Now we are partners in every sense: working together, riding together and training other people. It's our business and Laura moved in here in 2009.

We kept Nemo but sold the other three horses we'd bought on that epic buying trip. Over the winter of 2007 Laura had spotted, at Jorge Naeve's, a horse called Carlo, a seven-year-old grey who Jorge said was an excellent jumper. I'd seen him in action as a five-year-old and liked him. I told Gary about him. I asked Jorge to send Carlo to me in Florida so I could try him and that if he lived up to expectations Gary would buy him. So I rode Carlo that first week and liked him, rated him very highly. I sent Gary the video and he bought him. Carlo went well from the beginning; he won the seven-year-old classes at La Baule and was well placed all season, as he was in 2009 when I stepped him up a level.

Carlo was an out-and-out jumper, very careful. He had all the scope and was very rideable, but at home, and in the warm-up, he could be spooky. He was frightened of other horses. If a horse came towards him, he'd be ducking and diving. At home, he'd spook at all the jumps! You would never have thought he would be as good as he was, but as soon as he went in the ring and the bell went, he lost all that spookiness. It was funny. If you rode him at home you'd think, Christ, there's no way I'm going to get him round the ring! But as soon as he got in there, he was in his element, in his comfort zone.

Being a year older than Big Star gave Carlo his chance and kept me occupied. I felt fortunate to have such good horses thanks to Gary and Beverley. In 2010 I took him back to Florida again, where he won the grand prix. I don't think I'd ever had it happen before but Carlo and Nemo had a knack for coming first and second together. They did it in the Shrewsbury Flower Show grand prix, where Carlo won and Nemo was second, then in 2010 in Florida where Nemo got the edge over Carlo in the 1.50 Classic. It's pretty special, I think, to get a 'one two' in a class. It hasn't happened since.

The big championship was the World Equestrian Games in Kentucky and I said early on I wouldn't be aiming Carlo at that. He was only nine and I could already see him at the London 2012 Games. Carlo was brilliant at the Global Champions Tour in La Mandria, Spain, where he came second to Germany's Marco Kutscher and Cash by just two-tenths of a second.

Laura and I went down to the South of France for the Global Champions Tour at Cannes, which was followed by Monaco a week later. Gary and Beverley invited us to spend our week off on their boat, which was pretty amazing. US rider Lauren Hough came with us and we all went down to St Tropez. Coming into Monaco at the end of the week the party had got going on the huge top deck. Gary and I were doing our rock star impressions as 'The Inflatables' playing air guitar and air saxophone with these blow-up instruments to loud rock music. Lauren said it was the best week she'd ever had and did we have to go back and do show-jumping? We do this every week, I said, you should come and be on our team!

The spotlight on the following year's European Championships was especially strong in the lead-up to the 2012 Olympics in London. Our year started in Florida where Big Star jumped amazingly in the two-star series, winning two grands prix and finishing as 1.50m series champion. Carlo was second in the three- and four-star grands prix.

Carlo was the linchpin of several Nations Cup teams that year, even though he was still relatively inexperienced. We fought back from fourth in St Gallen to finish joint second with Switzerland, then Carlo jumped two amazing double clears to land the grand prix. I knew going into the jump-off that American Rich Fellers had set an incredibly fast time so we really had to go for it. Carlo was so careful and we got home half a second faster. That was a valuable class and that win put us firmly in the frame for the Europeans.

In Aachen the team was joint second again, this time with Germany, then we went on to Dublin with Michael on Amai, Scott on Intertoy Z and Robert Smith on Talan. We all jumped clear in the first round, apart from Scott who had just one down. When the Irish team ended up on the same score we were into a jump-off for first place. Rob Hoekstra, who had taken over as team manager the previous year, put me and Carlo forward in a head-to-head jump-off against Ireland's Billy Twomey and Tinka's Serenade, a mare by my old ride Tinka's Boy. It's a risky strategy but one I have often used to good advantage and would do in the future. Go first, and then watch the other make mistakes trying to catch you or play safe and go slower. Carlo rose to the challenge. Billy's horse made a mistake at the second fence. The Aga Khan Trophy was ours again and Carlo had put in one of the best performances of his career. I was over the moon with him.

Madrid was hot, scorching. Carlo was selected for the team alongside Ben Maher on Tripple X, John Whitaker on Peppermill and Guy Williams on Titus. The team was in fifth place after the speed leg. Carlo had jumped a copybook clear round over a difficult course and we were in eighth place individually. He jumped two more brilliant clears, going first for the team. Guy's Titus came into his own to finish the final round on just a time fault and Ben's stallion touched the oxer for four faults. John didn't get the round he wanted when Peppermill lowered two, but when the Dutch team crumbled we were on the podium and elated to be taking back the team bronze.

We started the individual competition in second place but Carlo's clear run was ended with an unlucky pole down in each round. I had to sit and wait then as the last three riders jumped. Sweden's Rolf-Göran Bengtsson had just a time fault on Ninja La Silla, one medal booked. Carsten Otto Nagel and Corradina, one down, another medal booked. I wouldn't wish it on anyone as I know what it feels like, but when Gerco Schröder had two fences down I got bronze. That's the game. Two medals, we hadn't done that in a while. It felt good.

That November, Carlo won the grand prix in Washington, where I finished as Leading International Rider. I also had another horse with me of Gary and Beverley's, Unique XVIII, who won the puissance at 7' 8". It had been a great year. Beverley was thrilled to be awarded the title of 'Owner of the Year' by the FEI and the International Jumping Owners Club. I was proud for her as she, Gary and Albert had put so much into the team's success and mine. They're all in it together, but Bev's the more decorative one! When the award was started in 2004, John, Pat and Lisa Hales won it two years running for Arko. It's a great way to give owners the recognition they deserve. Carlo was voted Horse of the Year for 2011 by the British Equestrian Writers' Association (BEWA). He was the first showjumper to win it.

Going into the Olympic year, I had two horses capable of going to the Games: Carlo and, even though he was only nine, Big Star. We went to Florida, where Big Star won three grands prix. He'd have eleven major wins on that circuit over his career. I'd never had a circuit like it, but then I'd never had a circuit as long as that.

When we came home I took him to Antwerp, where he won the 1.60m grand prix. There were only three clears out of forty-seven starters in the first round. Eric Lamaze went first and fast but had a rail, then Switzerland's Pius Schwizer took it steady for a clear.

A Big Star Emerges

I let Big Star go and he flew. We were ten seconds faster.

The Global Champions Tour in Hamburg was a serious challenge. Big Star rose to it. Whenever I'm asked what Big Star was like as a young horse I can only say, 'Same as he is now, only younger.' He was jumping like an experienced grand prix horse and nothing flustered him. He jumped on the Nations Cup team in La Baule, double clear, where Carlo won the grand prix. While we didn't win the Nations Cup there was some fun at that show.

David McPherson is a great guy but he's a real worrier. He gets passionate about doing the right thing, he never wants to let anybody down. His horse Chamberlain Z was always funny at the water and there was this one line of fences away from the collecting ring he was worried about. I said to David, 'When you jump the triple bar, just go. Miss the stride out, just go forward and the momentum should carry you, rather than going splosh straight into the middle of the water.' So we decided that's what he was going to do. I was first to go and Carlo went clear so I was out in the collecting ring, warming Dave up, telling him, 'Don't mess around, just go straight at the water.' Dave went in, we were all watching. What does he do but jump the triple bar, go for the water and splosh, Chamberlain goes straight in it. I was going mad at Rob Hoekstra, effing and blinding. Then Dave comes out of the ring and he says to me, 'What do you think?' 'What do I think?' I said. 'I think you've been in more water than fucking Nelson!' Robert Hoekstra's going at me to shut up because I'd upset Dave, but although Dave didn't have great second round, I think they did jump the water.

We'd been led out by Jennifer Saunders, who had become a British Showjumping ambassador. She came over with Maria Haig, the communications whizz at British Showjumping, and Judy Craymer, the brilliant film and theatre producer – she produced *Mamma Mia*, among others – another great ambassador who also has horses in training with Dan. Maria and Judy grew up less than a mile apart and were in the same pony club together. Judy was making a TV programme about Jennifer's love of horses. They also shared our love of partying and we made quite a night of it after the Nations Cup.

On 26 May we had a big celebration, Dan's marriage to Grace, a beautiful and proud day at the bride's family home in Somerset.

Carlo was going well but Big Star was unbelievable. I had always believed in him but for it to be happening like that was causing a stir. He had a big name and he was living up to it. In June that year, I got the news that I was to receive the OBE for services to equestrian sport in the Queen's Birthday Honours List. That was a huge honour. I was humbled. It wasn't just a great recognition for me but also for our sport.

In July I was selected for the Olympic team with Big Star. We had four good young horses for the team: Big Star at nine, and Hello Sanctos, Tripple X and Vindicat – all ten-year-olds. Scott Brash and Ben Maher were in their twenties, and Peter Charles and I in our fifties, me with two years on Peter.

A week later we went to Aachen. Beverley picked up her Owner of the Year award there. That I was going to the Olympics with Big Star was entirely down to the Widdowsons resisting the huge offers they'd had for him. He won the big class on the Wednesday for them. It was Carlo I rode in the Nations Cup. The team came fifth. Michael Whitaker had missed out on team selection with Amai, who'd had time off for injury, and wasn't too happy about it. We shared a few beers after the Nations Cup – quite a few, in fact. We were heading past the big roll of honour board for the grand prix. There's a tradition that the winner's name is written up temporarily after the class before being officially added by the signwriter. Michael decided to get a step ladder. He got up there and wrote in the 2012 winner's slot 'Michael Whitaker' . . . and for the horse he wrote 'Totilas'. It was hilarious that he'd done it, not least because Totilas was a bloody dressage horse! Anyway, next day, Michael only went out on Amai and won the Rolex Grand Prix!

As London 2012 approached I was sure we'd get a medal. I didn't think we'd win, to be honest, but I was sure we'd be in the first three. I wasn't being disloyal or an 'unbeliever', it was just that for the four of us it was our first time together as a team and I didn't think we were quite strong enough for a win. But we had the advantage of being at home and the people were so behind us; two brats and two old timers with injuries. Those loyal fans following us were not only hard-core showjumping fans but horse people, people who liked sport and people who were simply behind the Olympics taking place in London. All of those supporters and being on home soil did help. Going into the competition we were all calm and relaxed. Ben said it was the calmest team he'd ever been on, but then he hadn't been on as many as I have.

Greenwich Park looked amazing; the blue and purple colours everywhere, the flags and that setting mixing historic with modern as you looked out to Inigo Jones's Queen's House at one end of the arena, then to Sir Christopher Wren's imposing Royal Naval College with the backdrop of Canary Wharf and the City set against the skyline across the River Thames. The stables and set-up were all superb, as were the gamesmakers (as the volunteers became known) and the forces personnel who looked after security, always with smiles on their faces.

The first day was the qualifying event, which decided the order for the team competition and counted as qualification for the individual competition. I went first on Big Star, just where I like to be. Clear inside the time, we were followed by Ben on Tripple X, who did the same. Scott had one pole down with Hello Sanctos and

Peter's Vindicat had two down and two time faults. The crowd was the noisiest I've ever experienced. We knew we were going to get that as it had been the same for the dressage riders, but Big Star wasn't bothered. It got noisier as the class went on and we knew that, from then on, our horses would have to cope with it and so would we.

The first round of the team competition was the next day, Sunday. The way Big Star jumped was unbelievable. Bob Ellis's courses were a masterpiece of design, all sixteen fences depicting London landmarks from Big Ben to a red London bus. It looked amazing, it felt amazing and it was amazing. Big Star was perfect. As usual, he was quiet outside, then as he went into the arena he neighed and just lit up, shifted gear and gave me the most amazing feeling. Some of the lines were tricky but that didn't bother Big Star.

Tripple X went clear next, and then Scott looked on for a clear until Hello Sanctos touched a pole on the Trafalgar Square fence. It was only a rub and the pole fell late. The noise had bothered Peter's horse, but Vindicat was happier that day. He was unlucky in the middle of the combination and rolled a pole at the Penny Black vertical so proved the discard score, but as a team we finished the day in joint second place on four faults. But it wasn't just with one country, it was with three: Sweden, Holland and Switzerland. The Saudi team were in pole position on a single penalty, which shocked everyone. The Canadian team were on five penalties and Brazil and the USA qualified for the second round on eight each. Amazingly, Germany, the favourites, didn't make the cut and neither did France or Belgium, but it was all very, very close for the final eight nations.

The next day's course was big, technical and needed a lot of shortening and lengthening to cope with the tricky distances. In the stables we were all quietly confident and we believed we could do it. No one was getting flustered, which was a good sign. I had absolute faith in Big Star, that nine-year-old genius. I knew there was nothing he couldn't do.

He jumped a perfect clear. Tripple X rolled one pole at fence ten. Scott, at his first Olympics, produced the round of his life on Hello Sanctos, then Peter and Vinny were clear until the penultimate fence, ironically called the Olympic fence, a gate. They got home on five, including one time fault.

Now we had to wait to see what Dutch rider Gerco Schröder would do. He had one down on London (ironically, that was his horse's name). If he'd had another or a time fault we'd have been home and dry, but he didn't. A jump-off it was, a penalty shoot-out almost, between us and the Dutch team.

First to go, Big Star kept up his amazing record. Clear and fast. Job done. We were matched by the orange when Jur Vrieling went clear on Bubalu. Over to you Ben, job done, clear, pressure added. Maikel van de Vleuten's Verdi had two down. Our banner passed to Scott; great round but unlucky at the second. Four faults then the same for the orange team when Marc Houtzager felled one with Tamino. Banner to Peter and Vindicat; you could have heard a pin drop as they rode in. They took their time! They were nearly fourteen seconds slower than us, but that didn't matter, Vindicat had got his confidence. They were clear.

Sixty years after Harry Llewellyn and Foxhunter, Wilf White and Nizefella and Duggie Scott on Aherlow had made history winning Olympic gold at the Helsinki Games in 1952, a British team had again, at last, won the Olympic team gold in showjumping. We had done it, on home soil. With all the Olympic Games I had been to, the mistakes I'd made at previous games, to hold that gold medal, well, it just didn't get any better. The atmosphere was unbelievable, the crowd went crazy.

I still think we owe those gold medals to that fantastic crowd at

Greenwich Park, all 23,000 or more of them, and to the owners who'd kept those horses for us. And I owed Big Star, big time. The way he jumped in the team competition was just unbelievable. But I believed it, I believed in him.

There was a lot of hugging, tears; Laura had been there to support me all the way as she wasn't riding. All the owners played their part too, especially Gary and Bev, Lord and Lady Harris, and Lord and Lady Kirkham who had been and are so supportive of Scott (and need to watch out as he then said he hoped he'd be riding in his fifties!). The prize-giving was amazing, there is no feeling close to standing up at the top of the podium with your mates wearing gold medals. I was a bit premature and got on the podium early, only to be pulled off by Ben with the others saying, 'Not yet, Nick!'

Then it was off into media frenzy. Maria and the communications team at British Showjumping were working remotely so they could grab every opportunity without having to worry about being tied to the opening hours of the media centre. They'd been hoping we would get a medal, the gold even, and the media response was immediate. Maria and her team ended up working until 5 a.m.

We got changed into our tracksuits and headed to the Greenwich Tavern, conveniently sited at the entrance to the stables. Will Connell was going round telling everyone not to give us any drinks. We were supposed to go to the main media centre to do interviews with Clare Balding, but we were stuck, we weren't going to get out of there. I rang Clare and asked would it be a good idea to come to the pub to interview us all there? She thought it was a great idea, so we did the interviews in an upstairs room. Clare was asking us what we thought we'd get out of winning the gold. Scott's answer was that he hoped he would get some girlfriends. I told him he needed to win more than one gold to achieve that!

A Big Star Emerges

The next morning, nursing sore heads, we went up to the Olympic Park to be on Radio 2's Chris Evans breakfast show. Live on air, Chris persuaded the owner of Greenwich Tavern to rename the pub 'The Gold and Saddle' for the rest of the Games. Very appropriate!

For the individual competition, I was confident; Big Star was jumping so well. He flew the first round, he was great. In the second round we were last to go. Switzerland's Steve Guerdat had already jumped what was to be the only fault-free round, with Ireland's Cian O'Connor and Holland's Gerco Schroeder both with one time fault each. The atmosphere was incredible. The crowd were behind us and Big Star was jumping amazingly. We had to jump a pretty big combination then turn right-handed at the top of the ring. As Big Star came out of that combination clear, I distinctly remember the crowd went mad. There was a big bank of PA speakers at the top of the ring and as we turned and went past it, the announcer, Nick Brooks-Ward, said 'Shush' to the crowd and the crowd took up the cue. I felt Big Star light up at the noise, that wave of 'shushing'. He took hold of the bridle. As I turned right-handed back to the vertical, he was buzzing a little bit. I didn't have much time to settle him as the time was tight. I had a good shot to the fence but he clipped it behind. It was very, very unlucky. So that was that. The chance of an individual medal was gone. But that's what happens, that's the game. It was at the Cutty Sark fence, modelled on the world's only surviving tea clipper and fastest ship of her time. We went into it that bit too fast and the Cutty Sark sank us.

That amazing crowd were still kind enough to give us a standing ovation as we left the arena. Was I devastated? Maybe, at the time. I was annoyed for quite a while. But then, if it had all gone to plan, would I have carried on? What I did know was that Rio 2016 was the plan for me and Big Star.

The dressage team had got their first-ever gold the day after ours – Carl Hester said we'd spurred them on – then Charlotte Dujardin rode Valegro to individual gold and Lara Bechtolsheimer got the bronze on Mistral Højris. The eventing team had started off the medal haul with team silver. It was the best result ever – and not just for the equestrian teams. Team GB overall was third in the medal table at the end of the Games with a total of 65 medals. The whole country was celebrating with us, it was amazing. That people lined the streets for us as we paraded through London on open top buses was amazing. It was all just amazing, for our sport, all equestrian sports, everyone. The only thing that wasn't amazing was the state of my back. I was glad to be able to rest on the rails of that bus as we were driven around.

We did more media, the *Alan Titchmarsh Show* in September, I think we were all sober for that one. It went on right to Olympia where all the equestrian medallists were driven round the arena to massive cheers and hoots from the flag-waving crowd.

Earlier that December I had been to Buckingham Palace. To win Olympic gold in my own country, then to receive the OBE from the Queen, that made my year.

21

The Long Road to Rio

It was a long road and it was a struggle. I'll admit there were times when I didn't think we'd make the Rio Olympics. In the September after London we sold Carlo to the Spanish rider Sergio Alvarez Moya, who has done well with him, in fact they were in Rio. Unique had been a good 1.45m winner for us, he was another one of Gary and Beverley's, but after London I decided to play things down and not ride too many horses, so while I continued to ride a few others in the meantime I had pretty much decided then to stick with Big Star.

I will always be grateful to the air ambulance for both occasions they've picked me up, but especially for 2000 as I don't think I'd have come out of that fall without some sort of paralysis had it not been for them. So, I was delighted when the Midlands Air Ambulance Charity asked me to become an ambassador, along with Carl Hester and the Paralympian gold medallist Lee Pearson, who had also been airlifted after a fall. I do whatever I can to raise awareness for them. I was also delighted when the FEI announced Big Star and me as leading international horse and rider for 2012. That was for all of the team involved with an amazing horse.

Off we went to Florida again, where I took it easy with Big Star. In May we went back to La Baule for the Nations Cup with Scott on Hello Sanctos, Ben on a new ride, Jane Clarke's Cella, and Robert Smith on a new ride, the ten-year-old Viola. Big Star jumped a double clear, and the team was third, then Big Star finished third in the grand prix. Then we went on to Rome where Big Star again jumped double clear in the Nations Cup (the team was fifth) then he won the grand prix. He was jumping amazingly. There were fourteen clears so it was going to be a rush. The first two went fast and faulted, then Robert jumped a slower clear. We were ninth to go and I knew I had to let all the stops out to be in with a chance of winning. That's the sort of situation Big Star loved, he knew. The turns he made were unbelievable and he didn't touch a rail. After that we had to wait. The grandstands were packed and the atmosphere was electric. The Italian rider Emanuele Gaudiano was next in and he chased us, hard, but was a fraction of a second slower. In they came and faulted, the one remaining clear was slower. We won, Emanuele second, Robert third. Big Star had jumped six clears in ten days and I was over the moon. To win this big one, the grand prix I'd last won on Arko nine years before, incredible. I was running out of words to describe this amazing horse. Amazing does just fine.

The Global Champions tour came to London that June. It was to be held next door to the Queen Elizabeth Olympic Park and a month before it the then Mayor of London, Boris Johnson, was a good sport in getting on a horse for the media launch. He looked a bit out of place in a suit and a bicycle helmet! Big Star jumped another double clear in the 1.60m grand prix, but Ben Maher and Cella were faster for the top slot.

It is said that Aachen is the greatest horse show, and that the Aachen grand prix is the toughest in the world to win. It's the showjumping equivalent of Wimbledon, or ascending Everest – which I had done three times in the 1980s: once on Everest If Ever and twice on Everest Apollo! With Big Star's record, he could do it, I knew that. There was also the question of the new Rolex Grand Slam, a million-euro bonus for the rider who could win the grands prix at Aachen, Spruce Meadows and Geneva.

Forty, including three-quarters of the world's top twenty riders, were on the start list. Beezie Madden, the world's leading lady rider at the time, was first to go and jumped clear. We were seventh to go; Big Star flew round. There were only eight clears in the first round but the top eighteen went through to the second. Again, Big Star devoured that course. Three clears meant a jump-off. Switzerland's Janika Sprunger was born in the year I'd won the class for the second time. I sat on Big Star and watched her go on Palloubet d'Halong. Determined, fast, but they clipped the last element of the combination. In we went, turning tight but keeping a rhythm. Big Star stood off the big oxer and the crowd gasped. Clear, three seconds slower than Janika, but fast enough to put the pressure on Patrice Delaveau and Orient Express. I was sat on Big Star by the gate. Beverley, Gary and Laura were standing there with us. Patrice had to go for it. He was up on the clock. Then as a pole fell in the combination I stood up in the saddle and punched the air. We had done it! Laura, Gary and Beverley were jumping up and down with delight. We'd also pocketed 330,000 euros in prize money in the process. Big Star was my fourth Aachen grand prix winner and that prize money was a far cry from the 10k Deutsche marks I had earned when I won on If Ever thirty-one years before in 1982. Do the maths and it was at least one hundred times the money!

As we came out of the prize-giving, Gary got offered an

astonishing amount of money for Big Star. A bad time to ask to buy a horse which has just won the Aachen grand prix! He was not for sale and never would be.

After a lot of discussion with Gary and Beverley, Rob Hoekstra and Will Connell, we decided not to aim Big Star at the European Championships. We all agreed six rounds in seven days would not be in Big Star's best interests. Rio was the long-term goal.

We went to Estoril for the Global Champions Tour, where Big Star had one down in the jump-off. On to Chantilly where Beverley was delighted to be presented with the FEI Owner of the Year award for the second year running at the Global Champions Tour Show. Big Star jumped double clear, then had one down in the jump-off, finishing seventh. He was just showing the world he was mortal after all.

In August it was back to Dublin for the Nations Cup with Ben and Cella, Scott and Hello Sanctos and Robert and Viola. That was a bit of a battle but we won it.

On the first day we had the last fence down. Ben had one down, Robert had two. Since there were only six clears, we were in joint second place after the first round. But that was the first fence Big Star had had down after eleven double clears at Nations Cups. Big Star had a slight swelling on his leg. We got it scanned and were told it was OK, so we went on. Big Star jumped a great clear in the second round to the cheers of the British supporters. So did Ben, so did Scott; Robert was unlucky to be the drop score, but we held off the Dutch to lift the Aga Khan trophy again. Looking back, I think Big Star had that fence down as he didn't feel right, and when we got him home two days later he was lame.

Later that August Ben, Scott and their Dublin horses joined Michael Whitaker on Viking and Will Funnell on his home-bred Billy Congo to take gold at the European championships. I was happy for them. Ben went on to take individual silver and Scott the bronze behind Frenchman Roger-Yves Bost, 'Bosty' as he's known. Dublin was to be my last major win for a while – quite a while, in fact. Big Star wasn't right.

Meanwhile, I had been building on the Olympic legacy, literally. The idea of the racing yard had been in the back of my mind, the idea of giving Dan that start he needed. After the Olympics, it was time to start building. When I was in London I had asked what was going to happen to all the ground and the modular plastic boxes the surfaces had been built on. The organisers said it would all be sold, so I bought the plastic crates that were the base for the exercise gallop which had been set up for the eventers and the racing running rails that edged the gallop from Andrews Bowen, the surface people. They were all packed up and delivered here and we built the gallop on that hill where I'd planned it all out in my mind when I saw this place, so we have part of the Olympic legacy at Lodge Hill.

It took eight months to build everything before Dan moved in May 2013 at the end of the National Hunt season. It wasn't easy getting planning permission, but as time has gone on the planners have been very good to us. I think they're proud of what we've done at the yard and what Dan and Harry have done in the game, and that we've brought some recognition to the area. People enjoy coming here and it's all looking great and with my enjoyment of the building process it has all been extremely rewarding.

Dan had been assistant trainer to Paul Nicholls for nine years by then and the timing was right for him to apply for his own licence. His marriage to Grace had produced another reason to think about the future. Harry'd had a bit of a lean time of it when he lost his conditional jockey's weight allowance. It's a tough step up to join the big boys, so to come and be stable jockey for Dan as they were already such a good team seemed ideal timing all round. It would prove that and much more.

Dan's idea had been to start small, perhaps twelve horses. He saddled his first runner, with Harry up, at Stratford that August and they didn't have to wait long before Mister Grez became their first winner on 13 October. By November all forty-four boxes in the yard were full, then shortly before Christmas the boys had their first big race win, the Ladbroke Hurdle at Ascot. Harry rode Willow's Saviour to pip Paul Nicholls' runner and, generously, no one was more proud than Paul – apart from me, that is.

That autumn I featured in a Sky Sports documentary, one of the *Sporting Heroes* series, presented by Gary Newbon, which reminded me of my first encounter with Gary many years before. We were in Birmingham for the Horse of the Year Show and Gary was presenting for ITV. He interviewed me live on air and asked why I wasn't riding my best horse in the puissance. 'What the fucking hell has it got to do with you?' I replied. Gary looked horror-struck, his face was a picture. It was only when he heard the laughter from his crew that he realised we weren't on air at all, he'd been set up.

What wasn't funny was the situation with Big Star. But he was having stem cell treatment for the tendon injury he'd picked up in Dublin; those injuries always take time. While he was recovering, I was riding a few other horses including one bred and owned by the Hales, Aristio. He's also a graded stallion and just as beautiful as his dad, Arko.

When Big Star came back, I realised it was going to be a struggle riding them both, especially as Aristio was that much younger. So I suggested to the Hales that Aristio went to another rider who could do more with him and give him the experience he needed. So he went to the Irish rider Anthony Condon, who did well with him. Aristio went on to jump for the Irish team.

The Long Road to Rio

Meanwhile Dad and Janette had moved in two doors away. There had been a lot of talk about the HS2 train and the designated route was due to run straight through Odnaull Farm. All the talk about the train and the question of whether he would lose his home had worried Dad, so I'd said to him, 'Listen, if they're going to make a compulsory purchase, make sure you get in first, get paid and gone.' He took my advice, sold up and came to live here. He did find the move a bit of a stress, he had to go to hospital one day, but it didn't take him long to get settled in and it was the best thing he ever did. Every day he's up at the gallops, he walks up to the yard with his copy of the *Racing Post* and Janette enjoys her photography so it turned out to be the best decision whether the train had ended up going through or not.

Big Star came back to the ring in May and back to top level in July 2014. He was jumping with as much enthusiasm as ever after his enforced rest. But it didn't last long. Back we went to the lovely beachside show at Estoril for the Global Champions Tour. Big Star was third in the grand prix, which Scott won on Hello Sanctos. We'd jumped clear in the first round so in the jump-off we went fast, fastest in fact, but we had the last fence down. When Big Star put down after that last fence I felt him take a funny step as he landed. I thought it was odd but didn't think any more of it until the next day. Big Star was lame. He had a swelling on his left front leg. We got him home and got it scanned; a tear in his lower suspensory. It was going to take a long time to heal, I knew that, but I also knew Big Star was still only eleven, and Rio was two years away.

After treatment and nearly a year off, Mark rode Big Star for hours on the roads to get him fit. Steady walking on firm ground is the time-honoured way of strengthening a horse's leg muscles, tendons and ligaments in preparation for work. Then I jumped him at home for around three months before taking him down to Vilamoura in Portugal for his first show in sixteen months. He jumped clear.

Not long after our return came the news that Ronnie Massarella had died at the age of ninety-two. He had been unwell for some years and it was a great age, but the loss was very keenly felt by his close-knit family, friends, all of us he'd looked after over his three decades as chef d'equipe, and everyone who knew and loved him. There was a huge turnout for his funeral in Doncaster, and the wake afterwards. As Ronnie's coffin was driven away from the church, everyone applauded in the Italian tradition. Ronnie was a true gentleman in every way and the best ambassador the sport could ever have had. He was a great man to hold a team together and have you fighting to the last to win, a real team-spirit man. He had some terrific riders and we liked to ride for him. He had been like a second father to us.

That Christmas I got the best present ever. Dan and Harry surprised me with a new set of wheels, an exact replica of the three-wheel Reliant Robin Del Boy drives in *Only Fools and Horses*. Decked out with the legend *Trotters Independent Trading New York – Paris – Peckham* it arrived on Christmas Day, complete with a blow-up doll in the back seat and a set of furry dice hanging from the rear-view mirror. Well, I had to take it out for a drive. The horn-tooting and light-flashing responses I got from other drivers on the road was hysterical.

We went back to Florida after Christmas. Olympic year was upon us. The footing in the arenas there wasn't to Big Star's liking. I think I only jumped him in one class, but I trained him out there, jumping at different people's farms and around the park on the grass, so by the time he left Florida he was ready to go. We came home for the Cheltenham Festival.

Harry had been saying for a couple of weeks on the lead-up

that Superb Story would win. That kind of self-belief? Don't know where he gets it from! Cheltenham's the big one for everyone involved in National Hunt Racing, it's the pinnacle. The County Handicap Hurdle is one of the big races, the second race of the last day of the Festival, run over two miles and a furlong. Harry got the horse home first by two and a half lengths. It really was a Superb Story, for Harry, Dan, the owners, the whole yard.

In early April we were selected for the Nations Cup team in La Baule. Di Lampard, my teammate from the 1998 World Equestrian Games, had succeeded Rob Hoekstra as World Class Performance Manager early the previous year, so it would be my first trip with Di as chef d'equipe. In fact it was my first team call-up since Dublin 2013. The team was drawn eighth to go and I was going first. Big Star jumped amazingly. We went through the finish to huge cheers, not just from the British camp but everywhere. He always has drawn the crowds, people rush to the ring to see him and this was something special, the respect for him. Big Star was back.

Joe Clee jumped clear with the stallion Utamaro d'Ecaussines, then Ben Maher had an unlucky pole down with Diva II. Michael Whitaker jumped another super clear on Cassionato, also owned by the Widdowsons. He had started out with me but his style of jump and my back didn't get on, so when Gary suggested he went to Michael it was an easy decision. We had talked about Michael having Carlo before London as the team had looked lacking in horsepower but if anything had happened to Big Star that would have been me out, so it didn't happen.

We were on a zero score going into the second round but it didn't last. Big Star jumped with total enthusiasm, he felt great and happy to be back. Someone told me later the commentator described him as a 'wonder horse'. Spot on there then.

Joe and Utamaro had the pole over the water tray, Ben and Diva had one down early on, then another coming out of the double. Cassionato had trouble there too and was then unbalanced to the last, which also fell. Sixth, ups and downs, but I was on a high with the way Big Star had jumped. Gary and Bev were there to watch him and we were all on a high.

It didn't last. I came down to earth with a bump the next day. Big Star was slightly lame behind and the Rio Games were only three months away. It was what I call a 'niggle' on the suspensory ligament. Hind suspensory niggles are a bit like tennis elbow – good one minute sore the next. But we didn't need a niggling thing on the way to Rio.

Understandably, Di and the selectors were concerned. They wanted to come over and see Big Star with the team vet Rob Cnockaert, so I asked my vet to come over at the same time. I have two vets; Alex Rey my vet from America who has always looked after Big Star, and Ben Brain of Brain Partners in Gloucestershire, who looks after a lot of racehorses and had found the key to sorting out Big Star's suspensory injury when it first happened. He came with his father Jeffrey, who at ninety years old had seen more horses' legs than Bernard Matthews had seen turkeys and chickens.

Rob warned us he thought we might not make Rio, but Ben and his father Jeffrey were emphatic in their opinion that, provided we didn't over-jump Big Star and took every possible care, we had every chance of being there. So we followed their advice.

Big Star never stopped working, but we took it steady. We bought a salt spa and installed it at the racing yard. Salt hydrotherapy reduces swelling around new injuries and maintains the healing process by keeping any swelling down. It gets at any stresses and strains before they can develop into more serious problems. Every day Mark would hack him up there, to Lodge

Hill, to the spa, it was part of the routine. It was funny as Big Star hates walking through water, he'll avoid puddles, which is probably because he knows water is for jumping, but he's very happy to stand in the spa for an hour a day. Mark always had looked after him superbly but he took Big Star on now as a mission of pampering. He looked after Big Star's every need, nine hours a day, and made sure he got his favourite snack: bananas.

In June we took him to Knokke in Belgium, a nice show with good facilities. I jumped three rounds on Big Star over three days, he was ninth in the grand prix, then we went back for the three-star competition to jump him in the 1.40m and 1.45m classes. So on three rounds in La Baule, three in Knokke the first week then maybe another four in the second week we went to Rio.

I heard tittle-tattle on the grapevine questioning our selection; why was Big Star going to the Olympic Games when he hadn't jumped much, hadn't been seen much? I had said to Di and the selectors, and I knew they were concerned about him, 'If my horse is right and capable, I'll take him. But if I don't think he's right, there's no way I'm taking him.' My reasoning was that I'd been to a lot of Olympic Games and I knew what you needed to win. It's no fun being there on a horse that's not right or not good enough. I made it clear that if Big Star was right I would tell them and that if he wasn't, then I would tell them too.

They used to come and check him every week, which annoyed me, but I could understand they were only doing their job. To be honest, I wasn't that trusting by that point. There were a lot who had knocked me by saying the horse shouldn't go as he hadn't done anything, but they didn't realise how good that horse is. If we'd had five horses of Big Star's capability then probably I wouldn't have been going and I'd have understood, but we were in that space and time where we hadn't got those superstar horses and he far outweighed the rest. I knew I could not have done what Big Star and I did, on so few rounds, with any other horse I've had – no way, not a single one. But Big Star I knew inside out. I knew his mentality and I knew how brave he is. He was absolutely fine and all he was lacking at the time was top class, big jumping. If I had thought for one minute that he wouldn't hold up, there was no way I'd have taken him to Rio.

22

Gold

Mark flew out from Liège to Rio with Big Star and the rest of the team horses. Big Star is a great traveller, he is so laid back, but I was glad Mark was with him. I'd given Big Star a good jump at home two days before they left and he was fine, he felt great.

I'd been in the running to carry the Team GB flag at the opening ceremony but that honour went to Andy Murray. Just as well; I ended up missing it because I had another engagement before I flew out, at Lapworth show down the road. My granddaughter Florence went in the fancy-dress competition dressed up in all things Olympic on her pony Molly. She even had a torch.

The media had given Rio a bit of a bad name before we set off, saying the security wasn't up to scratch, the food was substandard, there were health warnings and so on, but it was fine. The venue for the horses was five-star; the rings, the ground, the stables, security, everything was first class. The village was probably the best we've ever stayed in, the accommodation was excellent and the transportation to all the venues was running well. There were two great big blocks of flats for Team GB. We were on the top floor – the fifteenth, I think. The showjumpers were on one side and the dressage and three-day eventers on the other. There was me, John and Michael, Ben, the travelling reserve Jessica Mendoza and Di. Both of Scott's horses had picked up injuries that season, which was a huge blow to Scott and his owners.

Laura was there too, as reserve for the US team. The Americans stayed in a hotel, so I was back and forth to both camps, sleeping with the enemy! Dan and Harry didn't come this time as they were busy riding and racing, but Gary and Beverley came – in fact, they had half the team as they also owned Michael Whitaker's horse Cassionato. Then there was Terry Spraggett, who has racehorses with Dan. Terry was our mascot. He's a great follower and good to the lads and a true friend – there's nothing he won't do for you. It was wonderful to have him along.

Big Star felt amazing in the warm-up. I was a bit concerned, him not having jumped those big courses, but in he went for the first individual qualifier with his usual neigh. This was the biggest course he had jumped since he won Aachen in 2013. He was going well until the last fence, and that was my fault. It was big square oxer, 1.55m, and as Big Star came out of the double so well I let him go on five strides when I should have held for six. He had the back rail, which is not something he would normally have done. He was OK, but he felt a bit rusty. That was all, just rusty, and maybe I was as rusty as him.

Michael and Cassionato were on four, having clipped a plank, and Ben and Tic Tac had two down. Only John went clear on the relatively inexperienced Ornellaia. The course caused a lot of problems and that round, which only counted for the individual qualification, was the time to have faults if you were going to have any.

On to the first round of the team competition: Big Star jumped an amazing round – he couldn't have jumped any better – but was given four faults at the water. He'd never been in a water jump in his life. The team did appeal, but it wouldn't have made any difference anyway. The water posed a lot of problems and either he just touched the tape or I probably took it for granted he was going to jump it. It was a big water with a bit of a flat distance to it and I probably didn't ride it strong enough. Michael's horse did the same and they got a time fault as well, then Ben's Tic Tac took the back bar off the oxer and John, with a lot of pressure on him, had a Horlicks of a ride when Ornellaia stopped at the treble and then had several rails down. That was that, no medal. The top eight teams went through to the second round and we didn't make the cut, but me, Ben and Michael would jump the second round as a qualifier for the individual, for which thirty-five would go forward.

Compared to back in the day when we'd get up to all sorts of tricks at shows, including Olympics, we were all pretty quiet. It was very serious. But that night when we got back knowing that from the team competition there would be no medal, nothing, Michael, John and I decided to drown our sorrows. There we were, John and Michael and me, sitting on the couch in our tracksuits, with the Olympics on the television, reminiscing about what we should have done, how we could have done it, how we didn't do it and going on and on and on. The more we drank, the more we felt sorry for ourselves. It was like going back in a time warp, thirty-odd years!

I went to bed about two o'clock in the morning as I was sick of listening to it: how unlucky we were, the same old thing. Next morning, I got up early to go and ride. There was Michael, still sitting on the couch, still with his tracksuit on, and he's still got a Brahma Brazilian beer in his hand. I took the photo to prove it: 10.08 on 17 August.

In that next round Big Star hit the middle part of the combination behind, something he never does. But that was the turning point. From that day on I wasn't worried. That's it, he's going to be fine, I thought. Why? I knew he felt he needed something to open him up, give him a blow, a wake-up call because he'd not jumped anything like it for so long. Big Star had probably never had five jumps down in his life, and he had three of them in Rio. He wouldn't have another.

We had a day off before the individual competition. Michael was probably right to have done some extra sorrow-drowning as he was out of the individual when Cassionato showed signs of colic and was taken to the veterinary clinic.

The course for the first round of the individual competition was big, which suited Big Star. There were thirteen clear rounds but he jumped it with so much ease I wasn't concerned. Second round, again he jumped well. I didn't feel for a moment that he was going to have a fence, not at all. From then on what I needed was the luck of the draw. I like to go first. I'm an impatient sort of person and I like to get in there, go as fast as I can and get the job done with the fences standing.

Nervous, anxious or whatever – I felt more of that in London than in Rio. I wasn't stamping around at all, and normally when it mattered so much I would have been pacing up and down. But I had this feeling; I'd told myself I was going to do it.

This began weeks before. I didn't tell anybody else, it was all in my own mind, but I kept going through it, day by day, running through what would happen, visualising myself on that podium. That was what I was going to do: win gold in Rio with Big Star.

Every day I went through it in my head. While I was riding Big Star, working him, I would be going through it. I kept telling myself over and over I was going to win, seeing myself standing on the podium, getting the medal – and how I was going to do it. I jumped every Olympic course I had ever jumped, only in my head, on Big Star. No mistakes, clears, and fast. It was my private vision, no one knew. I totally engulfed myself in Rio and my goal for myself and Big Star: gold.

Even in the jump-off, when the bell went, I was fine. I knew I was sitting on a horse that was no mere mortal and I knew at that point that provided I didn't mess it up, Big Star certainly wouldn't. I knew he was ready to go and do the job he was born for.

Big Star hadn't been against the clock since he won in Aachen in 2013. I had said after Aachen the aim was to go to Rio and win. Throughout that time off, getting him back to fitness, and the whole year before Rio, the focus was not winning any other class, not jumping a Nations Cup, it was all about Rio.

We had to walk around a bit when we went in and it gave me time to collect my thoughts. The bell went just as Big Star decided to have a crap. He is mortal after all. I got him cantering and as I turned him to the first fence on a right hand I thought to myself, Right, this is it, go!

That amazing horse. Big Star was at his brilliant best. There was no way he was going to touch a pole and he was fast. He turned when I asked him and he was on to the next fence. When you're in first and you've set a good goal – it was fast but it wasn't ridiculous – the others can't make a mistake, they know that. I thought I would be in the first three for sure but, to be honest, I didn't think I'd been quite fast enough.

Steve Guerdat's Nino de Buissonnets hit the first, Sheikh Ali Al Thani's horse hit two. We were still in the lead. 'So long as you're not fourth,' said Gary. Kent Farringdon's Voyeur had two. The least we'd get was bronze. 'I don't want a rusty one,' I said to Gary. Sweden's Peder Fredricson went clear but nearly a second slower, then there was Eric Lamaze left to jump.

You can say I was lucky but it fell my way, I got the right speed and everything went like clockwork. Eric Lamaze was unlucky he had that one vertical down, but he took the chance – I was sweating, watching him and Fine Lady – and it didn't come off for him. In the end, I think it was probably just meant to be. All that preparation, all that believing. 'You've done it!' said Gary. 'I could have told you that this morning,' I said to him. 'I wish you had!' he replied.

Going to so many Olympic Games (seven) and not winning, Big Star being injured then coming back, me being injured then coming back, doing it at my age – it was a fairy tale. Yet I had believed it.

It was amazing, and I knew there was no way I could have done that, or even thought I could have done that with any horse other than Big Star. I also knew I wouldn't be doing it again!

The medal ceremony was one of the most, if not the most, emotional moments in my entire life. To be standing there on the podium, for real, who wouldn't let it all come out? It was overwhelming, my sheer pride in hearing the British national anthem. After all that mental preparation, all that belief, there we were. Me up there and Mark holding Big Star just behind me; if I could have got them up too, I would have. Eric Lamaze was emotional too. He told me it couldn't have happened to a nicer guy. That was very touching and generous of him.

I'd always dreamt of that day. After such a long career, to win gold at that stage was unbelievable, no matter how much I had believed we could do it. To actually win Olympic gold at my age and to be lucky enough to get Big Star to Rio meant a lot to the whole team. That amazing horse, we all trusted him, he wanted to do it and, well, Big Star is the best horse I've ever had.

After the individual they take you off to do a dope test, that means a pee, and then it's off to the press, off to see the BBC and Clare Balding at the Olympic Park. By the time we got back, it was 10.30 p.m. They put on a bit of a party at the Team GB Equestrian house, which was great, but the next day at 7 a.m.

I knew they'd be picking me up to do more TV.

I have always loved the Olympics and that's why my motivation was so tuned to getting it right in Rio. The motto Baron de Coubertin came up with when he proposed the idea of an Olympic Games was 'Faster, higher, stronger'; who could do that better than Big Star? The fact is, no one had done it better than Big Star. In the next day's papers, they were calling him the Usain Bolt of showjumping. I was glad we'd had the chance to see Usain Bolt out in Rio.

We flew home the day after. Rio wasn't a long trip for the horses, with no quarantine needed, or for us. I flew back with Gary and Beverley. It wasn't an athletes' flight, but there were lots of Games people on it including Jonathan Agnew, the cricket commentator, who'd been picked to do the BBC radio commentary because his wife had a horse! He thanked me for his being able to finish his equestrian Olympic experience on such a high. Then we got down to planning the party.

The next morning I went straight to the British Showjumping headquarters at Meriden. They had organised a reception for me. I didn't know quite what sort of reception until I got there to be greeted by full camera crews from ITV and Sky Sports, complete with their outside broadcast units. From then on it was non-stop requests for interviews for the next month or more, a total whirlwind.

Maria and her team had pulled another all-nighter to deal with all the requests that first day back. They'd put out banners and all sorts. It was amazing. Over the coming months, Maria would be fielding requests for me to go on almost every game show. I resisted those challenges.

When Mark brought Big Star home, that horse bounded off the lorry as if he'd just been to pony club camp. He jumped off the end of the ramp and headed straight for the grass. We were all there to welcome him home, all the lads and lasses from the racing yard and my dad. Big Star might have won against the odds but the odds had made for a tempting bet at 16 to 1 and the lads had backed him.

We held the party in the indoor school. The numbers were well on the way to four hundred people. Everything was Rio-themed in green, yellow and black. We even had Brazilian dancers. So many people came from the showjumping world; John was away but Michael came, there was David Broome, Malcolm Pyrah and all my old friends like Sally Mapleson, Lindsay Vaughn, who I used to ride with on young-rider teams, Nikki Caine, the Scottish contingent Tricia Fraser and Janet Hunter, who I used to ride with years before. These were people I hadn't seen in ages and many of them hadn't seen each other for thirty years, so they had a great time.

We had a band and disco and there was even a Del Boy lookalike who came and did some jokes on the stage. That was Saturday night into Sunday morning and into Sunday lunchtime, as a lot of people were still here, especially the Irish boys: Noel Meade, Enda Bolger, Con Power, whose son Robbie is an excellent jockey, Eric McNamara, who rode for Ireland as a young rider and is now a trainer, Louis Murphy of the Dunraven Arms in Adare. And Ludger Beerbaum. It was real *craic*, as the Irish say.

The fun continued when I helped Frankie Dettori, A.P. McCoy and Victoria Pendleton with their jumping for a celebrity challenge class at Olympia in aid of the Injured Jockeys' Fund. Frankie claimed never to have jumped anything bigger than a foot and Victoria had never sat on a horse until eighteen months before. They did well and once again it was well attended by the media. Later, A.P. came back and rode Big Star for a *Horse & Hound* article. They got along well together and jumped some quite big fences, but then A.P. is a great horseman.

The awards flooded in and I was proud to receive all of them, and humbled too. The Horse & Hound Lifetime Achievement, British Showjumping Lifetime Achievement, I was inducted into the BBC Midlands Sporting Hall of Fame to join previous winners like Sir Stanley Matthews, Dennis Amiss, Gordon Banks, Dave Moorcroft and Richie Woodall. Then there was the BBC Sports Personality of the Year. I didn't for one moment think I'd get nominated, so to end up third was an amazing honour for someone from showjumping, which is probably a minority sport. I had a great night there and it was great to get it, especially as Andy Murray's wife Kim voted for me. It was brave of her, considering Andy said she ought to be careful as Christmas was coming!

It had been an amazing year. Then, on my birthday, I got the news I had been awarded the CBE in the New Year's Honours List.

23

The Biggest Decision

When we'd finished in Rio and Big Star and I had the gold in the bag, some people were already asking whether I would stop then and there, while others were saying we'd be looking forward to Tokyo. Fast-forward four years and Big Star would be seventeen and I'd be sixty-two, so realistically I thought that was pretty unlikely. I know there are riders like Canada's Ian Millar still going at the age of seventy – he made history as the oldest showjumper back in Beijing at the age of sixty-one and would probably have been in Rio had his horse been fit – but that wasn't in my sights. I do suffer with my back and have to work very hard to keep it right, so my immediate thought was that Tokyo was a no-go.

Could I have retired right at that moment? Yes, I could have. Thinking emotionally, at that point I had achieved everything I had ever wanted to. But looking back, having given it a bit of thought, the main reason I didn't retire then was because it had taken quite a while to get Big Star to Rio, in a condition to do what he did there and achieve everything he had, and I thought it would be a shame for him to stop. He's a horse who loves to jump, he really does. People would still go running to the ring to watch him, as they always did, as Laura had way back when she first laid eyes on him in Holland. He does everything so perfectly and he's exciting to watch, he gets the blood going. Stopping then seemed somehow unfair on him.

When we came home and things had settled down, I took Big Star to Barcelona for the Nations Cup Final. He jumped amazingly there, just as he had in Rio a month earlier. With Team GB and Germany both finishing on a zero score, we had to jump off head to head with the Germans. I was first to go on Big Star but I was jumping off against Marcus Ehning and I knew, whatever I did, however fast I went, he was going to beat me. At that point I needed to be clear. Big Star jumped as his usual brilliant self, he never touched a fence. Then at Toronto, the Royal Agricultural Winter Fair, which was indoors, he was third in the World Cup qualifier then second in the grand prix – and that was the last time he jumped at a show. I had planned to go on to Madrid, then Geneva to have a crack at the Rolex Grand Slam. The million-euro bonus that winning the grands prix in Geneva, Aachen and Calgary brings was obviously very attractive and that's on top of the prize money for each class. The gold meant I was automatically qualified to start in any CSI or CSIO grand prix. It was another challenge, a huge one, but Scott Brash had become the first rider ever to do it two years earlier in 2015 so it could be done. Then Big Star sustained a new injury.

It was a joint sprain this time. It wasn't serious; he must have done it in the paddock or the stable, I don't know which, as he was good one day then the next he had a bit of heat in the leg. So we didn't go to Madrid, Geneva or Olympia in London, which would have been great for the home fans who would have loved to have seen him jumping.

After Christmas at home with the family, turning fifty-nine and seeing in the New Year, the 2017 season began. Laura and I went to Florida as usual while Big Star stayed in England. I did a lot of thinking in Florida. Big Star went to stud for January and half of February. He was back in work and Mark was going over to Twemlows to ride him and get him fit. My intention was to win the Grand Slam, starting with Aachen in July, Calgary in September and Geneva in December. Big Star came home from stud and Harry started working him and jumping him. Harry was sending me videos every day and Big Star was looking great. He was jumping well. When I came home for the Cheltenham Festival and rode and jumped him for three days he felt fantastic.

I went back to Florida and kept thinking how good he'd felt, but instead of thinking about the Grand Slam, the seed of another thought had entered my head. Wouldn't it be crazy if something happened to Big Star when he was jumping in competition? What about the extreme pressure that I'd have to put him under at the likes of Aachen? After being on top form, in really good order, the thought of something happening at a show or even in the ring made me stop and think no, it would be silly and not nice for Big Star. The thought had nagged at me, the seed had taken root. One morning I just came out with it and said the last thing I would want is for him to go to a show and come out of the ring lame, or get another injury which would set him back again. I talked it over with Laura and the boys, with Gary and Beverley, and came to the conclusion that it would be best to stop. Big Star had given me so much; I didn't want to ask him for more.

As for me, I always said that when Big Star stopped I would stop too, so there was no going back. I knew once I had made the decision I wasn't going to change my mind. The last few years had been hard for me and it wasn't getting any easier. My body had taken a few poundings with injuries and my back wasn't in great shape. All the times during my career when I didn't have those top horses it was always an effort. I had absolutely 100 per cent faith in Big Star, but I no longer felt comfortable going into the big league on any other horses.

When you're older and you've had a few falls, you start to think that, if you have another, this is going to hurt. I'd had big problems with my back and put a lot of work into it. It's OK at the moment, but the minute I stop putting the work into it the problems start. Ironically it isn't the neck injury that nearly ended my career in 2000 that's to blame; the damage was done by that fall from Flambeau at the City of Chester show. When all the bruising and swelling had gone down and the 'black shorts' had faded, I was left with what felt like a step on my back, even though nothing was broken. From then on my back gradually got worse, and worse, and worse. Over six to seven years it kept on deteriorating until the back pain I was getting was just horrendous.

Back in 2011 when we were in La Baule with Gary, Beverley, Gary's dad Albert and Scott Brash, we'd decided to go out for a meal. Walking down to the restaurant on the beach, I kept having to stop every two hundred yards and sit. Albert, who was in his eighties, said I looked like the one in his eighties. In 2012, at the London Olympics, I was in so much pain I couldn't walk round the opening ceremony. In fact, I couldn't walk a hundred yards, so I stayed in the village. I realised then I had to do something.

Dr Ian Beasley was part of Team GB's Performance Services team and was on call in the village. He told me to come in and see him. He injected my back. I had to get wheeled out and back in a wheelchair to our accommodation, where I lay down for about eight hours. Then, miraculously, the pain was gone. I was fine. Whatever Ian did, he did a brilliant job. He's medical advisor to the Royal Ballet, spent many years in football including heading Medical Services at the Football Association and being team doctor to the men's team. Before that he put hockey players back together, so I was in excellent hands. It was thanks to Ian that I could ride at the Games.

My back was fine for a month or so after London 2012, then it started to deteriorate and the pain returned. I called Ian to ask could I get the same treatment. He wasn't available but referred me to Mr Otto Chan in London, who did the back injection and again it was all fine. I went to see him two or three times and each time it worked for a couple of months. Then in the middle of that course of treatment I was in the US with Laura. We were 'on tour' in Washington, Toronto and New York, but before that there'd been a bit of a world tour in search of medical solutions including a visit to Germany.

Basically, what had happened was that a disc had ruptured; the one that had taken the impact after that fall in 2002. It had gone, and the two bones were pressing on the nerve. The pain was getting worse and worse and I had sciatica down my leg. I went to see a few surgeons but I didn't like the sound of the treatment involved: another operation and the aftermath. In New York we were training Jessie Springsteen; her dad Bruce took me to his doctor. Bruce has been through the career-threatening surgery – damaged discs in his neck were causing numbness in his fingers, making it difficult for him to play guitar – so he and I understood each other on that front. But his doc said the same thing: they'd have to operate and it would mean a cage and support rods. I'd been there, done that and wasn't at all keen on the idea.

When we got back to the UK, I went to see Mr Chan. Otto Chan isn't a surgeon, he's a brilliant radiologist who has specialised in sports medicine. He said my best hope was Colin Natali, a consultant orthopaedic surgeon in London. Given my history with the prospect of surgery it took a while, but I eventually arranged a meeting with him. I took all my scans and to my amazement he said he wouldn't operate on it and what I needed to do was go to the gym and get a strong core to hold it all together!

I couldn't see how I'd be able to do that as I was in so much pain. I couldn't stand, bend, invert or anything, so how was I going to go to the gym? But Colin said he'd get rid of the pain and have me working out in the gym with a detailed exercise plan. So he made a hospital appointment for me where I underwent a general anaesthetic. He injected my back and two hours later I was pain-free. It was amazing. So then I started going to the gym, doing the exercises he recommended to strengthen my core and hold my back together. It got better and better as I went on; the more work I did, the better it got. After that, I went back for an injection every six months or so.

I think it was around November when I had it done. After Christmas 2013 we went to Florida, where I met Ed Smith, who helped me throughout that time we were Florida. Now, Laura and I go to him every time we're there. Ed helps a lot of riders with physio – he's a specialist in post-operative rehabilitation for athletes – and work in the gym. He trains American footballers too, having started out with the Tampa Bay Buccaneers. Ed has designed a special programme for riders to help us be strong in the position you need to be, sitting on a horse. The core is core, you might say. He's a funny little guy, Ed, he looks a bit like a gnome, not something you'd expect from a personal trainer, but he's not your typical personal trainer. You can also have a right laugh with him, he's a real case.

The Florida facility, Athlete's Advantage, is massive, with every possible type of equipment for strength and conditioning work. I do lots of work with cable-wire weights, on the medicine ball, with free weights. Ed also comes to the shows and watches. If there's something not quite right, he'll spot it. When I was preparing for the Olympics in Rio he was on it all the way, he was a massive support. Ed sent me a message on the morning of the individual in Rio. It just gave me that bit of extra confidence on the day.

Even now, I still feel I need to do those exercises, partly to keep my weight under control, but also so I can be out and about all day. I had an injection three weeks before Rio, just as a precautionary measure, as I'd have been mad not to dot all the 'i's and cross all the 't's, especially thinking back to London, but I've not needed one since. All through the Florida season I'd been at Ed's, doing all the stuff and having a laugh, and on Tuesdays, from two until four, I'd go to see Linda Umla, a physio/masseuse and expert in acupuncture. She did a great job relieving tension in my back, and seeing Linda also meant I got two hours off from working – she'd wake me up when she was finished and tell me it was time to go home!

I still go to the gym every morning when I'm home here. Yes, my back's good, as good as it can be, but it did affect my thinking about retirement. At Aintree, standing all day, I was aware of it, even if not in pain. If I go to bed at night and lie still it's fine. But three days at Aintree and four at Cheltenham do take their toll. It's not at a critical stage now, but I am still trying to keep my weight down and stopping competing doesn't mean stopping. I'd be scared to do that. And I am still going to be riding at home. Frankly, if I stopped going to the gym and stopped riding and just decided to be retired, I'd be fat and useless – and I'm not going to do that. I am going to be as strong as I can be for as long as I can.

Has it been emotional? The thought that I'm never going to put a team jacket on and ride through a start, jump clear and relish the applause, ever again? Yes. I have always loved going into the ring, I have loved winning. I've loved doing what I did and, yes, it's going to be hard going to competitions and not riding, not going in to win. But there comes a time when you have to say 'stop'. The older you get, the harder it is to bounce back from the falls, and the more you find yourself having to take chances. I think that's even more true nowadays than back when I started. There are so many good riders out there, the jump-offs are all fast and they've got faster, so you have no choice but to take chances. And when you get older, your movements aren't as quick, your reactions aren't as sharp.

I competed in the same *Stübben* saddle for thirty-five years, including in Rio. It's so old Mark is almost afraid to clean it. It's not anything to do with superstition, just that, like Big Star, I am a creature of habit. I've got my old velvet hunting cap on display in the trophy room; I rode in that, ripped velvet on the peak and all, for twenty-three years until the chinstrap rule was introduced. And I've ridden in the same spurs ever since I was at the Edgars'. I bent them to be exactly how I like them but, for competitions, it was time to hang them up.

I worked out over the last few years that I needed a better horse than everyone else just to stay equal with them, whereas twenty years ago I could perhaps have got away with being on a bit less of a horse because I could ride well. Nowadays, to beat the likes of Scott Brash, Ireland's Bertram Allen, Italy's Lorenzo de Luca – actually, Scott's the oldest of those at a mere twenty-eight years younger than me – and the young, up-and-coming riders, I realised I'd need to be on a better horse than theirs to beat them. I thought ages ago that unless I have Big Star it's going to be a struggle, and I didn't ever want to just ride around for the sake of it. I love winning too much. There are still a lot of horses at home and we have young horses that I'll ride and produce. That, after all, is our business. So I'll carry on schooling them at home, I just won't be doing any riding in the ring. Laura can do that.

I had already made it public knowledge that when Big Star stopped I would too, so when I came to the decision to call time on us competing, I naturally spoke to Gary first and told him how

I felt and why I thought this was the time – pretty much everything I've just told you – and he said 'fine'. He was completely behind me. Gary and Beverley have been very good, the best owners you could wish for. They'd had a great time as owners, though they never sought the limelight. One year in Florida, Mark Bellissimo, the man behind the Wellington Festival, invited Gary and Beverley to join his table at the show as he had a guest coming. It was Donald Trump. Mark introduced Gary and Beverley, saying to Trump: 'They own the best horse in the world and even you haven't got enough money to buy it.'

For years before and certainly after the Aachen win in 2013, they could have sold Big Star for a huge amount of money – and I mean huge – but they didn't sell him. They believed in the Olympic dream as much as I did, even though at times it seemed not much more than a pipe dream. When we teamed up again after all those years, Gary and I were on the boat and we talked about the aim, the Olympics, and shook hands on it. We'd win or lose together, and that suited us.

There is something about winning the Olympics. Years and years ago, starting out, the Olympics were something I was aware of, watched on telly, heard about, but it wasn't part of my agenda. That changed when I went to Seoul in 1988. Then I realised that this was the most unbelievable experience; with so many countries and such a sports extravaganza, it's like nothing you've ever seen. From that moment I knew this was where I wanted to win. Seeing the likes of Carl Lewis, Michael Phelps and Usain Bolt winning gold medals, it dawned on me why those medals were so important to them. An Olympic gold is the highest thing you can win . . . The chance only comes around every four years. Nothing else can compare – no big class money, no million-euro challenge, nothing gets close to the highest prize and honour you can win, that Olympic gold medal. To do it in London was great, amazing, but to do it as an individual in Rio, after a forty-three-year career? That was the highest achievement ever for me. It was also an achievement never to be repeated by me and Big Star, and I'd known that since the day I stood on the podium in Rio with tears streaming down my face.

This country makes a lot of sports stars – I think so, anyway. The reason so many people followed my success was not because they were hardened fans of showjumping but because of my age and the story of my comeback, the injuries I've had and how it all came right that day in Rio in spite of all the pain and the battles to get there. That I did it at my age inspired people – I know, because they come up and tell me that they've taken up walking or cycling or whatever as a result of my story. It helped that the Rio Olympics were the perfect timing to watch on TV here. No having to stay up all night like I did during Sydney when I couldn't sleep in that torturous halo. Rio was broadcasting at the perfect time in the afternoon for people to watch, and that helped it all go berserk. It was a great day. It's been a great life. There is more to come. The day the announcement was made, by British Showjumping, that Big Star and I would both retire at Royal Windsor, Dan had his hundredth winner of the season when Listen to the Man crossed the line first in the mares' handicap hurdle at Wincanton. Dan and Harry go from strength to strength and I can go racing more now to support them.

Big Star might produce big or little stars, and that'll be great to see. But for me there will never be another like him. He's the ultimate, the best, and my best friend and partner. Together we achieved my ultimate ambition: Olympic gold.

Gary and Beverley have a house on Tortola, the largest of the British Virgin Islands. It's a beautiful place, with lots to do: island-hopping, eating and drinking are at the top of the list. Gary and Bev and Justin and Kathleen, their son and daughter-in-law, stayed there after London 2012. There's an island across from Tortola called Jost van Dyke and on that island there's a beach bar called One Love. They were all there having drinks and eats and partying one afternoon. It's a quirky place, full of character, and people write all sorts of things on any surface they can find. Kathleen got up – probably after she'd had a few drinks – and wrote 'Big Star Rio 2016'. After Rio, in November 2016, I went out there with Laura, Gary and Beverley, Will and Pippa Funnell, David and Karin McPherson and our non-horsey friends Sean and Corinne. After all the excitement and commotion of Rio, the endless round of press interviews, appearances and what have you, it was real relaxation and fun with friends. Naturally, we went to the One Love Bar. There was something I had to do. I got a marker pen, found where Kathleen had written her bit and added my contribution:

Mission Accomplished, Nick Skelton.

Praise for Nick Skelton

Graham Fletcher

However successful a top sportsman has been in their chosen sport, when they retire they only have a small window of being remembered before they are all but forgotten.

It could have been the same way for Nick Skelton. For sure myself and his fellow pros and supporters would always have remembered all his great Grand Prix wins and Team Gold in London. I was there when he set the high jump record at Olympia; the laughs and stories I could tell from many nights out together; but for most people, remembering those victories would have ebbed away as they looked for younger riders to support.

But all that changed in 2016 with that brilliant individual gold medal in Rio, because in winning it, it encapsulated the British public's admiration for a man they heard had come back from a career-threatening broken neck. They saw in that win all that's been great about Skelly. His determination, his bravery, his flamboyance and, above all, his professionalism.

It's been a huge pleasure to have known him throughout his career. The name Nick Skelton will never be forgotten.

Laura Kraut

Who would have thought that day when I first saw Big Star would lead to two gold medals and the accomplishment of a lifetime for Nick. We never could have known the impact that day would have had on both our lives. It has been an amazing journey and I am just so extremely proud to have been part of the brilliant final chapter of Nick's career.

Sir Anthony 'AP' McCoy

I know he wanted to, but Nick's over-qualified, has too many brains and is too good a rider to have been a jockey. When you ride a racehorse you don't tend to think about it, there isn't time. I think where Nick and I are the same is that – and this is putting it politically correctly – we both had to learn early on that our standard of performance had to be better than that horse's, not the other way round.

I was very lucky to have been able to ride Big Star. That made me wish I'd gone back twenty years, been around the people Nick was and done it. The idea and the concepts are similar, even little things like timing. That was one of the only times I've ever felt nervous, riding that horse in front of Nick and what he's achieved on him. I got such a buzz I really thought I wouldn't mind having a go at this – the power of that horse!

To achieve that longevity in sport needs a bit of obsession, a bit of selfishness, for that period of time you need it. And walking away at the highest point is the best thing he could have done. Look at Usain Bolt. Nick did it right. The hardest thing to do is to walk away. I know all about that.

Mark Beever

It's been a journey and a half, an amazing journey. Not all roses, mind you, but if I hadn't worked for Nick I would never have been to practically every country you could ever go to. Nick can do anything with a horse and he's brilliant at everything he does, even grooming. He expects the highest standards but he can DO everything to the highest standard – if he mucks out a box there'll not be one bit of shit left in the shavings! I've learned a lot from Nick, including about grooming, which is annoying really, and you don't normally get that from a rider. As well as being a great horseman and a great rider, he's the tidiest person in the world.

David Skelton, 'Dad'

Nick was a winner from the beginning. I'm unbelievably proud of him. If his grandparents had been alive they'd have been so proud; the OBE, CBE and since then lunch at the palace with the Queen, that was a real honour. I think one of the best things was when the Queen asked him to take Big Star up to the Castle, and of course the retirement ceremony the next day was out of this world.

I don't know what his next goal is but he can't go much further! When people asked me what Nick was going to do when Big Star retired, I'd always say there's another 180 up the road to look at, at the racing yard, and he's so dedicated now to Harry and Dan. And to see him so devoted to Flo; the first thing he does when he gets back here is bring her, on her pony, to visit Great Grandad.

When some local children came to visit after Rio and found Nick wasn't there, as soon as he got back he went to their house and said: 'You came to see Big Star, well, come on then.' He wouldn't let anyone down.

Geoff Billington

I'm one of the few that can say I was there at the beginning and I was there until the end. Nick would have gone to the top of whatever profession he decided to take. His attention to detail and pure horsemanship are second to none.

Travelling the world with Nick, John, Michael and Robert was like one long lads' weekend in Benidorm; best mates, all watching each other's backs, having lots of fun but, don't forget, fierce competitors. I was lucky to be part of a team that could beat the world on its day.

I don't think there is anybody who has won more grands prix on more different horses than Nick. I remember Nick turning up at a show, aged eighteen, with six horses, no groom, and every one of those horses turned out to perfection. You don't see that with modern-day kids. But there is one thing for sure; Nick was always going to be an Olympic champion!

Scott Brash

Nick has been and is an amazing idol of mine. Growing up, to know someone who had not come from a privileged background gave me hope and determination to make it in the sport I love. Nick showed it is possible to be top of the sport no matter where you start from.

Nick has had such a glittering career and it really is incredible what he has won. He has made records in the sport that I know will never be matched. He can win on any horse in any circumstances and he's proved time and time again that he's not only a top rider in the ring but an out-and-out horseman. The way he plans his horse for an event, the way he educates horses, and the way he knows how to get the best from a horse is truly admirable.

To come into the sport to compete alongside him was one of my biggest dreams. To be in London alongside Nick, someone who had experienced so many Olympics, was not only a dream come true for me but a big influence. The team spirit was fantastic and the drive and determination throughout the team to win gold was incredible. Nick was the main force behind this.

When I won Spruce Meadows for the second time last year he phoned me up and said: 'Well done, mate, you've only got another two to win to match me.' This, for me, is Nick to a T; he congratulates you but motivates you more at the same time, and reminds you that you've never made it so keep working hard. Great advice! He has been a great motivator, great adviser and a great friend to me. Some of the best experiences of my life have been because of Nick Skelton.

Gary Widdowson

We were two sixteen-year-old boys jumping on our first International Team in Dublin. I went on to have success in the business world and Nick went on to have great success in the showjumping world. Who would have thought that forty-five years later we would team up through Big Star to achieve our greatest dream in showjumping, but we did in London and again in Rio!

Nick was never just our rider; he has always been our friend.

Ludger Beerbaum

The first time I met Nick was in 1985 when I started to compete internationally. He was winning everything with Apollo and St James. These two horses couldn't have been more different in type and character. I was extremely impressed by Nick's competitiveness and also his horsemanship.

We have shared many highlights and struggles over the last thirty-two years of our careers. On the rare occasion of conflict, there was always an underlying respect. Seeing Nick win the individual gold with Big Star last year really touched me because once again he proved his unbelievable horsemanship, not only in the delicate preparation with his horse but also how he kept himself motivated and focused beforehand.

Beverley Widdowson

We would always wind up Nick by saying what a legend Ludger was in showjumping.

When Nick won the individual gold, I ran up to him, gave him a big hug, and said to him: 'Nick, you're a true legend now!'

Liz Edgar

I was there at the start and there at the end, at Royal Windsor. Nick made the decision to retire at the right time for him and it couldn't have been better. The nicest thing about it is all the young people coming up who have seen Nick and appreciate what he has achieved; that's what he will be remembered for. Some go on too long and youngsters wonder whether they were ever any good. Nick was never toppled off the top.

It's the way he had done it all his life. He was always a planner, and he's never done anything 'ad hoc'. I think he got the taste for gold in London and it was a four-year plan to get to Rio. Nick, Big Star and the plan? I would never have doubted it.

Nick Brooks-Ward

I have been fortunate to have known Nick all my life and I am honoured to call him a friend.

His preparation is immaculate, his perseverance is unparalleled, his talent is unbounded – and that is why he is the most successful showjumper the world has ever seen. When he came back from a broken neck to compete in Athens, and just miss out on Olympic Gold on Arko, it was incredible, and then to go on and be the lynchpin in London securing Team Gold, and then go one better with individual Olympic gold in Rio, is a testament to his sheer brilliance. But, above all, his dedication to Dan and Harry is what is so inspirational for us all – a true family man at heart and double Olympic champion – it doesn't get better than that.

Rodrigo Pessoa

Nick is inarguably one of the greatest our sport has ever seen. He has won every grand prix in the world on multiple occasions, countless Nations Cups, so many championship medals and, to top it off, the Olympic Gold was matchless.

His style was unique, his speed was incredible and his accuracy was perfect. He was a tough guy to beat and didn't leave much to chance. Nick has been one of my heroes and idols since childhood. I was thirteen when I watched him jump Jappeloup and that round convinced me I would be a showjumper and nothing else.

Malcolm Pyrah

The best number one in Nations Cups ever. Cool and organised.

Eric Lamaze

Nick is a rider I have looked up to throughout my career, and it was an honour to stand next to him on the podium at the Rio Olympics. He has always been strong in his convictions, and never afraid to speak out for the good of our sport. He is a great ambassador, and I have always admired his commitment to protecting the sport's best interests.

Simon Brooks-Ward

It takes guts to do what you know is inherently dangerous. I was in the Olympia collecting ring, as a very junior steward, when Nick had piled through several attempts at the high jump record. As he was being persuaded to go again by a very persuasive Ted Edgar, he was showing the strain. His 'sod you' attitude came through that night in spades as he finally re-entered the arena and went on to famously clear that enormous fence. However tough it was, or is, Nick is courageous in his outlook and one of the most determined people I have ever met. Talent aside, this is why he is one of the greatest showjumpers ever to grace these shores.

David Broome

When Nick started out with my sister and brother-in-law (Liz and Ted) he had 150 per cent tuition in every round he jumped. As he matured, his attention to detail was unbelievable. He was always difficult to beat as he was so organised, he was ready for anything.

I remember walking the course with him at Dublin when he was riding Hopes Are High. When we came out he gave me the exact assessment of how he was going to ride that course down to the last half stride. He rode it to perfection and won it, and that's what he did all his competitive life.

That organisation and attention to detail is Nick, he's the business. It's part of racing too and he's so dedicated to that. I know Nick's very enthusiastic that the gold medal should be used to propel the sport forward. So am I, and I hope it is.

Praise for Nick Skelton

John Whitaker

There are lots of stories I could tell but most of them are un-printable. Nick and I first met as teenagers. We did our first championship together in 1980 and winning the silver was a bit unexpected, as he's said in this book. I always knew he was good but at that point I knew he was very good. He's unbelievably org-anised, to the finest detail. Ronnie put him in first, in the middle of all the chaos, and Nick went in and jumped clear. Going on to European championships medals, knocking on the door for world championships – they were good times.

Nick is second to none as an individual winning all the big grands prix and not always with superstar horses. As part of the same era, he has been an inspiration to me and many others with his will to win.

He likes everything his own way, though, and he's very tight!

Michael Whitaker

The thing about Nick is his determination. When he sets his mind on something so often it happens. He bought Big Star with Olympic gold in mind and it happened, in London and Rio, and to have won the likes of Aachen and Calgary four times each, and more – getting it right on the day when it matters that many times – is not easy. It is Nick's character to be that single-minded, that determined. Mind you, he can be a pain in the arse with it!

To have Nick on your side as a teammate, to be in it together on a winning team, he brings that will to win which is obviously very good. He was always very helpful and I've learned a lot from him. With his attention to detail he could pick up on the things that make a difference and tell you – often with f's and b's in it! That he had a plan and stuck with it is why he's been so successful.

Harry Skelton

We are ever so close. Dad brought me and Dan up without a mother for most of our childhoods and he has literally been there for me since day one. I had a lot of good ponies, and while Dad said I always thought I knew a bit better than him I watched him and learned, even at an early age. If one day I have kids, if I could give them what he's given us, well, that's one of my aims in life.

He realised school was a waste of time for me as it had been for him. He's not just taught us with horses, he's been the perfect role model. Of course he hasn't been perfect in life – who is? – but knowing how the Edgars were hard on him to take pride in keeping everything spick and span, that's a life lesson I have learned from him. I go out mowing the lawns and keeping my place looking very tidy. Dad's taught me to look after everything I've got and work for everything I have.

Rio, when Dad won the gold, was the best day of my life without a doubt. To reach a childhood dream like that. I texted him to that effect and he texted back saying the best day of his life was when me and Dan had our first Cheltenham win with Superb Story. Dad's is a superb story.

John Hales

Prior to Nick winning the gold medal in Rio, Nick had agreed to throwing a party to recognise the achievements of his sons. In only their third year of Dan training and Harry as his stable jockey, Dan had trained over a hundred winners and Harry had ridden over a hundred winners. Reaching that milestone was a remarkable double achievement. Unfortunately for that plan, Nick went and won the gold medal in Rio and the party was held quite rightly to recognise Nick's achievement. Nick told me that it had cost him £xxxx. I have reminded him that he must now pay a similar sum to celebrate his sons' achievements!

Grace Skelton, with Bridget Andrews (Harry's partner and fellow jockey) and Florence Skelton

Sitting in the Royal Box for Nick's retirement ceremony at Royal Windsor, we were trying and failing to hold back tears. Florence was worried. I tried to explain to three-year-old Flo that this was a happy day when we got to celebrate all the special things Grandad had done, that he would stop riding Big Star and going to all the shows now. As he would be at home more, he would be able to give her riding lessons as he wouldn't be jumping in competitions. Flo seemed satisfied with this. After the ceremony and all the accolades had been received, Nick returned to the box, which our family had been given for the day. As he walked in, Flo ran into his arms. He picked her up and Flo whispered into his ear: 'You're all mine now, Grandad.'

Acknowledgements

To my late mum, Norma, for finding Oxo, and to her and my dad, David, for taking me to all those shows in the early years. To the late Kenneth Clawson, then Ted and Liz Edgar for the grounding. As for all the owners and wonderful horses I have been very lucky to have had during my career, a big thank you to them, and to my sponsors and the staff who have looked after my horses, especially Mark Beever for sticking with me for thirty-two years. To everyone who has contributed to my competitive career, to my team mates and the lads I've competed against who have kept me on my toes: You are all part of this story.

To our agent Johnny Whitmore of Stellar Group for guiding us to the brilliant team at W&N books; Alan Samson who has kept a steady hand on the reins throughout, the ever-calm Lucinda McNeile, Anne O'Brien and publicist Leanne Oliver.

When you've jumped as many rounds as I have, it can be a bit of a challenge to recall dates and times, so to all those who have helped Bernie in her detective work, sorting dates, checking facts and sourcing pictures a huge thank you; Maria Haig at British Showjumping, the team at HPower, Simon and Nick Brooks-Ward, with a special thanks to Clare Gussin, Hannah Rawdon-Mogg, Byron Massarella, Ben Brain, Jenny MacArthur, Grace Skelton, Beverley Widdowson, and Ella and Lucinda at Dan Skelton Racing.

I've known 'Bernie-the-book' a long time, she promised me she'd have my back and make it easy – and she has. When I'd made the decision that Big Star and I would retire she texted me: 'Thanks, I've got the ending'. Glad I was able to oblige! It took some convincing to get me to do this and without friendship and

Acknowledgements

trust we couldn't have done it. Thanks, Bernie, for all of this, and to Keeley Durham for spurring you on in the first place.

If I hadn't had Arko, there would never have been Big Star; thank you, John, Pat and Lisa Hales. If Laura hadn't found Big Star this story wouldn't have happened. To her, Gary, Beverley and the late Albert Widdowson for Big Star, and to Big Star, who is everything a rider could ask for.

I could not be more proud of my sons, Dan and Harry, it's over to you, boys, now to do the winning.

Nick Skelton

Picture Credits

The author and publisher are grateful to the following for permission to reproduce photographs:

Bob Langrish: p.3 (above right); p.3 (below); p.4 (top); p.4 (middle); p.4 (below); p.5 (above left); p.6 (top); p.6 (below); p.8 (above); p.8 (middle); p.9 (below); p.14 (above)

Cealey Tetley: p.10 (above); p. 10 (below); p.11 (top left)

John Carter / Mail on Sunday / Rex Shutterstock: p.6 (below right)

Stephen Davies: p.9 (top); p.15 (top); p.15 (right)

Times Syndication: p.7

Olympia The London International Horse Show / Kit Houghton: p.9 (above)

Beverley Widdowson: p.8 (left); p.11 (top right); p.11 (opposite below); p.12 (top); p.12 (below left); p.12 (below right);

Royal Windsor Show / Peter Nixon: p.16 (below)

Grace Skelton: p.13 (right)

Royal Ascot / Annabel Hannam): p.14 (left)

Index

Index

Index

Index

Index